THE

# AD/HD

# PARENTING

# HANDBOOK

THE

# AD/HD

# PARENTING
# HANDBOOK

## Practical Advice
## for Parents from Parents

### Second Edition

## COLLEEN ALEXANDER-ROBERTS

TAYLOR TRADE PUBLISHING
Lanham • New York • Boulder • Toronto • Oxford

Published by Taylor Trade Publishing
An imprint of The Rowman & Littlefield Publishing Group, Inc.
4501 Forbes Boulevard, Suite 200, Lanham, Maryland 20706

Distributed by NATIONAL BOOK NETWORK

Library of Congress Cataloging-in-Publication Data

Alexander-Roberts, Colleen.
    The AD/HD parenting handbook : practical advice for parents from parents /
Colleen Alexander-Roberts.— 2nd ed.
      p. cm.
    Includes bibliographical references and index.
    ISBN-10: 1-58979-283-1 (pbk. : alk. paper)
    ISBN-13: 978-1-58979-283-8 (pbk. : alk. paper)
    1. Attention-deficit hyperactivity disorder—Popular works. 2. Child
rearing—Popular works. I. Title.
    RJ506.H9A58 2006
    618.92'8589—dc22                                              2005034631

™
∞ The paper used in this publication meets the minimum requirements of
American National Standard for Information Sciences—Permanence of Paper
for Printed Library Materials, ANSI/NISO Z39.48–1992.

Manufactured in the United States of America.

# Contents

# Foreword

O MATTER what I read, whether it is some longhair academic paper from ivory-tower land or a book directed to the general public, I always have a few standards by which I judge the content: Does this material make sense? Does it have real-world application?

In *The AD/HD Parenting Handbook: Practical Advice for Parents from Parents* by my friend Colleen Alexander-Roberts, the answer to both questions is a resounding Yes!

The first thing that leaps out at me, as a trained physician and psychiatrist, is that this book is *accurate* in its descriptions of AD/HD and related psychological and psychiatric conditions. (I am particularly pleased to have been invited to write the chapter on medications, so I am certain that the material on medications is as accurate and up-to-date as possible!) The second, and probably the most important, thing is that for all its technical accuracy, this book has practical, everyday techniques for application and changing both child and parent behavior. It clues the reader in to what the life journey with a child with AD/HD might be like, what it *could* be like, and how to advocate for your child, and yes, even how to enjoy some of the journey together. In that sense, it is a very positive, proactive, and hopeful book.

I have a somewhat unusual and privileged position to write this foreword and endorse this book. I have known your author for more than a decade. We first met on the CompuServe ADD forum at the dawn of the Internet age, even before web browsers were available. All communication was handled by text windows on CompuServe. Talk about the old days!

As Colleen and I got better acquainted, I invited her to speak at three community-wide seminars on AD/HD, which I hosted, several years apart. She graciously accepted each time, and my patients' families talked about her "straight from the heart" style of presentation long after she departed from the scene. Just like everyone else, I heard her stories about how she was in the process of raising two children with AD/HD, one of whom was so wild and out of control that he ran from bathroom to bathroom in the house, stuffing the toilets with toilet paper and then flushing them to make them run over because it seemed like such a wonderfully creative idea! And as Colleen was cleaning up one bathroom, he was on to the next to continue his creative scientific experimentation. She has subsequently raised both of these children successfully. Her book includes over a decade of experiences and insights that were learned in the University of Hard Knocks.

Having Colleen review her real-life experiences, as well as those of so many other parents, brings some common sense and a balanced perspective to what otherwise would have been the all-too-typical book recounting psychiatric symptoms and cookbook-style approaches. With the real-life examples and anecdotes, this book sparkles with warmth, personal investment, and an immense caring for this challenging and frequently brilliant and gifted population.

My patients' families and I have all benefited from the wisdom contained in this book. I know that you will too.

Colleen and I both wish you the best of success on your life journey with your child with AD/HD. Although challenging, it can be a grand adventure with a happy and thrilling outcome.

*Louis B. Cady, MD*

# Acknowledgments

**I** AM EXTREMELY grateful to Louis B. Cady, MD, a psychiatrist in Evansville, Indiana, for writing the foreword for this book and the chapter on medications, enabling me to provide my readers with the most current information on medication therapy for AD/HD. Louis, you have been a friend for over a decade and you have always been there when I needed your expertise. Thank you from the bottom of my heart for all the help you have given me over the years.

I am also grateful for the assistance of Bruce A. Pasch, MD, FAAP, who reviewed and edited the manuscript and offered numerous suggestions and tips. He also shared his expertise, spent countless hours working on the manuscript, and supported this project. Not only was Dr. Pasch a great pediatrician to my children when they were younger, but his work with children who have AD/HD and their families is to be commended. Thanks to Mary D. Squire, PhD, for her assistance in reviewing the manuscript, offering suggestions, and sharing the joys and frustrations of parenting children with AD/HD.

I want to thank my dear friend Judith Gilbert for the numerous pages of tips she provided, for the parts of her family life she shared in this book, and for her encouragement and belief in this project. I am grateful for the insight Janet Robinson, RN, PhD, provided on parenting adolescents with AD/HD and for the advice she shared on working with educators. I also wish to thank Kathy Galbreth, a former teacher at Maumee Valley Country Day School in Toledo, Ohio, for reviewing parts of the manuscript and Donna Waghorn, information specialist at the National Dissemination Center for Children with Disabilities, for clarifying the Individuals with Disabilities Education Act (IDEA) and Section 504 of the Rehabilitation Act of 1973.

In writing this book, I relied heavily on the experiences of more than two hundred parents who offered their insight, suggestions, tips, and words of advice. My thanks to all these parents who took the time to fill out questionnaires. I would especially like to thank all my friends who have children with AD/HD who shared their stories, especially Debra Graf, Gary and Joanie Hoffer, and Dianne Gladieux (now deceased) and the many members of Adoptive Families of America and CHADD who graciously shared their thoughts and suggestions, frustrations and fears, and joys so that this book could be written.

My children were the inspiration for this book. Thanks to my sons, Christopher and Blake (you both are awesome and I am so blessed to have you in my life!). They taught me to be more patient, compassionate, and forgiving. Because of them I learned to be an effective, loving parent—not a perfect parent, which I strove to be for years. I would also like to thank my parents, Joanne and Stan, for the interest they have shown in this book and for their love and support over the years.

# Introduction

ATTENTION-DEFICIT hyperactivity disorder (AD/HD) is a disorder characterized by age-inappropriate levels of inattention, impulsivity, and hyperactivity. AD/HD currently is a popular diagnosis, constituting the largest single reason children are referred to child mental health clinics. Because of its popularity, it has come to be viewed as the Yuppie diagnosis, and many people are not taking the diagnosis seriously. Consequently, the child with AD/HD and his family are often misunderstood by friends, extended family, teachers, scout leaders, and Little League coaches. The child becomes labeled as a behavior problem, lazy, irresponsible, and disorganized. Parents are often accused of failing to control and discipline their children. The developmental tasks of childhood and parenting, which are difficult under normal circumstances, are compounded by AD/HD and by society's misunderstanding of the disorder. Parents are left with the task of educating those around them, coping with the associated behavior, advocating for their child with AD/HD, and protecting themselves and their immediate family from the disapproval of others.

In spite of the view of many, AD/HD does exist, as any parent who has a child with the disorder will attest. It has been shown to have a biological cause, or etiology, which appears to be inherited, although other etiologies (such as lead poisoning, perinatal difficulties, and maternal drug use during pregnancy) may account for a percentage of cases of AD/HD. Estimates of AD/HD's prevalence vary from 3 to 5 percent; some sources suggest it may be higher.

AD/HD symptoms may be mild, moderate, or severe. Symptoms are considered mild when there are few, if any, in excess of those required for diagnosis and when there is little impairment in school and social functioning. Severe symptoms are present when they markedly exceed the number required for diagnosis and when there is a significant and pervasive impairment in home, school, and social functioning. Symptoms falling between mild and severe are considered moderate.

Each of the three primary symptoms of AD/HD—inattention, impulsivity, and hyperactivity—is multidimensional. Thus problems with attention can manifest themselves in difficulties with alertness, arousal, selectivity, sustained attention, or distractibility. Impulsivity, also referred to as behavioral disinhibition, is manifested in children with AD/HD in their inability to delay gratification, their failure to consider the negative, even dangerous, consequences of risk-taking behavior, and the careless and destructive handling of their own and others' property. Similarly, children with AD/HD often experience difficulty waiting for instructions to be completed, resulting in careless errors. Hyperactivity may be manifested either through excessive motor movements or verbalization.

Manifestations of AD/HD occur in varying degrees in most situations the child participates in, including home, school, and social situations. Nonetheless, ability to focus in highly stimulating or novel situations is not uncommon. Because of the impulsive nature of children with AD/HD, aggressive acting out is common. Difficulty with peer relationships also is common. Noncompliance with parental requests and directives is often observed in home situations. Children with AD/HD often have low self-esteem, are emotionally labile and prone to temper outbursts, and have low frustration tolerance. Many children with AD/HD have academic difficulties or are academic underachievers due to difficulty concentrating and staying on task to complete assignments.

The behavioral characteristics associated with AD/HD are often sources of conflict between children with AD/HD and their parents and siblings. Researchers have found interactions with and reactions from parents and siblings of children with AD/HD to be different than those in normal families in that they are more negative and stressful to all family members. Moreover, there is considerable evidence that parents and siblings of children with AD/HD are more likely than those of non-AD/HD children to suffer psychological distress and psychiatric disorders.

The effects of AD/HD on family members have been demonstrated in a number of research studies. These studies have found that mothers of children with AD/HD often report significantly lower levels of parenting self-esteem and higher levels of depression, self-blame, and social isolation than their counterparts who have non-AD/HD children. Marital disturbances are more common among families with a child who has

AD/HD; some studies show separation and divorce rates are three times that of couples without a child with AD/HD. Similarly, strained relationships with extended family appear to be more common among families with a child who has AD/HD. Consequently, young parents often are deprived of needed emotional support from family and friends, resulting in a sense of social isolation that is detrimental to emotional well-being.

It is no surprise that the entire family system and the way the family functions together can be affected by AD/HD. The family systems theory is based on a general systems theory, which maintains that a change in one part of the system results in a change in the entire system. Thus a family can be thought of as similar to a mobile. When one portion of the mobile moves, all other parts move as well. When a family experiences stress in one subsystem, whether it is the marital, sibling, or individual subsystem, the entire family reacts with attempts to adapt or cope with that stress. Some of these adaptations may be functional; others may be dysfunctional. Healthy families are those that are able to make appropriate or functional adaptations in reaction to stress.

To cope with the behavioral manifestations of AD/HD and the accompanying parenting stress, most families with a child who has AD/HD make a variety of attempts to adapt or change the way they react to and handle the child. Some of these attempts are functional and successful, and others are not. Oftentimes parents are at a loss for how to successfully adapt or cope with the behavior of their child with AD/HD. This difficulty is compounded by children with AD/HD often being impervious to rewards and consequences. Moreover, rapid habituation to reinforcers, a common characteristic of children with AD/HD, means that just when you thought you had the key to coping with a behavior, the technique you are using becomes old hat to your child with AD/HD and is no longer effective. Consequently, parents must constantly be creative and remain one step ahead of the child to successfully cope with the behavior.

Resources for learning to cope with the behavioral manifestations of AD/HD can be hard to come by. Pediatricians are often helpful in prescribing and monitoring medication but may fall short when it comes to additional suggestions for behavioral interventions. Medication, unfortunately, is only one piece of the puzzle required for dealing with AD/HD. Psychologists and family therapists who specialize in the treatment of families and children with AD/HD may be helpful. However, many are not specifically trained in this area and may even fail to recognize the symptoms of AD/HD, particularly when symptoms are mild. Others may confuse severe symptoms with family dysfunction and view the child with AD/HD as the family scapegoat, a position he can fall into very easily. Unless one is fortunate enough to be referred to a psychotherapist or pediatrician who specializes in the treatment of AD/HD, few resources for coping with AD/HD behavior may be available.

Colleen Alexander-Roberts offers parents a rich source of parenting techniques and sound advice on adapting successfully. She addresses a wide variety of problems at all age levels, from preschool to adolescence. She has enlisted the help of many parents of children with AD/HD and adds her own sensitivity and parenting successes to their advice. As the parent of two children with AD/HD, she is uniquely qualified to understand and communicate the pain, frustration, and—yes!—joys of parenting challenging children.

*The AD/HD Parenting Handbook* is solution focused and offers hope to parents of children with AD/HD. Through Ms. Alexander-Roberts's suggestions, parents will discover how to anticipate problem situations, how to become advocates for their children, and how to make appropriate adaptations to cope with AD/HD. Parents undoubtedly will find this book an invaluable tool in their quest for a healthy family.

*Mary D. Squire, PhD*
*The Martin & Johnson Group, Inc.*

# Getting Started:
# What You Need to Know

VER 2 MILLION children in the United States have a medical condition called attention-deficit hyperactivity disorder (AD/HD). AD/HD is a disorder characterized by developmentally inappropriate chronic levels of inattention, impulsive hyperactivity, or both. Onset usually begins in late infancy or early childhood, often by the age of three, but many times it is not recognized until the child begins school. Not all children will manifest the same symptoms. Some, not all, children with AD/HD will have one or more learning disabilities along with their attention difficulties. Extreme motor activity is seen more often in males than females, which means girls may be diagnosed at a later age than boys, or not at all. Many will have social, emotional, or family problems also, often resulting from the numerous stresses the child experiences daily because of AD/HD.

For about 30 to 70 percent of the children, AD/HD symptoms will continue into adulthood. Symptoms like hyperactivity may decrease (sometimes replaced by restlessness), but the impulsivity and attention problems will persist. Although AD/HD is not related to IQ, it impairs to some degree a child's ability to learn, behave, and socialize, no matter how bright the child is. (Children with AD/HD fall into the same IQ ranges as the general population, including giftedness.)

Some professionals use the term ADD (attention deficit disorder). In this book, however, the term attention-deficit hyperactivity disorder (AD/HD) will be used to refer to this group of children. In the past decade, the terms ADD and AD/HD have been used synonymously in the media, publications, and in public policy even though AD/HD is technically the correct term.

## Characteristics of AD/HD

The most recent edition of *Diagnostic and Statistical Manual of Mental Disorder* (DSM-IV-TR), 2000, provides criteria for diagnosing AD/HD. It specifically defines three types of AD/HD:

- AD/HD, predominantly inattentive type
- AD/HD, predominantly hyperactive-impulsive type
- AD/HD, combined type

Children who have AD/HD, predominantly inattentive type, find it difficult to pay attention to details, follow instructions, or follow conversations. The child has difficulty with organizing and finishing tasks and is forgetful in everyday activities, is easily distracted by extraneous stimuli, and often does not seem to listen when spoken to directly. Often these children will answer a question with an "I don't know" because they may not really know—their inability to pay attention gets in their way.

Children who have AD/HD, predominantly hyperactive-impulsive type, often fidget or squirm when seated, have difficulty waiting their turn, and are often on the go or act as if they are driven by a motor. They often run about or climb excessively in situations where it is not appropriate, often talk excessively, and have difficulty engaging in quiet leisurely activities. They often act without thinking, which can lead them to engage in risky behaviors.

Children who are diagnosed with AD/HD, combined type, present symptoms of the two types listed above. Children have symptoms of both inattention and hyperactivity-impulsivity. (It is important to note that many "useless movements" that appear somewhat constant—playing with earrings, tossing things in the air and then catching them, or leg shaking while seated—are subtle, less pronounced forms of hyperactivity.)

## Prevalence

Approximately 10 million people, including adults, have AD/HD in the United States. Studies indicate that between 3 and 9 percent of school-age children are affected. Other studies have shown that the incidence of AD/HD may be as high as 20 percent. One study estimates that the incidence of AD/HD among children who were adopted may be as high as 25 or even 40 percent.

AD/HD is a disorder that affects children of all races and ethnic groups. Although media reports and publications have often stated that AD/HD appears to be limited to the United States, studies have shown that in Japan 7.7 percent of school-age children have AD/HD; Germany 8.7 percent; and China, where incidence is even higher, 8.9 percent. Other countries that have studied this population are showing similar results. The diagnosis in boys far outnumbers the diagnosis in girls, most likely because boys are more apt to exhibit a higher level of motor activity or aggressive behavior, or both, than girls and thus are more likely to be seen by a professional when parents become concerned.

## Causes of AD/HD

AD/HD is thought to be generated by a chemical imbalance in the brain that is either inherited or due to head injury caused by trauma, prenatal or perinatal insult, or exposure to toxic agents. Technology advances enabling study of brain structure and functioning show that some adults with AD/HD have reduced metabolic activity in those areas of the brain that control movement, emotion, and attention. Many questions remain regarding the cause of AD/HD, but one thing we do know is that AD/HD runs in families.

## Diagnosis and Treatment

If you suspect that your child has AD/HD, the evaluation should start with a consultation with your child's physician, who then sets up a plan for an assessment. Some pediatricians may do the assessment themselves, but often they refer the family to an appropriate mental health specialist (table 1.1) they know and trust.

## Table 1.1. Specialists' Qualifications and Services

| Specialty | Can Diagnose AD/HD | Can Prescribe Medication if Needed | Can Provide Counseling or Training |
|---|---|---|---|
| Psychiatrists | Yes | Yes | Yes |
| Psychologists | Yes | No | Yes |
| Pediatricians or family physicians | Yes | Yes | No |
| Neurologists | Yes | Yes | No |
| Clinical social workers | Yes | No | Yes |

*Source*: National Institute of Mental Health (NIMH).

Knowing the differences in qualifications and services can help you choose someone who can best meet your child's needs. Several types of specialists are qualified to diagnose and treat AD/HD:

- **Child psychiatrists** are doctors who specialize in diagnosing and treating childhood mental and behavioral disorders. A psychiatrist can provide therapy and prescribe any needed medications.
- **Child psychologists** are also qualified to diagnose and treat AD/HD. They can provide therapy for the child and help the family develop ways to deal with the disorder. But psychologists are not medical doctors and must rely on the child's physician to do medical exams and prescribe medication.
- **Neurologists,** doctors who work with disorders of the brain and nervous system, can also diagnose AD/HD and prescribe medication. But unlike psychiatrists and psychologists, neurologists usually do not provide therapy for the emotional aspects of the disorder.

To assess whether a child has AD/HD, specialists consider several critical questions: Are these behaviors excessive, long term, and pervasive? That is, do they occur more often than in other children the same age? Are they a continual problem, not just a response to a temporary situation? Do the behaviors occur in several settings or only in one specific place, like the playground or in the schoolroom? The child's pattern of behavior is compared with a set of criteria and characteristics of the disorder as listed in the DSM-IV-TR. (Some children may display eight or more symptoms, others may exhibit less.)

The evaluation process for making the diagnosis usually includes obtaining a thorough medical and social history through interviews with the parents, the child, and the child's teacher; a complete pediatric medical examination; observation of the child by the evaluators; behavioral assessments, which are questionnaires completed by the parents, teachers, and often the child (if over age thirteen); and educational and psychological testing (the latter when academic performance suggests the possibility of a learning or developmental disability).

Rarely is just one professional involved in the management of a child's AD/HD. Successful treatment of the disorder depends on continual input from parents, teachers, physicians, other professionals, and sometimes the child if old enough and may include a relevant educational plan, the use of medication, behavioral management techniques, self-skills training, and counseling and support for the parents and child.

## Co-morbid Conditions

(*Source*: National Institute of Mental Health.)

It has been said that rarely does AD/HD travel alone, meaning that most children (and adults) with AD/HD will have a co-existing, or co-morbid condition—and sometimes more than one condition. The following are some conditions that have been specifically associated with AD/HD in children, but others do exist:

**Anxiety and depression**. Some children with AD/HD often have co-occurring anxiety or depression. If the anxiety or depression is recognized and treated, the child will be better able to handle the problems that accompany AD/HD. Conversely, effective treatment of AD/HD can have a positive impact on anxiety as the child is better able to master academic tasks.

**Oppositional defiant disorder**. As many as one-third to one-half of all children with AD/HD—mostly boys—have another condition, known as oppositional defiant disorder (ODD). These children are often defiant, stubborn, non-compliant, have outbursts of temper, or become belligerent. They argue with adults and refuse to obey.

**Conduct disorder.** About 20 to 40 percent of AD/HD children may eventually develop conduct disorder (CD), a more serious pattern of antisocial behavior. These children frequently lie or steal, fight with or bully others, and are at a real risk of getting into trouble at school or with the police. They violate the basic rights of other people, are aggressive toward people and/or animals, destroy property, break into people's homes, commit thefts, carry or use weapons, or engage in vandalism. These children or teens are at greater risk for substance use experimentation, and later dependence and abuse. They need immediate help.

**Learning disabilities.** Many children with AD/HD also have a specific learning disability (LD). In preschool years, these disabilities include difficulty in understanding certain sounds or words and/or difficulty in expressing oneself in words. In school-age children, reading or spelling disabilities, writing disorders, and math disorders may appear.

## "National Co-morbidity Survey"

In May 2004, at the ADDA conference held in St. Louis, Thomas E. Brown, PhD, presented information from the "National Co-morbidity Survey." The results of this study were obtained by face-to-face interviews with 9,282 families. Dr. Brown's comments and statistics are extremely informative as they relate to AD/HD:

- **A mood disorder** afflicted 45.4 percent.
- **An anxiety disorder** afflicted 59 percent.
- **An impulse disorder** afflicted 69.8 percent.
- **One or more psychiatric disorders** afflicted 88.6 percent.

This information is offered not to frighten you but to make you aware of possible co-existing conditions that your child may be experiencing, or may experience as he or she matures. To treat just the symptoms of AD/HD and not treat the symptoms of depression, for example, or any other co-existing disorder, would be a great disservice to your child. I believe, based on personal experience, it is far better to be forewarned of possible co-existing conditions than to struggle for years wondering why the medication your child is taking for AD/HD is not working. For this reason, your child must be accurately diagnosed.

## Medication

Many parents find the thought of medicating their child for attention or hyperactivity problems frightening. "When the pediatrician, pediatric neurologist, and the psychologist all agreed that Andrea should be placed on medication, my first reaction was to fight the decision," explains Chuck, the father of a five-year-old. "I was willing to try almost anything, but medicating my daughter was not something I wanted to do." The pediatrician gave Chuck and his wife, Sharon, information on the most commonly used stimulant medications and suggested that Andrea be placed on Ritalin. (Ritalin is often the first choice of many physicians.) Chuck and Sharon decided they wanted to learn more about the medication first, so after reading some books and discussing the medication with their local pharmacist, Andrea's parents decided to try Ritalin.

Within a few days they noticed a remarkable improvement in Andrea's behavior. Chuck says, "Her temper tantrums were shorter and fewer than before the medication. She was following directions for the first time, not arguing with us over every little thing, and able to sit through meals. We were astonished."

Cathy, of Los Gatos, California, had a similar experience. "I tried to hold off using [medications] for AD/HD," she recalls. "I really thought that if I just had more patience and I accepted my daughter as she was—a bundle of impulsive energy—that everything would be all right. I watched her day after day in preschool (she was four) pushing kids off swings, throwing sand, knocking over children's block structures, spitting water, etc.

"I realized that a large group setting, with lots of children and choices of activities and little structure was not the best setting for her," Cathy adds. "I hired a babysitter to stay at home with her and there was an immediate change. Even though she was still impulsive and very active, she was not as anxious at home and we could monitor the stimulation. When she was about to start kindergarten I was scared to death that she would repeat the behaviors, as it was also a large group setting with lots of choices. It was a week before kindergarten that I told the pediatrician that I wanted to start her on medication. What a miracle! She got the praise and encouragement she needed; she was able to cultivate friend-ships and concentrate on lessons."

As one parent explained it, "Once my son began taking medication, his quality of life improved greatly. Before medication, all he ever heard was, 'No, no, how many times do I have to tell you no? Why can't you ever listen to me? Why can't you learn not to touch things that don't belong to you? Why can't you sit still in school? Why can't you keep your hands to yourself?' Everything we said to him was negative. With med-ication all of that changed. Suddenly, we found we were giving him a lot of positive feedback. His schoolwork improved and he actually made some friends. Most important, as a family we were all much happier."

Many parents hesitate when drug intervention is recommended. Fathers are often more reluctant than mothers, possibly because they may spend less time with their child on a day-to-day basis. By the time par-ents approach professionals about their child's behavior, mothers are often at the end of their rope and willing to try anything legitimate that sounds promising. Many parents I interviewed, who were initially hesi-tant to try medication, said their child's physician suggested a trial period. "Our doctor told us to try Ritalin (a psychostimulant medica-tion) for two weeks," explained Julie from Billings, Montana, "and if we didn't like what we saw, then we could stop the medication. Our daugh-ter responded favorably to the medication and all of our lives are so much better now." ("However, a successful trial period does not mean that the child has AD/HD—'normal' children respond favorably also," cautions Bruce A. Pasch, MD, FAAP, director of the Children's Center for Learning and Development.)

Stimulant medication is not, however, a miracle drug; medication does not cure AD/HD. Instead, it helps control the symptoms of AD/HD. An important aspect of using medication, one that parents must remem-ber, is that many of the symptoms are still evident even when a child uses medication. Stimulant medication helps *improve* alertness, concentra-tion, and attention span; *reduce* impulsive and disruptive behavior; and *decrease* noncompliant behavior, but the symptoms continue. All chil-dren with AD/HD benefit from medication, but some children cannot tolerate these types of medications because the side effects outweigh the benefits at the doses needed. Don't despair, as other medications or com-binations of medications can be used.

Not all children need to take medication. But for those children who do, not all will benefit from the same medication or the same dosage. All who are involved in the care of the child must carefully monitor the child until the proper dosage is attained and the desired effects achieved. The continual, successful use of medication relies on parents', teachers', and physicians' constant observation of the child because dosages sometimes need to be increased or medications changed as the child grows and develops. Please remember that medication alone is not the only answer for the child with AD/HD. When recommended, it should be used, but only as a part of a complete treatment program aimed at supporting the child psychologically, medically, educationally, and behaviorally.

For an excellent discussion on medication therapy, please read chapter 9, written by Louis B. Cady, MD, a psychiatrist in Evansville, Indiana, who is extremely knowledgeable on the medications used to treat AD/HD symptoms as well as the medications that a child may need to treat a co-existing, or co-morbid condition accompanying a diagnosis of AD/HD.

## Acceptance Can Be Tough

Whether you gave birth to or adopted your child, learning that something is wrong with him or her is tough. Most parents rarely consider the possibility that the healthy infant they brought into their lives may someday have special needs. When your child becomes a child with extra needs, you feel a loss. You have lost your dream child. For those who adopted an infant because of infertility, the loss may be even greater because you have already suffered the loss of a child dreamed of but who could never be.

Most parents of children with AD/HD (or any other medical condition) eventually reach acceptance and learn to cope and live with their child. Some parents will attain acceptance much faster and easier than others. This is normal because we all react differently to loss.

However, the sooner parents reach acceptance and gain an understanding of AD/HD, the sooner they can begin working for their child. Seek to learn more about AD/HD from books, videos, newsletters, trustworthy Internet sites devoted to AD/HD, parent support groups, and professionals. You can appropriately advocate for your child only when armed with a strong knowledge of the subject.

"AD/HD is frustrating and it can drive you crazy at times," acknowledges Mary Squire, PhD, the mother of two children with AD/HD, "but in the grand scope of things there are disabilities that are much worse [and more devastating]." However, if you find you are having difficulty coping, please speak with your physician.

## Where to Find More Information on AD/HD

Several national organizations offer free information for parents on an array of disorders, including AD/HD, anxiety, bipolar disorder, conduct disorders, depression, and ODD. A few are listed here, but many others are listed in the appendix. Visit their websites or contact organizations directly.

Center for the Advancement of Children's Mental Health
Division of Child and Adolescent Psychiatry
Columbia University
1051 Riverside Drive
New York, NY 10032.
212-543-5334
www.kidsmentalhealth.org

Children and Adults with Attention-Deficit/Hyperactivity Disorder
    (CHADD)
8181 Professional Place
Suite 201
Landover, MD 20785
800-233-4050
301-306-7070
www.chadd.org

National Alliance on Mental Illness (NAMI)
Colonial Place Three
2107 Wilson Blvd.
Suite 300
Arlington, VA 22201
800-950-6264
703-524-7600
www.nami.org

National Dissemination Center for Children with Disabilities
  (NICHCY)
P.O. Box 1492
Washington, DC 20013
800-695-0285
www.nichcy.org

National Institute of Mental Health (NIMH)
Office of Communications
6001 Executive Boulevard, Room 8184
MSC 9663
Bethesda, MD 20892
866-615-6464
301-443-4513
www.nimh.nih.gov

National Mental Health Information Center
P.O. Box 42557
Washington, DC 20015
800-789-2647
866-889-2647
www.mentalhealth.org

## How This Book Will Help You

Even with the help of the many professionals (pediatricians, psychologists, child psychiatrists, social workers, teachers, therapists, etc.) involved in the management of children with AD/HD, many parents are still unable to find answers to the many questions they have about parenting the child with AD/HD. What you are holding in your hands is a compendium of successful tips and suggestions from over two hundred parents of children with AD/HD; parents willing to share what worked for them. This book is for parents whose children have already been diagnosed with AD/HD, which is why you will not find entire chapters devoted to evaluations and diagnosis of AD/HD. These topics are covered extensively in other excellent books, most of which you will find in the bibliography.

**2**

# The Symptoms That Characterize Your Child

P ARENTS MUST become familiar with the characteristics of AD/HD, specifically the particular symptoms their child exhibits, to help their child along the challenging path that lies ahead.

Although there have been many theories on the causes of AD/HD over the years, and controversies over special diets and the use of medication, professionals do agree on one thing: no two children with this disorder display the same combination of symptoms. One child may display eight or nine symptoms of AD/HD, whereas another may exhibit many more symptoms than those required to diagnose AD/HD. Each child with AD/HD displays a different pattern—symptoms that may change in different situations or even change from one moment to the next. Some children, for example, may do quite well in school while others may display behavior or learning problems in the classroom. If you have ever attended a support group meeting for parents of children with AD/HD you know exactly what I mean. Every parent present describes a child with a different combination of symptoms.

As a parent of a child with AD/HD, it is your responsibility to identify (with the help of other professionals such as teachers, physicians, psychologists, etc.) the symptoms that characterize your child and determine the best way to approach those problems. Only with the knowledge of the problem areas can you help your child effectively; knowing and understanding these characteristics provides a framework for expectations, management, and foresight.

## Primary Symptoms of AD/HD: Inattention and Hyperactivity-Impulsivity

Typically, the child who displays hyperactivity-impulsivity is the child who experiences behavioral problems at home and in school. Some parents of hyperactive children say, with all seriousness, that their children never crawled. One mom recalls, "He just stood up and walked one day and by the next was running through the house, going through drawers, and taking apart the stereo system. As a toddler and a preschooler he was like a tornado releasing his fury in his small world. Actually, he's not much better now at age seven, even when medicated. He has learned to control a few symptoms in some circumstances, but we face new challenges at each age."

Children who display the symptom of hyperactivity are often risk takers. Nothing seems to frighten them. No cupboard or bookcase is too high to climb. No situation is too dangerous. You can't tell them that something is hot; they must experience it for themselves. Even after a serious burn, they'll often return to the burner on the stove because of their impulsivity. They commonly have difficulty controlling their behavior and examining the consequences of that behavior. Therefore they end up in the emergency room for stitches, burns, or broken bones more frequently than the average child.

"No," "Stop," and "Don't touch" appear to mean nothing to some children with AD/HD (due to their poor self-monitoring skills). Their intense curiosity compels them to explore everything, even though that curiosity (which is a wonderful trait when channeled properly) sometimes invites trouble. One father reported telling his son not to touch the computer many times a day. "Every time I turned around he was playing on the computer, opening and closing files, moving from one program to another haphazardly. One day he erased everything. He immediately denied that he was responsible for the lost files." It is common for children with AD/HD to not accept responsibility for their own actions.

Children with AD/HD are sometimes overbearing with peers. They can't keep their hands to themselves and tend to poke, grab, and touch other children. This aggressive behavior may result in physical fights on the playground with classmates, neighborhood children, and siblings. When asked who caused the fight, the child may place the blame squarely on the shoulders of the other person. He seldom sees any relationship between cause and effect, whether he's burnt himself on the stove, deleted a computer file, or caused a fight on the playground.

Some children with AD/HD create other problems within the home setting. Some have no respect for closed doors and are forever walking in on a parent or sibling who's using the bathroom. Oftentimes this is not done intentionally. The child simply does not stop to think before he pushes open that door, so locking doors is usually a necessity. But don't be surprised if your child knocks on the door repeatedly demanding entrance, especially if he has a low frustration tolerance. (My son once became so frustrated that he couldn't get into the bathroom because I was in the shower that he took a metal toy and began hitting the wooden door. The damage was so extensive that the door had to be removed, sanded, and refinished.) Other children will listen in on telephone conversations, ask inappropriate questions at embarrassing times, take items from siblings and forget to return them, and badger you for explanations when you've said no and then won't accept the explanation you've given.

In the classroom, children who have AD/HD with hyperactivity may be noisy and disruptive. Or they may make numerous trips to the pencil sharpener or restroom. They may fidget, squirm, tap their feet or fingers, or swing their legs. (Hyperactivity can also be displayed as just excessive fidgeting. "This is the hyperactivity most underdiagnosed: hyperactivity manifested as activity without purpose," says Bruce A. Pasch, MD, FAAP, director of the Children's Center for Learning and Development.)

Interestingly, children with hyperactivity react to negative feedback in the opposite way most children do (negative feedback becomes a positive reinforcement). A child without AD/HD may quiver when you raise your voice or stop the offending behavior immediately at the threat of physical punishment. But threats of physical punishment may mean nothing to the hyperactive child. And resorting to punishments such as putting soap or hot sauce in a child's mouth will *not* teach compliance. Raise your voice at your hyperactive child, and he may scream back at you. Spank a hyperactive child for misbehavior, and his misbehavior may escalate rapidly, sometimes reaching violent levels (aggressiveness kicks in). Or he may just turn around and continue the activity you have just forbidden. (If you had his attention when you told him to stop, this is not AD/HD but plain old-fashioned defiance.)

Parents and teachers are usually frustrated by an overactive child on a day-to-day basis, but consider how wonderful it is to have an over-abundance of energy. Think of what a child could do with all of that energy if the child is taught to channel it properly while maturing.

Many children with AD/HD have great difficulty paying attention. This means that they have difficulty filtering out unimportant stimuli. In the classroom they may hear not only the teacher talking but also the truck driving by, the child in the seat behind flipping pages in a textbook, and the church bell ringing halfway down the block. They may also notice the flock of birds flying past the window and the squirrel running up the tree. Children with AD/HD who are easily distracted have many stimuli competing for their attention and they are unable to filter out and pay attention to what they should be attending to in school, at home, or anywhere else they may be. Although hyperactivity is annoying and frustrating, the inability to pay attention can be far worse. In fact, children who are severely distracted and do not display hyperactivity often go undetected for years. Distractible children frequently experience school failures and may be labeled lazy or space heads. They suffer in silence and are not identified easily because, unlike overly active children, their behavior does not disturb others. Children with AD/HD may be predominantly hyperactive-impulsive, predominantly inattentive, or they may be diagnosed with AD/HD, combined type—the symptoms of the other two types equally prevail in the child. Most children are diagnosed with the combined type of AD/HD.

Inattentive children are usually unable to stay focused on one activity for any length of time, unless it is something she chooses to do. One may observe this in a preschooler or a lower school–age child, for instance, who becomes bored in a room full of toys. A complaint commonly heard by parents is, "I'm bored. There's nothing to do." The parent looks around at all the toys and wonders how the child could possibly be bored. But bored she is! Not one of those toys is able to hold her attention for more than a few minutes and she therefore becomes bored.

Do you find that you have to tell your child two or three times or more to complete a chore? Does he need to have directions repeated several times? Does he start projects but fail to complete them before moving on to another activity? Does he have difficulty keeping track of his possessions? Does he have difficulty paying attention in school? Does he have problems taking messages, keeping the facts in order? Is he frequently late for appointments or never shows up? Does he have difficulty concentrating or paying attention except when he's doing something he particularly enjoys? When you are speaking with him, does he often have a blank look on his face as if he hasn't heard a word you've said? You're witnessing the inability to pay attention.

## Social Difficulties

Many children with AD/HD tend to act younger than their chronological age. They usually are immature and, as a result, tend to play better with younger children, often because they cannot successfully do what their peers do. An eight- or nine-year-old child who has AD/HD and co-morbid (co-existing) fine-motor-skill challenges may not be able to play certain sports but can run, jump, and climb (gross motor skills) successfully— typical play activities for younger children. Therefore, the eight-year-old may feel more comfortable with a five- or six-year-old than a child his own age. Sometimes the child with AD/HD will even prefer toys made for younger children. Rarely does he understand why he fits in better with younger children, but his perceived immature behavior often separates him from others his own age. As one mother stated, "He's like a square peg trying to fit into a circle [of peers]. He can't fit in no matter how hard he tries." Yet the immature child often successfully maintains friendships with younger children.

Some children with AD/HD are bossy (telling others how to play the game, and insisting it be done their way), pesty, and annoying (teasing and harassing). They may throw temper tantrums when they don't get their way and be prone to fighting, arguing, lying, and cheating. They may attract and make friends but are usually unable to keep them. Unlike other children in their age group, children with AD/HD often have difficulty picking up on social cues, such as facial and verbal expressions or body language. The child is often unaware of the negative messages being sent from peers and seems surprised to learn that others are upset with them. (Children with social skill deficits, without AD/HD, may also do these same things.)

A child with AD/HD may grab toys away from others, not wait his turn in games, or not follow the rules—all irritating behaviors to playmates. Yet this same child may also have wonderful creative-play ideas and find that he has many friends who are willing to tolerate his bossiness because he is able to organize fun activities (the ability to organize and take the lead are valued skills). Another child with AD/HD may consistently interrupt conversations (because he's afraid he might forget what he wants to say) or not pay attention to what others are saying. While friends sit around talking and laughing, he may be staring out into space, inattentive to those around him. So while one child with AD/HD might attempt to play with other children and fail miserably, another may be totally oblivious to those around him, thus also failing to make and sustain friendships. Still others, because of their gregarious nature, may have no social difficulties. In fact, they might be seen as some of the more popular students in school.

Some children are great negotiators. If you offer them fifteen extra minutes of play time, they'll negotiate for more. Before you know it, your offer of fifteen minutes has been upped to thirty minutes. Other children with AD/HD are also extremely persistent. If they enjoy a particular activity, or want to learn a specific challenging concept, or want to tackle a difficult game, they'll stick to it until they've conquered it. They don't give up easily. In the same light, if they desire something, they are not hesitant to go after it. Many children with AD/HD have sharp observation skills and notice things that others frequently fail to notice. This is a wonderful trait, until you witness your child darting across the street to take a closer look at a bird's nest in the peak of a neighbor's roof. Although these are all marvelous attributes for adults, parents often think these characteristics are overbearing when displayed by their children.

Many children have little appreciation of how their negative behavior leads to adverse consequences. They have no idea what they have done wrong or why friends have ostracized them. They do not feel personally attached to an incident or consider themselves responsible for causing the problem, so they blame others for being angry with them and feel that they are being treated unfairly. However, children with attention deficits often are able to feel genuine remorse for their actions in retrospect. This is a key point because it distinguishes AD/HD from conduct disorder. This creates confusion in the minds of those closest to them. "If he understands now what he did wrong, why didn't he recognize it at the time?"

is a question that often stumps parents and teachers. The answer: although the child now recognizes the consequences of earlier behavior, it does not necessarily mean he can prevent it from happening again in the future. Remember that children with AD/HD are frequently impulsive, insatiable, and often lack the ability to control themselves in many situations.

## Emotional Difficulties

AD/HD is a physiological, not a psychological, condition. If emotional difficulties (depression, anger, anxiety) are evident, they are the result of AD/HD or co-morbid, not the cause. This is extremely important for parents, teachers, and other caregivers to understand. Children who exhibit signs of emotional difficulties often have low frustration levels, explosive tempers, and difficulty accepting no for an answer. They experience frequent and rapid mood swings, are especially self-centered and have little or no regard for the feelings of others, and sometimes have an I-don't-care attitude.

One mother sums it up quite well: "Whenever my son is punished by losing a privilege or being sent to time-out, he screams out, 'I don't care what I lose. I hate you and I think you are stupid.' Usually he apologizes later, so I know he has given thought to what he said to me. When he loses control like this because he doesn't get his own way, he's very angry and I feel very frightened for him. I wonder if he'll ever be able to control himself. I wonder if he really doesn't care. I wonder if I am the cause of the behavior and if he really hates me." Children with AD/HD usually forgive and forget quickly, but they are sometimes moody and unpredictable. Employ a trained professional to help your child with anger control if it becomes a problem.

Children with AD/HD are unusually hard to please. For instance, one mother bought her son a video game for which he had been begging for months and remembers, "He played the game for about twenty-five minutes and then came to me looking for something to do." They can also be extremely negative and oppositional. "My daughter complains about everything. Nothing is ever good enough," says Kelly from Austin, Texas. Children with AD/HD may also be irresponsible, negligent, and argumentative as is evident in the lighthearted approach they take to completing homework, for instance. Point out an error to them and you're apt to hear, "Who cares?" or "My teacher won't care if one problem is wrong."

Clearly, poor self-esteem is a common emotional difficulty many children with AD/HD suffer from and one area that parents need to help their children with. Poor self-esteem is the result of many things these children experience, such as frustration with getting school assignments completed and handed in on time, distress in not being able to follow directions, difficulties in organizing themselves, stress from trying to control impulsive behavior, and the constant struggle to stay on task. Often they feel they are being treated unfairly compared with non-AD/HD siblings or friends. As a result, their self-esteem plunges even lower. They hear the frustration in their parents' voices. They regard themselves as bad, or troublemakers, and often see themselves as stupid (sometimes because a parent implies or tells them they are) and different from other children. These feelings usually begin to develop about the time they enter lower school and often continue to get worse as they age, resulting in troublesome behaviors, such as getting in trouble with the police as teens. Some children are bombarded with "no" and "can't you behave?" from parents and caretakers. As a result of the constant criticism, some children may develop a cavalier attitude. Once a child reaches the point of not caring, he has lost a relevant incentive for adhering to society's rules.

Poor self-esteem can exhibit itself in the form of depression, but the depression is secondary to chronic failure. The child may be gloomy, saddened, and detached. He may cry easily or appear angry at himself or the world in general. Some children may act out their depression in destructive ways, such as trying to hurt themselves or someone they love.

The common symptoms of depression are the following:

- I-don't-care attitude (about things that used to matter)
- Irritability, anxiety
- Loss of interest
- Loss of zest (fatigue and diminished energy for normal activities)
- Diminished appetite or increase in food intake
- Feelings of sadness, hopelessness, and despair
- Preoccupation with death, suicide, or running away
- Disturbed sleep
- Hopelessness and despair
- Inability to concentrate or make decisions

If your child (or you) experiences these symptoms, please seek professional help.

One excellent defense mechanism against depression, and a way to release anger, is exercise. Studies prove the benefits of exercise in both children and adults. Hyperactive children and children with AD/HD who do not display hyperactivity can profit from regularly scheduled exercise programs. Exercise promotes relaxation and helps build stamina and confidence. It is pleasurable, fun, and distracting. It can be a wonderful family activity, or your child can exercise alone with proper guidance. Specifically, karate has been shown to help improve self-discipline. If your child has coordination problems, you may want to avoid team sports in which his peers will judge his performance.

## Physical Difficulties

Children with hyperactivity are in constant motion, whether they're bouncing off the walls, talking nonstop, wandering aimlessly, or moving from one activity to another. You may observe them picking their nails, cuticles, noses, or scabs; pulling on their hair (one boy I know has a bald spot from pulling his hair out one strand at a time); pulling up their socks, or tugging on an earring. Attempts to break the child of such idiosyncrasies are futile, and another peculiar, distressing trait often replaces the previous one.

Sleeping difficulties are apparent in many children with AD/HD who are also hyperactive. Many times, they require less sleep than the average child, so don't expect your child to take a nap or fall asleep peacefully at 8:00 p.m. like your friends' children do. Many children don't fall asleep until 10 or 11:00 p.m. and are awake by 5:00 or 6:00 a.m., but they usually sleep through the night, often quite soundly. Others may fall asleep without much of a problem, but they sleep lightly and often awake during the night. One mom said her child used to fall asleep every night by 9:00 p.m. but would wake around 1:00 a.m. and not fall back to sleep until 4:00 a.m. Because she couldn't trust her child when left up alone, she would stay awake to make sure he didn't get into trouble. Whether your child goes to bed at 10:00 p.m. and sleeps until 6:00 a.m. or is awake much of the night, sleep deprivation is a common complaint among parents, especially mothers who are usually with their children the majority of the time.

Children with AD/HD may have difficulties with either fine motor skills (small-muscle coordination) or gross motor skills (large-muscle coordination). Children with poor fine motor skills may have problems with writing, drawing, and coloring, for instance. It is not unusual for some fourth graders to be still drawing stick people, much like the ones four-year-olds draw. Their coloring may still be uneven and they can rarely stay within the illustration's lines. Their ability to print and write may be limited. They have difficulty forming letters and may actually form letters differently than the way they were taught. They may always have poor penmanship, but their handwriting often improves with age as small muscles develop. Many parents report that their child's handwriting actually improves when they begin taking medication for AD/HD.

Children who face challenges with co-morbid gross-motor-skill problems may have difficulty riding a bicycle, running, skipping, and hopping on one foot. They appear clumsy and uncoordinated and often have difficulty with team sports that require an ability to hit or catch a ball. Children who experience difficulty playing certain team sports like football and baseball usually do much better in sports like golf, swimming, bowling, horseback riding, fishing, diving, and karate. AD/HD motor difficulties that are not caused by a co-existing condition are due to poor self-monitoring skills and, consequently, improve with medicine. It is important to note, however, that such difficulties can occur without AD/HD.

Some children with AD/HD have a high tolerance for pain. As previously mentioned, coupled with their impulsive behavior, this means they are more likely to have accidents that require trips to the emergency room. Your responsibility as a parent is to literally keep your child alive. Supervise your child constantly. Some children will climb bookshelves in a matter of seconds if something they want is on the top shelf. If the bookcase is not bolted to the wall, the unit will come tumbling down. Their curiosity and determination (another great trait to have when channeled properly) are so intense that if they want to see how power tools work, for example, they'll test them without your help. My son once turned on a power grinder, but when he turned it off he stuck his wrist right in the grinder. Because he did not find it particularly painful, he bandaged it himself. When it was discovered, he was taken to the emergency room, where he received fifteen stitches. They can scale a tall tree in seconds and fall to the ground in even less time. Pain is felt for only a few seconds (because of their attention span), so they don't learn from past mistakes. They will climb that bookshelf, test that power tool, and scale that tree again, no matter how serious their injuries were.

Toilet training is often difficult. It is not uncommon for children with AD/HD, especially boys, to still be in diapers during the day at age four (sometimes they just don't want to take the time to use the bathroom and interrupt their play). Often boys, and sometimes girls, will still experience occasional nighttime wetting when they reach lower school age or still be in diapers every night, having never experienced a dry night. Bedtime wetters are often sound sleepers. If their nervous systems are not fully developed, as is often the case, they should not be punished for what they cannot control. Sometimes patience, understanding, and time is all that is needed. If bedwetting is still a problem after age seven, speak with your pediatrician as there are interventions that do work, including waking the child during the night until he learns to wake himself.

Last, children with AD/HD appear to have a higher number of physical ailments than other children, such as ear infections; allergies; speech, hearing, and vision problems; and stomachaches and headaches. Headaches and stomachaches may be caused by medication or result from anxiety. Your child may develop a stomachache or headache when facing a test or just from the fear of having to confront a new situation.

## Academic Difficulties

Without a doubt, most children with AD/HD have academic difficulties. Children with hyperactivity may not be able to sit still in school. They may appear restless, fidgeting and squirming in their seats, or they may not be able to stay seated more than a few minutes. They may be disruptive in class or even assume the role of the class clown. Their ability to pay attention is often limited even when medicated.

Other children, those without hyperactivity, may be compliant. So compliant, in fact, that they never get into trouble for talking or misbehaving in class. They sit still, but are often found staring out the window or into space. As a result of their inability to concentrate and sustain attention, they also experience academic failure. They may be unable to focus and listen to the teacher when directions are given for assignments and may do the assignment inaccurately or not at all. Often, they start an assignment but never complete it. Timed tests are often impossible for some children because they work much slower than the average child. It takes them longer to get started on a project, to process the information, to organize needed materials, and complete assignments. They need more time simply because they are not able to attend to the task in the same manner as the student who does not have AD/HD. Perhaps the most frustrating aspect of inattentiveness is that the student may be able to attend successfully one day, but not the next. A teacher who does not fully understand the inconsistencies of AD/HD may see the student as lazy or unwilling to do the work.

One child told me, "As class began, I would tell myself over and over, You must pay attention. You must pay attention. Before I knew it, the class was over and I hadn't heard a word the teacher said." This eighth-grader was not considered a problem in school, but she had the same difficulties in school as the hyperactive child as far as learning was concerned. Her problem was not hyperactivity in the classroom but daydreaming. She simply was not able to pay attention.

Consequently, the child without hyperactivity often slips through the cracks. She is not disruptive in class, or overly active, so her attention problems are not easily identified by her teachers. Usually, by sixth, seventh, or eighth grade (or even later), her problems will catch up with her (or her AD/HD problems may never be identified). After years of frustration and disappointments, children without hyperactivity may come to the attention of teachers only because of behavior changes. They may become withdrawn and depressed. The length of time before the AD/HD is detected may also depend in part on intelligence level. Those children who have high IQs are usually working at grade level or above. Deficits are often masked. Children with average or below-average intelligence are at a greater disadvantage. A percentage of children with AD/HD will also have other learning disabilities. The actual percentage varies between 30 and 60 percent, depending on which doctor, psychologist, or psychiatrist you speak with or what study you read.

Problems may arise with class work and homework, beginning in lower school and lasting throughout the child's educational career. Children with AD/HD may be slow in completing classroom assignments because they sense a need to overmonitor as they go. Or they may do their work quickly, making numerous errors because they hurried through it to move on to something more enjoyable. Others may be impulsive and overlook details, such as addition or subtraction signs, or they may fail to stop and read the directions before beginning the assignment. Additional problems children with AD/HD may experience in school are wandering from the classroom, not focusing on a group activity, poor organizational skills, poor short-term memory, talking out of turn, and bothering classmates who are attempting to complete class work.

## Keep in Mind

AD/HD is difficult to understand, but it is important that parents keep the characteristics of AD/HD in mind when dealing with their child. While many children with AD/HD will not exhibit symptoms as severe as some of those outlined here, it is imperative that parents identify those symptoms their child displays. Parents and other caregivers simply cannot compare a child who has AD/HD with other children. It is unfair to the child with AD/IID. Parents must keep their expectations of themselves and their child realistic. Never forget that AD/HD is a developmentally disabling condition, which in many cases will last a lifetime.

**3**

# Chronological Patterns of AD/HD in Children

**W**HETHER YOU suspected your child had AD/HD from the time he was born or learned of it later, you now know that your parenting role is different from other parents'. You know, because you are reminded of it every day by your child's actions and behavior, from the time he awakes each morning until he retires for the night. Even when you are out alone, the reminders are there. You observe other families in restaurants, in places of worship, at the mall, and you note the differences.

As the popular saying goes, children do not come with instructions. However, each of us enters parenthood with preconceived ideas of how our child will behave, speak, and to an extent, dress (even when the child is not biologically related to us). But children do come with their own temperament, personality, likes and dislikes, abilities, and challenges. For many families, this is not a problem. However, for families dealing with a child who has special needs, preconceived notions are just that, and it then becomes necessary for the families to make adjustments in their lives. We must first look at our child objectively and determine his talents and abilities, his strengths and weaknesses. To do this effectively, parents must often rely on the expertise of many professionals, such as pediatricians, pediatric neurologists, psychologists, psychiatrists, teachers, social workers, and therapists. They also must open their private lives to relatives and friends because they, too, will be with the child and will provide the parents with assistance and moral support. With help, most parents eventually learn coping skills and find extra patience, new ways to discipline, and different ways to teach their child.

As your child grows and develops, you will find that each age brings different concerns and unique challenges, and what works one day or one year may not be appropriate the next. Naturally, all families must learn to adapt as parents and children grow and change, but a family with a child who has AD/HD will experience more confusion and challenges than the average family. You must learn to expect the unexpected.

Grandparents, other relatives, and friends also have preconceived ideas about your children. They may also experience a mixed bag of emotions when confronted with difficult or unusual behaviors exhibited by your child. Some may be very straightforward with you, telling you clearly what you are doing wrong. Others may offer suggestions using the backdoor approach, "If I were you . . ." And still others may just shake their heads in disapproval.

However, some relatives and friends will offer you support and help. I encourage you to accept all of the assistance you are offered because there will be many days when you will need a shoulder to lean on for moral support. Families and friends can provide a tremendous amount of support, but only if you share information with them about your child.

This is not meant to imply that all the days ahead will be dismal and bleak; they will not. You will have some wonderful times with your child. But children with AD/HD can be so unpredictable. One week they are great, the next two weeks they are awful, and then suddenly they're great kids again. The highs and lows are tough to handle; most parents feel as if they're riding an emotional roller coaster. A supportive person can help even out feelings of anger, bitterness, shame, pride, joy, and love.

With these feelings in mind, let's take a look at some extra parenting challenges you might experience at different stages of your child's development and how you might begin to cope.

## Infants

"My parents kept telling me I must be doing something wrong when Drake cried continuously," says Kathy, a twenty-eight-year-old mother of a difficult baby who rarely slept and physically resisted affection and cuddling. "She made a point of telling me that I scarcely cried when I was an infant because she met my needs. She also reminded me that all babies love to be held and cuddled, implying that I was doing something wrong."

Kathy's mother did feel her daughter was an inadequate mother. Instead of looking at the baby as a possible source of the problems Kathy was experiencing, she was quick to blame Kathy. She had her own thoughts, which she shared freely, about how babies (Drake in particular) should behave. Clearly, Drake did not fit her expectations.

## AD/HD Symptoms in Infants

A small percentage of babies display AD/HD symptoms. These infants are not easy babies to care for from day one. They often have sleeping and eating problems. They are rarely on a dependable schedule and often wake up during the night every hour or two for as long as two or three years. They often display sharp mood swings and an intense response to stimuli. Babies may spend many of their waking hours crying or fussing, and efforts to calm them are ineffective. Most babies enjoy being held and cuddled, whereas the baby with AD/HD frequently resists holding. Parents report that their babies actually turn away from them, pushing and squirming in their effort to break loose. Many resist being held, wiggling and crying frantically, even for routine bottle feeding, preferring instead to take their bottle propped or holding it themselves while in an infant seat. Once the parent puts the baby down, the crying usually stops immediately. Parents feel rejected and frustrated and report difficulty bonding with their new son or daughter during the first year or even longer.

These babies are generally very alert, active, curious, and often display remarkable strength by turning over at two or three weeks of age, for instance. Some reach milestones well before other babies. Other children do not reach milestones by the appropriate ages.

These symptoms do not necessarily mean that a baby has AD/HD. But they do identify babies who are at risk, especially when a family member has been diagnosed with AD/HD. Some children with AD/HD show signs as infants and are identified at an early age, usually by age two or three. However, some children who are diagnosed with AD/HD at a later age may not have shown any subtle signs as infants. Some parents remark that their children seemed "normal" until they began walking.

"It was like a dam had broken," said one parent, "and he was the rushing water. Nothing was safe from destruction."

Adoptive parents of difficult babies should be open to the possibility that their baby may have inherited this disorder from his or her birth family. Adoptive parents should always make an effort to obtain as much background information on their child as possible. They should not be afraid to ask if AD/HD or learning disabilities are evident in the medical history of the birth parents and their families.

## Admitting Something Is Not Right

What can you do if you are experiencing parenting difficulties? First, you have to be able to admit that your baby is not like the average baby. Once you can accept that your baby is different, and difficult not because of anything you have done or not done, you should seek the help of a health professional. Usually, this will be your pediatrician. However, if your pediatrician tells you these behaviors are normal, get a second opinion.

Supportive professionals can offer suggestions and techniques to help you manage your baby. Some hospitals have a child-evaluation program for difficult babies and can offer techniques for coping with your baby on a day-to-day basis. Call your local hospitals for information.

**Establish Routines** You can take steps immediately to begin modifying some of the difficulties you are experiencing. Start by establishing routines. Give baths at the same time each day, right after breakfast or before bedtime, for example. Feed your baby at approximately the same time each day. If you cannot hold your baby to feed her with a bottle in the normal manner, try laying her on your lap with the heels of your feet resting on a coffee table or footstool. Your knees will then be propped up so she can't roll off your lap. Then hold the bottle but not the baby, or let her hold the bottle. This will (almost) give you the desired closeness with your baby, without causing her to feel restrained.

According to Bruce Pasch, MD, FAAP, a pediatrician and the director of the Children's Center for Learning and Development in Toledo, Ohio, difficulties in breast-feeding an infant who does not like to be held are rare. Unlike the bottle-fed baby, Dr. Pasch says, breast-feeding appears to calm the infant when held in the cradle position. If your infant is under six months of age and you are experiencing difficulties with breast-feeding, he recommends talking with your pediatrician or a breast-feeding consultant or nurse educator at a local hospital. Some mothers may choose to terminate breast-feeding. Others may prefer to express the breast by using a pump and then feed the breast milk through a bottle. For infants over the age of six months, Dr. Pasch recommends placing the baby on your lap in an upright position facing you with your hand on his bottom. If this method doesn't work for your baby, your choices are the same as for the infant under six months of age.

**Avoid Overstimulation** Try not to overstimulate your baby. Although many babies love to be gently tossed around and many dads, in particular, enjoy doing so, this type of exciting play will only stimulate your baby more. Although using a rocking chair is calming for most babies, my youngest child hated the rocking motion. He cried when I rocked, yet stopped crying when I ceased rocking. He also cried because he didn't like the feeling of being restrained on my lap. As soon as he could sit up on his own, we then sat next to each other, but I usually had to be sure there was at least one inch between us so our bodies didn't actually touch. Often, we could sit like this for five minutes—not much time, but the closeness helped with bonding. Gradually, the sitting-close time did increase, but not by much. Take whatever closeness you can and feel grateful. Continue to look for other activities you can enjoy together that permit some degree of closeness—like bathing your child or brushing his hair—without stifling him.

**Keep Things Soft and Quiet** Use soft colors in the nursery rather than bright or primary colors. Keep a night-light on in the room at all times, so you never have to turn a bright light on during the night or in a room that is naturally dark during the day. This way you won't startle your baby by turning on a light.

Use smooth-textured blankets in the crib, one or two soft, cuddly stuffed animals, and only one toy (even one toy may be too much for your baby). Some infants respond to soothing music at bedtime. Try a special tape, but realize that some infants will wake when the tape player turns off, in which case you may need to use a radio. My youngest son, who rarely slept as an infant and toddler, would wake at the slightest noise. At nap time, I turned the phones off and used the answering machine. I also had a fan going in his room day and night to make white noise to block out all sounds. Eventually we had to disconnect the doorbell and leave a note on the front door with other instructions for visitors.

## Babies Who Don't Sleep at Night

When tending to a baby who frequently awakens during the night, follow the same routine. Do not turn lights on (this won't be necessary if you use a night-light), and do not pick up the baby. Your goal is to check on his safety, settle him down, and leave. Of course if the baby is wet or it's time for a feeding, care for him, but follow the same procedure night after night.

If your baby never sleeps more than an hour or so, ask your pediatrician for a mild sedative. Once the baby can sleep several hours with a sedative, you will be able to stop the medication because the infant usually will have established a routine. Some doctors recommend using Benadryl, but always check with your doctor before administering any over-the-counter medications to learn what dosage would be appropriate for your baby.

## Time Away from Baby

Whenever possible, spend time away from your baby outside your home. These babies can drain you of every ounce of energy you have. If you can afford a babysitter for a few hours a day or every other day, then hire someone. One woman hired a babysitter for two hours a day; one hour she used for running, the second hour she took an extra long bath and read. This gave her the time she needed to pull herself together. If you can't afford a babysitter, find another mother you can trade babysitting time with.

Don't forget about your husband. He, too, needs time away from the baby. Make time to go out together. If you can find a babysitter only for during the day, then meet your husband for lunch.

## Difficult Babies May Become Difficult Toddlers

Many babies who are suspected of having AD/HD may become even more troublesome as toddlers. These toddlers may exhibit distractibility, hyperactivity, or both; get into everything; exhibit a low frustration level; become accident prone; and have unusually long and intense temper tantrums. Some professionals believe that it is possible to identify 60 to 70 percent of all children with AD/HD (only if hyperactivity and impulsivity are the main traits) when they are toddlers or preschoolers.

## Toddlers and Preschoolers

Daniel was an easy baby. He ate and slept well and was a good baby overall. As an infant, he loved being held and cuddled. At fourteen months, however, Daniel became extremely active. His mother, Janet, described the next two years: "It was as if he became a different child. Suddenly he was climbing on the furniture, climbing up on the kitchen counters to reach into the cabinets, sneaking outside when I was trying to do laundry. Toys no longer interested him. He found electrical appliances to be much more entertaining. We couldn't keep him away from anything electrical, including the outlets. Attempts to child proof the house were in vain. He would literally break off the child-proof locks we had placed on drawers, cabinets, the refrigerator door, and on electrical outlets. He would throw towels in the toilet bowl, flush the toilet, and I would find him in the bathroom laughing with delight as the toilet bowl overflowed. Once, when he was supposed to be napping, I found him trying to climb out of his bedroom window.

"Three times before his second birthday, he received stitches. Once at twelve months he was trying to stand on his head while on a chair and he fell out of the chair and hit his head on the end table. The second time he ran and tried to jump onto a rocking chair. He missed and hit the arm of the chair. The third time he climbed a bookcase that was not bolted to the wall. The bookcase fell on top of him and he cut open the back of his head. At four years of age, Daniel was diagnosed with AD/HD."

### Risk Takers

Many toddlers and preschoolers with AD/HD are accident prone because they take risks that most children wouldn't. They are often destructive, often noncompliant, and forever getting into things the average child wouldn't even notice or be interested in. They are unable to see a relationship between cause and effect. When Daniel required stitches after falling off the chair, he surprised his parents by immediately returning to the same chair after coming home from the emergency room. Much to his parents' dismay, he was ready to try the same stunt again.

## Speak with Your Child's Doctor

Again, there are things you can do to reduce stress during this age period. If your child's behavior is not like that of other children of the same age (extreme temper tantrums, noncompliance, low frustration level, abnormally high energy level, etc.), talk with his physician. Obtain a second opinion if necessary. You may want to contact a local mental health center or a university, if it has a mental health center, to have his learning and behavioral problems assessed. You also can contact local hospitals to see if they have child evaluation services. Whatever you do, don't give up. If you suspect your child has AD/HD, it is important that you find appropriate services for him as soon as possible.

## Transition Times

As with a difficult infant, keep your child on a schedule so he knows what to expect daily. When you must break the routine, tell the child that day what to expect ahead of time. Give him a five- or ten-minute notice before changing clothes, leaving the house, or arriving at your destination. Remind him of what you expect his behavior to be like several times during the drive. For example, on the way to Grandma's house you might say, "Nathan, when we arrive at Grandma's, I expect you to get out of the car quietly." Once in Grandma's driveway, "Nathan, I want you to hold my hand (or I will carry you into Grandma's house), but we must do this quietly." Always tell your child what his behavior is to be like once you are inside, for example, "Nathan, give Grandma a hug and say hello. Then sit on the floor and play with your toys." In other words, don't surprise your child with breaks in routines. Always give warnings. And remember, not all children respond to changes in routines and warnings equally. Some children will always react negatively to change, which becomes an extremely difficult and embarrassing problem for parents to handle. For many, these problems do diminish over time or reduce in intensity on their own and often dissipate completely when the child begins drug therapy.

## Ways to Cope

First, understand your child's temperament. Temperament is your child's natural, innate tendency to behave in certain ways. Is he stubborn? Impulsive? Does he throw temper tantrums? Is he shy? Inattentive? Fussy? Defiant? Overactive? Now, when you witness certain frustrating behaviors remember that you cannot *change* your child's temperament, because it is inborn. You can, however, learn ways to cope with his behavior.

"When I see Michael getting upset about something and know a temper tantrum is just seconds away, I immediately distract him by offering to play a game or read to him," explains Jennifer from Sacramento, California. "Distraction is a management solution to some problems parents face with young children who have AD/HD. Bring out a toy your child enjoys. Offer to take a walk outside with him. Suggest a treasure hunt. Sing a song together."

Be consistent in your disciplining techniques; always praise your child's acceptable behavior. In fact, watch for appropriate behaviors and praise as often as possible. Try to praise your child several times a day. Set a goal for yourself and keep track of the positive remarks you make to your child until it becomes a habit.

"Too often parents get caught up in seeing only the negative," says Sue from Cincinnati, Ohio. "If you find yourself constantly saying, 'No,' 'Don't,' 'Stop,' then you're missing the positive qualities your child displays. Praise your child each time you see her doing something right."

Children in this age group are not receptive to long talks about appropriate behavior. All small children have a short attention span, but young children with AD/HD are especially unreceptive. Make explanations simple, and calmly say what you must in as few words as possible.

Child proof your house, including covering electrical outlets. Lock up cleaning products and lock other cabinets necessary to keep your child from getting into things he shouldn't. Even if your child manages to break the child-proof locks, he probably won't break them all in one day. Keep extra locks in the house, including ones for the refrigerator and toilet bowls. For climbers who enjoy getting into kitchen cabinets, reserve one cabinet at floor level just for them. Let them climb in and out of this cabinet, but be sure to keep some interesting items in there for them, whether it's toys they particularly enjoy, pots and pans, or plastic storage containers. Let them know this is their area and that they will not get into trouble when they play in that cabinet.

For a child who strays out of the house, add a lock at the top of the door that he can't reach. While his temper will soar for a few days after installation, he'll learn that he can't go outside unless you let him out. This frustration usually lasts about a week, but you will no longer have to worry about him leaving the house without your consent.

Remove glass items, priceless keepsakes, and plants from your child's reach. These items appeal to all small children, but children with AD/HD won't leave them alone until they are broken. Don't bring these items out again until you are sure they'll be safe from your child's hands, usually around age six or seven.

If your child is always getting into one particular type of item, as Daniel did with electrical appliances, find something similar for him to play with. Daniel's parents gave him an old clock, a broken radio, and an old toaster— all minus the electrical cords. Always be cautious with items that have small parts for children under the age of three. As Daniel grew older, he became greatly attracted to computers and electronic games and is now extremely proficient in both. In this case, the child's interests were carefully monitored and channeled in a direction that proved productive and acceptable.

When you ask your child a question, allow ample time for the answer. Your child may need extra time to process the information. If your child doesn't comply with the request or answer the question, rephrase it. A child with AD/HD may not understand the question or the request you have made. The best way to handle the hyperactivity level in this group is to supervise your child constantly. Most parents have no choice but to follow their child around, unless they hire a mother's helper. If you are in tune with your child, then you certainly know what attracts him, whether it's electrical appliances, the refrigerator, the stereo, toilet bowls, mom's cosmetics, the home computer, or water. To help him with trouble areas, engage your child in other activities he enjoys and keep those little hands busy. But even then, keep your child in sight because you never know how long it will be before he abandons the coloring book or the television show he's watching. *Never* just tell your child to go paint a picture or watch a video. Instead, get the paints and paper out for him and lead him to the table or turn the television on. Most children will give almost any activity a try if everything is laid out for them.

If you are going out, put your child in the bathtub while you get ready—just make sure you are in the same room together. While fixing dinner, let your child play with water in the sink, play with pots and pans on the floor away from the stove, or work on a special project (gluing pasta on construction paper) within your sight. Always check on children who should be napping. In a matter of minutes they can destroy their rooms or remove screens from bedroom windows if left awake and unattended. Most parents develop a sixth sense with their children, but parents of children with AD/HD must develop a seventh or eighth sense.

One mother, realizing that the house was awfully quiet, found her three-year-old backing her car down the driveway. The car stopped when it hit a tree. The child had always shown an interest in cars and, unbeknownst to anyone, knew exactly where mom kept the car keys. The next day, mom and dad bought their child a battery-operated car. Yes, they are expensive, but this child drove that car in the snow, rain, and sunshine for three years and now their youngest child is enjoying it. These parents accepted that their child's impulsivity would likely lead to another experiment with the family car; they concluded the play car would cost far less than repairing the family automobile.

As you know, children with AD/HD can be a handful, but they are also delightful toddlers and preschoolers. They are creative, bright, curious, and have a boundless supply of energy—qualities we admire in adults. As parents, we need to direct these qualities to generate positive experiences for our children.

## Elementary School–Age Children

Half of all children with AD/HD are diagnosed during the lower school years. Learning disabilities also become more evident in lower school. However, not all children with AD/HD will have learning disabilities. There are children with AD/HD who are gifted. Anthony, who has been on Ritalin since age four because of hyperactivity and impulsivity, began reading at age three. Now eight years old, Anthony is reading at the eighth-grade level and his comprehension is at the ninth-grade level. He began playing around with computers when he was eighteen months old. In third grade now, he excels in computer science. Everything he knows about computers he has learned on his own. He also speaks two languages. Still other children with AD/HD have average or slightly above-average IQs and do not have learning disabilities, while other children have one or more co-morbid learning disabilities.

Andrea was in third grade when her teacher approached her mother. Andrea was having difficulty paying attention in class, never completed her class work on time, and seemed unable to follow directions. The teacher also noted that Andrea seemed withdrawn and isolated and did not have friends to play with at school. Andrea's teacher suggested that she be evaluated for AD/HD. When Andrea was diagnosed with AD/HD, her mother blamed herself for not recognizing the symptoms. Andrea's older brother had been diagnosed with AD/HD when he was in kindergarten, but his symptoms were more obvious because of his hyperactivity. Andrea was fortunate in that she was identified at age nine. Many girls are not identified until they are older, usually they are quiet and shy and sometimes withdrawn.

David's grandfather had waited for the day when he could play baseball with his grandson. The problem was that every time he tried to play with David he was greatly disappointed. "David always seemed excited about playing ball, but he became bored with the game. It was also difficult for him to take turns with the other neighborhood children. He often got confused about the direction in which he was supposed to run," says his grandfather. "One time I kidded David about falling down, and he became extremely angry, verbally lashed out at me, and then lost total control of himself. I was shocked. When I finally summoned the courage to confront my daughter about David's behavior, she admitted that David had always been like that at home and recently was displaying the same types of behaviors in school."

Eventually David was diagnosed with AD/HD. Grandpa was disappointed and saddened to learn about David's disorder. David's parents, also saddened, were relieved to find there was a name for David's problems.

School-age children will continue to display many of the characteristics they exhibited as toddlers and preschoolers. Many children with AD/HD are immature for their age, often two to three years behind their peers. Children in this age group may also display poor social skills. Tasks performed in school and at home often indicate inconsistent performance.

## Establish Rules and Set Up a Reward System

As a parent, you should clearly state the household rules for your child, your expectations, and the repercussions if those rules are broken. If there are two parents in the home, both must be clear about these rules and consequences, so when your child acts inappropriately you both deliver the same results in the same manner. Be sure your child knows and understands the house rules. Discuss them with your child when he is calm and able to sit and listen. Write them down and post them where your child can easily review them.

Before discussing house rules, be sure you have made eye contact with your child. Then begin the discussion. For a child who always puts his feet up on the chair at the table you might say, "John, we need a new rule in our house. The rule is that no one may ever put their feet up on their chair at the table during meals. We hope you will abide by this rule, but if you can't keep your feet off the chair, you will be excused from the table whether your meal is finished or not. This rule has been written down on the blackboard in the kitchen and the bulletin board in your bedroom." Have your child repeat the new rule so you are sure he is listening and understands it. Always decide ahead of time which behaviors bother you the most and begin with no more than three inappropriate behaviors to work on at one time. Even three behaviors may be too much for some children. If so, reduce the number to two or even one.

Do not expect the behavior to change overnight; it may take months. Give positive feedback immediately on those days he can keep his feet off the chair. You can acknowledge this accomplishment by verbal praise, a hug, a kiss, extra television time, or another appropriate activity.

The reward system is another approach that works well. For it to work successfully, however, parents must make a commitment to use it. Here's how this system works: Let's say that each day your child comes home from school he drops his belongings on the floor right at the door. You become more frustrated every day as you remind your child to pick up his backpack, hang up his coat, and put his boots in the utility room. Following the previous suggestions, you would sit down with the child and establish the new rule. Only this time, you and the child will choose the reward he will receive after remembering to put away his things for three days (the time period may be extended to five days or more for older children). For every day he remembers, you give him a small token, a sticker perhaps, that he places on a chart. When he accumulates three stickers, he is then entitled to receive the reward, an hour playing at the park or a board game with you, for example. The three days do not have to be in succession for the child to receive the reward. For younger children, even three days may be too long to wait for a reward. If this is the case with your child, you may need to give the reward daily or even in half-day increments.

In our home we used play money. We had a chart with household rules on it. Each rule was worth a specific amount, anywhere from one dollar to twenty. Every time our son followed a rule, he receives the agreed amount. The money he earned was placed in an envelope for one week. During the week he had to spend this money. We charged him five dollars an hour to play a video game, two dollars an hour to ride his bike, ten dollars an hour for playing games on the computer, three dollars to watch a rented video, and two dollars to watch an hour of television. Every Saturday, he turned in what was left of the money he earned. For every ten dollars in play money he turned in, he received one dollar in cash. He was able spend this money as he wished or save it for something special he wanted to buy. In this case, once we gave a reward (the play money, for instance) we never took the reward away. Instead, for noncompliance we used time-out, took away a privilege, or assigned an extra household chore. We never took away what he had already been rewarded.

We used this play-money system very successfully for quite sometime. The original household rules were replaced by new house rules two months after we initiated this system; we had achieved the desired effect. However, no reward system works forever, so be ready to substitute another system when needed. Always seek professional help if reward systems do not work with your child.

As with infants, toddlers, and preschool children, establish a daily routine. Children do best when they know what to expect—whether it is on a school day or on a weekend, in the morning or at bedtime. Plan a daily routine together, allowing for his input, and put it in writing. For instance, when he gets ready for bed at night he can have a snack, brush his teeth, and use the bathroom before he puts his pajamas on. Whatever the planned routine, he must follow it. On the nights he cooperates, you might allow him fifteen minutes reading time in bed before he turns off his light.

Devise a routine for mornings and provide a token reward (for every three or five stickers he receives a pack of baseball cards or she receives a new hair ribbon). Follow the same routine as closely as possible for every day of the week, including Saturdays and Sundays. The times may vary, for instance, on a weekend he may stay up an hour longer or he does not have to do homework on Friday and Saturday nights, but the basic routine stays the same. On weekends, he must still get up, brush his teeth, eat breakfast, and then get dressed—the same daily routine.

Although some professionals will tell you to reward only those positive actions that require no verbal warning, parents should assess their individual child. If your child has short-term memory problems or difficulty with concepts of time, a verbal warning may be necessary until a routine is established. With some children, daily reminders are always needed.

## Avoid Physical Punishment

Unless your child is an infant, you may have already learned that physical punishment does not work with your child. Many parents today prefer not to use physical punishment, yet most parents of children with AD/HD have tried it at least once—often out of frustration and desperation. If you are one of the few parents who have not administered a spanking at least once, here's an example of what may happen. "I struck my six-year-old one time," admits Jessica, "and couldn't believe what happened next. Bobby became more aggressive and verbally abusive. He actually displayed more strongly the very behaviors we were trying to eliminate."

For Bobby and other children with AD/HD, physical punishment becomes a positive reinforcement. If a child is seeking attention, your reaction to a particular behavior, whether it is a positive or a negative reaction, will give the child the attention he is seeking. Thus the behavior, whether positive or negative, will increase because it has been rewarded. Physical punishment also teaches aggression, the very behavior that many parents of children with AD/HD are trying to eliminate. For instance, spanking a child teaches that it is acceptable to hit others when angry. Remember, you are a role model for your child. If you hit, he learns to strike out. If you scream at him in anger, he learns that this is also a satisfactory way of handling feelings of anger. When angry, if you lose control of yourself and throw objects, you can expect your child to react the same way, since many forms of aggression are learned from others.

In addition to the risk of physical punishment causing extreme negative behavior, many children are extremely tolerant of pain because of their short attention span. The pain they feel is there one second, gone the next, unlike the average child who may feel that sting for several agonizing minutes. Remember the mom earlier in this chapter whose son, Daniel, received stitches several times before his second birthday? On each occasion, Daniel never cried—not when the accidents happened or when he received stitches. If an injury that requires stitches doesn't hurt, how can we expect a swift smack to the rear to hurt?

## Time-Out

Besides using a reward system, what are other ways can we deal with noncompliance? Many professionals suggest using time-out, and many parents use this system effectively. However, some experts believe that time-out should be reserved for the more severe noncompliance you experience with your child. As with all suggestions in this book, always consult with your physician or other professional who helps you with behavioral management techniques before trying something new.

Time-out is an easy concept to understand but may be difficult to enforce at times. A child is sent to time-out when he displays inappropriate behavior, such as casually walking by a sibling and striking her. Time-out is always carried out in isolation from other members of the family. This might be in the kitchen, a bathroom, the child's bedroom if there are no toys in the room, or a guest room. Time-out can be used for children two years and older. The time spent in time-out depends on the child's age. Parents often use one minute for each year of age until the child reaches the age of five. After that, some professionals feel five minutes is sufficient time because by then many children will have forgotten why they were sent to time-out in the first place. However, other experts advise that you use one minute for each year of age regardless—for a ten-year-old, time-out would be ten minutes.

This is how time-out works: Billy walks by his sister and strikes her. You see this behavior and say, "Billy, striking your sister is unacceptable behavior. Go to time-out and get yourself under control." No other comments should be made, including any conversation the child may initiate. Set a timer that the child can hear go off in five minutes, or in five minutes tell your child he may leave time-out.

Issue only one warning. If your child does not comply, then physically carry him to the designated time-out area. If your child does not stay in time-out during those five minutes, restart the time-out. With children who really test limits, you may physically have to place the child in time-out any number of times. One mom says she had to put her four-year-old daughter back into time-out thirty-six times before the child finally realized that mom meant business.

When parents initially learn about using time-out for children with AD/HD, their first reaction is usually, "We've tried everything and you're telling us our child will just walk off to time-out just like that?" Well, it may not be just like that, but if you haven't tried it before, you may be surprised. For some children, the first time they receive this command issued by a *calm* parent they may go immediately to time-out. The difficulty begins later because children with AD/HD, and all children in general, *hate* time-out. It means leaving a room where everyone else is to go to another room isolated from others. No fun!

If your child comes out of time-out and is still not under control, immediately send him back to time-out. Once he comes out and is under control, reissue your request if he was told to do something and failed to comply, for example. If he does not comply, then send him back to time-out.

After using time-out effectively for a length of time, don't be surprised when you tell your child to go to time-out and he immediately begins to apologize saying he won't do it again and how sorry he is. Accept his apology, but he must still spend his designated minutes in time-out. You might say, "Billy, I accept your apology, but you did not do as I requested. Go to time-out for five minutes." For children who absolutely refuse to stay in time-out, take away all privileges until the child serves his time. This means he loses access to toys, telephone calls, friends who stop over, television, games, outside play, etc. until he complies. Once he serves his time, he immediately regains full privileges.

You are probably thinking, okay, great, but how can we enforce time-out when we are not at home? Believe me, parents have found ways. "I recall one occasion when my seven-year-old was totally impossible in the car. I pulled into the first parking lot I saw, and he found himself outside of the car sitting on the ground for five minutes," says

Sheri from Atlanta, Georgia. "That was absolutely the last time he ever tried that stunt."

If you're shopping, try the floor in a corner away from foot traffic. In a mall, use the seating areas provided but not the ones down the main aisle. Older children will usually march to a seat and sit down. Younger children may need to be physically carried to time-out. Do what you must, but follow through with time-out. When visiting others, just ask for a place to use for time-out. People will be quite obliging, especially if the child is being disruptive. Time-out can be used anywhere as long as you use your imagination.

## Natural Consequences

Natural consequences also work. For instance, it is thirty-five degrees outside and your child refuses to wear a coat even though you have explained how cold it is outside. You could, of course, send him to time-out for noncompliance or you could let him experience the cold himself. Sometimes a natural consequence is a great way to learn. Of course, you should never use natural consequences as an option if it severely jeopardizes your child's health or safety.

## Adolescence

Adolescence is a difficult time for most teenagers, but especially for teenagers who have AD/HD. If hyperactivity was a problem in the childhood years, parents may notice that it is no longer a problem in adolescence or only a minor one displayed by a sense of restlessness, such as leg wiggling, finger tapping, or getting up every ten or fifteen minutes to sharpen a pencil or get a drink of water. However, other common characteristics—such as impulsivity, poor judgment skills, learning problems, and troubles with friendships—may be still evident. Later, we'll take a more in-depth look at the adolescent with AD/HD.

## Parents during These Stages

With a fleeting vision of their dream child in mind, parents are quick to realize that despite all their repeated attempts at normalcy their child is unable to meet their expectations. As the child tries to meet these expectations and fails, parents become confused, frustrated, angry, depressed, and often feel a sense of failure and guilt. As relatives and friends observe, they too become frustrated and saddened by what is happening. Many will empathize and offer their support and love. Others may simply withdraw from your life, believing you have done something wrong to create such a difficult child, or they may prefer not to socialize with what they perceive to be a dysfunctional family. Parents will need to make an extra effort to explain to others that their child has a disability and how it affects his behavior, so they will know that he is not just a bad child. For some parents this will not present a problem, but for those who are embarrassed that their child has a medical problem or is not a perfect child, the process of telling others will be difficult. In the next chapter, we'll take a look at those people who should know about your child's disability and why.

CHAPTER 4

# So Your Child Has AD/HD

**A**S A PARENT of a child with AD/HD, it is your responsibility to learn as much as possible about this disorder, not only for your child's sake but because you will be explaining AD/HD to family, friends, babysitters, teachers, and others caring for your child for many years to come. As you look for information and reference materials, don't forget to utilize medical libraries at nearby universities, textbooks that teach educators about AD/HD, and by all means make use of Internet websites, but be sure the site is trustworthy as there is a lot of misinformation available online. (See the appendix for all sorts of resources.)

Barbara, a thirty-four-year-old mother, was, like many parents, unsure about what and when to tell others. "My husband doesn't want anyone to know," she says. "He doesn't want people to judge Eric and feels they will if they learn he has AD/HD." The chances are good that people are already judging Eric, especially his babysitter Sue, who sits with him two days a week, and his preschool teacher who sees him three days a week. Grandma and grandpa are probably wondering also, as are Eric's neighbors. Eric is a hyperactive child who throws extreme temper tantrums whenever Barbara must leave him. Transitions are very difficult for Eric. He is also a child who is constantly on the go and always getting into things he shouldn't. Undoubtedly, the people who are with Eric weekly have already asked themselves, "What's the matter with this child? Can't he ever sit still? Why can't he control himself like most children his age? Why don't his parents do something about his behavior?"

Some parents have little trouble telling others about their child, but other parents feel that the fewer people who know about it the better. Ironically, most people who come in contact with your child already know something is not quite right because children with AD/HD usually act differently than other children. If you don't tell them about your child, they will speculate.

Remember, AD/HD affects every part of your child's life. It affects his behavior and his ability to learn, socialize, and make and keep friends. It affects him at home, in school, at camp, and at religious services and when you are out shopping, on vacation, or visiting friends, family, and neighbors. If people don't understand why he is the way he is, they will most likely judge him and you. Consequently, your child may be labeled as a troublemaker, a spoiled brat, a space-head, weird, or whatever name people may choose to use. If your child hears people using such labels, his self-esteem will plummet. Fortunately, this scenario can usually be avoided if the people who know your child understand AD/HD. Instead of ridiculing, most people will offer support to you and your child.

Who to share this information with, when, and how much to share is a relevant concern of most parents. When you elect to speak with others, you must be prepared to explain AD/HD in a simple manner. Your main goal is to elicit the support of those who love and care for your child and those who work with you in a professional capacity. Remember, the majority of the population still knows little about AD/HD despite the widespread media coverage.

## Physicians and Other Professionals

All professionals who work with your child should be told of his AD/HD. Even a simple dentist appointment will be easier for your child and the dentist if he or she understands that your child has AD/HD and may not, for example, be able to sit still long enough for a routine examination and cleaning. It's helpful to choose a pediatric dentist or a dentist who routinely works with children. Most understand AD/HD and can handle your child tactfully without humiliating him.

A speech or occupational therapist, although used to working with children with special needs, must still be told about your child's short attention span or his difficulty following directions. This knowledge gives all professionals, including teachers (see chapter 7 for a discussion on teachers), the ability to approach your child in an understanding manner and will make the experience less stressful for all involved.

## Journals

All parents need to keep accurate medical records on their children, but especially for their children with special challenges. Keep a journal and record unusual behavior. Note the date and child's age at the time the behavior became evident. Be prepared to give detailed reports to your child's doctor and other professionals, addressing the behavior you are concerned about such as extreme motor activity (how he displays the hyperactivity; whether it's a problem at home, in school, or at school and home; the effect it is having on the family, on classmates, etc.) or the inability to pay attention.

Write a brief history of your pregnancy, delivery, and when your child reached significant milestones, and update it continuously. Every time you visit a new doctor or other professional you will be asked the same questions, again and again.

Adoptive parents may not have information on a pregnancy or delivery, depending on the type of child they adopted (a child born in another country may not arrive with this sort of information), but an American-born infant may have this information in his hospital records. Although adoptive parents can share only what information they have been given, they can keep accurate records from the time the child is placed with them. Many adoptive parents routinely keep accurate records of their child's milestones, knowing how important these records will be to their child when he is older since adopted children usually arrive with little social and medical history.

## Making Good Health-Care Choices

### Questions to Ask about Referrals to Specialists

(*Source*: "A Parent's Guide: Doctors, Disabilities, and the Family," volume 1, number 2, May 1990, published by NICHCY.)

1. Specifically, why is this referral being made? Is this a second opinion or are we seeing the specialist for a diagnosis?
2. Are there records I should take with me or will they be sent in advance?
3. Is this specialist comfortable with children like mine? Has he or she been fully informed about my child's disability or would it be useful for me to give him or her a call?
4. Who will get the reports of this evaluation? Who will be interpreting them? Who will be discussing these reports with me?
5. What are this specialist's rates? Can arrangements be made to help cover these expenses?

## Questions to Ask When Scheduling an Appointment for Your Child

1. I will need a longer appointment than most families. Can we schedule a time when we can have a double appointment?
2. My child has difficulty waiting patiently. Is the first appointment of the morning available or one right after the lunch break?
3. If you don't make appointments, what times of day or which days of the week are least busy?

## What Should a Family Do Before the First Visit to Another Doctor?

The new doctor will need information about your child and his/her medical history. Before the first appointment, be sure all medical records are either mailed or delivered to the doctor's office. It would be useful for these records to arrive at least a week before your visit so that the doctor has time to look them over.

If your child has already been seen by a specialist, have these reports sent to the doctor, too. If your child has educational assessments, send these along as well. The more the doctor knows about your child, the better able he/she is to discuss your concerns.

Requesting that medical records be sent to another doctor is routine. You should not feel uncomfortable requesting your child's records. If your child has already been seeing a doctor, it is always acceptable to request an additional opinion without insulting the first doctor.

You should write to the first doctor's office (most physicians require written permission to send records) and say, "I am interested in discussing my child's situation with another doctor to get additional opinions. Please send a copy of my child's records to Dr. (fill in the name) at (give the mailing address)."

You might also make a list of topics for discussion with the new doctor. Since many children are shy around doctors, especially ones they've never met before, you may need to bring up problems that the doctor cannot readily see. For instance, if you suspect your child may have a language delay, say so. Then the doctor can try to initiate more conversation with your child to better observe your concerns. If you are worried about possible developmental delays, make a list of things your child does or doesn't do to give the doctor concrete examples of behavior he/she may not be able to observe in the office. If you would like a referral for a hearing screening or vision tests, be sure to mention this. Doctors can conduct preliminary visual, hearing, and speech screening in their offices to help to determine if a specialist is needed. [Never think a doctor is all-knowing. There is no formal board certification for those who specialize in AD/HD.]

## What Should You Look for When You Get to the Doctor's Office?

Look around. Is this office child proof? Are there toys for your child to play with? Are there many things he/she should not touch, climb, or get into? Can you let your child move around in this room without undue restraint? Are well children separated from children who may have contagious illnesses?

How helpful is the office staff? Do they seem open and friendly, or do you feel out of place here? Are the nurses who weigh the child, conduct eye exams, and perform some of the examination functions comfortable with your child? Are they pleasant to you? Are they supportive of your needs? Does your child seem comfortable, or at least as comfortable as any child feels in a doctor's office? If he/she is frightened, is the staff warm and reassuring?

After the doctor has examined your child, you might ask if the nurse or receptionist could take the child out of the room for a few minutes so you can talk to the doctor alone. Children who are very active can make conversation difficult for both you and the doctor. If this is not possible, ask if the doctor can phone you later in the day to discuss your child and pick a time when you can talk on the phone uninterrupted.

## Questions to Ask about Tests

1. What do you expect to learn from these tests? Always ask a physician to explain in layman's terms what a specific test is for and why it is being ordered.
2. Have these tests been given to my child before? Can we coordinate any of the earlier results with these?
3. Does the school or public health clinic also do these tests? Is there any reason not to have them done there to save on expenses?
4. How long will these tests take and what is involved in them?
5. Is there anything I should tell my child about these tests that will help prepare him?
6. Can he eat before coming?
7. Are there any precautions I should take before or after these tests?

## Questions to Ask about Medications

If the physician prescribes medication, be sure you know what it is for; ask for clarification of anything you don't understand and report any reactions to your physician immediately.

1. When should I give this medication?
2. When the prescription says "three times a day" does that mean every eight hours even during the night, or three times during the daytime while awake?
3. Should the child take this medication before, during, or after meals?
4. Are there any foods that should not be mixed with this medication?
5. How long should he take this?
6. (If your child has other medications he is currently taking) My child is currently taking (name of medication). Can he take this medicine at the same time?
7. Are there any possible side effects or allergic reactions I should be aware of? How will I recognize them? What should I do if I think he or she is having a reaction?

8. Does this medicine need to be stored at a special temperature? That is, will it go bad if the medicine gets too hot or too cold?

Between visits, write down any questions or concerns you have. When you visit the doctor next, take your notes along with you. Be sure to take notes during this, and all, doctor appointments. If you need an additional appointment to cover concerns that were not addressed during this session, make the appointment before leaving the doctor's office.

## Family Members and Friends

Discuss AD/HD with your family and friends. Because many people believe that hyperactivity in children results from poor parenting, it is vital that the child's grandparents, aunts, uncles, cousins, and siblings realize that AD/HD is a medical disability. In many ways, AD/HD is a hidden disability so parents may be reluctant to share something that they feel is not readily apparent to others. Other parents may hide their child's disability because they are disappointed that their child is not perfect or embarrassed that their child has this disorder.

Adoptive parents are often especially disinclined to share their child's medical information because they want to be seen as perfect parents of perfect children. Unfortunately, this attitude is perpetuated by society's attitude that adopted children are not the same as other children. Prospective adoptive parents often hear such comments as, "Why do you want to adopt? You never know what you'll get." Parents who adopted their child as an infant may fear hearing, "What did you expect? It's not like you gave birth to him." As if any parent, biological or adoptive, can look at a child and see what the future will hold! Whether your child is biological or adopted, you must remember that *no* child is perfect. As parents, we must look beyond our personal feelings and do what is best for our child.

You can help your child greatly by giving family members fact sheets and books on AD/HD to read. While some family members may be willing to take the time to read such materials, not all are. If your family is unwilling to read about the disorder, then share your thoughts and knowledge with them. Eventually, they will learn about it whether they want to or not. In the meantime, do not expect your family to adjust immediately. If you entertain ambitious expectations, you will be greatly disappointed when a family member reacts negatively to your child or makes an insensitive remark. Remember, many people know little if anything about AD/HD and their remarks are often made out of ignorance, not lack of concern. Learning about AD/HD is a daily process for you, but you must be patient with others.

"I've told my father at least fifty times to never yell at Brad when he does something wrong, yet occasionally he does," says Brooke, Brad's mother. "Then my dad becomes livid when Brad reacts violently to the yelling. The angrier my dad becomes, the worse Brad behaves." If family members sometimes care for your child, be sure you provide them with positive disciplining techniques to use when your child displays inappropriate behaviors. If necessary, write them down. Never concede to pressures from relatives who try to convince you that all your child needs is a good spanking!

Remember that close relatives, especially grandparents, are affected by your child's situation. They may feel guilty, especially when they learn that AD/HD can be inherited. They may wonder what part they played in their grandchild's problems. They may experience fear that future grandchildren will inherit AD/HD and confusion about the disorder in general. The method you choose for interacting and sharing information with them will affect the way they support you and interact with your child for years to come. (My oldest was the first to be diagnosed in my family, then his cousin, followed by my other son.)

Invite grandparents to attend workshops and conferences on AD/HD with you. This is particularly relevant if grandparents are extremely critical of your parenting style, vehemently oppose the use of stimulant medication, or both. They must be educated. One parent combined a conference with a short family vacation and invited her parents along, at her expense. ("It was worth having to eat on a strict budget for several months," says this parent.) Introduce grandparents to your friends who also have children with AD/HD. If possible, let them meet other grandparents who have grandchildren with AD/HD. This gives them the opportunity to discuss the disorder with their peers.

Provide special opportunities for grandparents to interact with your child so they, too, can learn to know him as a person, not just as a child who has special challenges. Choose activities that will not overly excite or stress your child. Grandparents can take grandchildren to the park, for an ice-cream cone, fishing, bowling, out to eat, to a movie (they can always leave if the child can't sit any longer), or to story time at the library. They can read to the child, initiate craft-making sessions, or attend Grandparent's Day at school. Children usually do well when with grandparents because they are the center of attention.

Finally, don't dwell constantly on the problems associated with AD/HD. Relatives, grandparents in particular, like to hear positive stories and feedback about their grandchildren. Always share your child's achievements and milestones with them. Be sure they understand that despite the special parenting problems you encounter, your child is still a unique individual with his own set of talents and abilities and is also an important member of your family.

## Siblings

A child with AD/HD will affect a younger brother or sister, as all older siblings do. Toddlers and preschool-age children often find their older brother or sister funny when the child displays inappropriate behavior. Because many children with AD/HD are immature for their age, the younger sibling often sees the older child as someone on his or her own level. Therefore, the younger sibling is quick to imitate the child with AD/HD, even though mom and dad constantly point out that the behavior is unacceptable. Removing both children from the scene and placing them in time-out (in separate isolated areas) is one recourse for parents.

Younger siblings need to be exposed to other children so they can learn appropriate behaviors. If there are no younger children in your neighborhood or you live in a rural area, your child is especially vulnerable because his older sibling with AD/HD may be his only role model. You may want to enroll your child in a day-care center or a preschool class either on a part- or full-time basis if you can afford the extra expense.

Some therapy programs and school programs have a special group for siblings who have a brother or sister with special needs. Such groups help siblings understand their brother's or sister's disability and teach the child how to interact with his sibling. Many groups also encourage role playing so the child can learn what it feels like to have a disability such as AD/HD. These groups also provide the opportunity for the non-AD/HD sibling to be with children who do not have special needs. If you cannot locate such a group, consider starting one with other parents of children with AD/HD who have younger siblings. Since children with AD/HD often embarrass their siblings, it is important that your child realize that he is not the only child with a brother or sister who appears to be different.

Explain AD/HD in terms your other children can understand. The best time to do this is when you are alone with your other children. Young children do not require long explanations, so keep it simple and clear. For example, you might say, "It is difficult for your sister to follow directions and pay attention. We all need to help her." Or "It is hard for your brother to sit still. We need to help him." Check your local library or bookstore for children's books that address disabilities in siblings.

If a child asks for more information, give age-appropriate facts. Older children will need a more detailed definition for AD/HD so they can try to help their siblings. Never explain AD/HD when you are frustrated and disappointed with your child, especially if the inappropriate behavior was displayed in front of your other children. You will be apt to explain the disorder in negative terms and make statements you will later regret. Be sure your younger non-AD/HD children understand that they cannot "catch" this disorder and that children do not die of AD/HD.

Talk about your child with AD/HD with your other children. Let them tell you how they feel about him. "After one particularly difficult morning, my four-year-old son and I sat down exasperated after my child with AD/HD finally left for school," says Sally from Fairfax, Virginia. "Ben just looked at me and shook his head slowly from side to side." When Sally asked Ben what was the matter, he replied, "I'll never act like that, Mommy, when I go to school. He was awful this morning." Sally admits that sometimes Ben does find the behavior irritating, yet he usually does follow his older brother's example. "That's why we enrolled him in school next fall," adds Sally. "He needs to be around normal behavior as much as possible."

Many siblings harbor jealous feelings because parents tend to give more attention to their child with AD/HD. Parents need to make a harmonized effort to spend quality time with their other children. Strive to strike a balance between the children so all energies are not inadvertently directed toward one child. This is often not easy because children with hyperactive-impulsive behaviors can deplete your energy levels quickly.

Although it is often easier to ask your non-AD/HD children to help with chores, it is not fair to the other children to have responsibilities while the child with AD/HD contributes nothing. Always give your child with AD/HD a list of chores that are his responsibility and be sure he completes them, even if it means you must supervise. Be sure the chores you designate are ones he is capable of handling so that you can give positive feedback on a job well done.

A younger sibling may taunt and tease an older sibling with AD/HD if he surpasses his older sibling in abilities. For example, toileting problems (particularly bedwetting) linger longer in some boys with AD/HD. "Our oldest son is seven and still in diapers at night. Our youngest son is four years old and has been out of diapers for over a year now," explains Troy, their father. "Unfortunately, our youngest son points this out almost daily to our oldest son. He's still too young to understand the problems his older brother has." Situations such as this one do improve as the younger sibling matures, but it's a difficult situation for the child with AD/HD to be harassed by a younger brother or sister. Assure your child that (1) he is not to blame for the bedwetting, (2) he will not wear diapers forever, and (3) his sibling is too young to understand why this is happening.

## Neighbors

Before you send your child off to play at neighbors' homes, be sure your neighbors understand that he has AD/HD and what this means in relation to your child (is he hyperactive, impulsive, a risk taker, has difficulty following directions or keeping track of time?). They may not want the responsibility of supervising your child, which means you may find the neighborhood children in your yard on most days. The majority of parents feel most comfortable with this situation. They can supervise the children and interfere, if necessary, before their child alienates himself from the entire neighborhood. Invite only one friend at a time to your house and limit the time they spend together. Tell your child your expectations ahead of time. For example, "Andy can stay one hour, as long as you and he can play well together. Then it will be time for you to come in and start your homework." Be sure the other child's mother is aware of the restrictions you have placed on play time, and always let the children know at least ten minutes beforehand that play time will be ending soon.

## Babysitters

A babysitter certainly deserves to be told that your child needs constant supervision and the reasons why. If he is impulsive and often gets into dangerous situations while playing outside, or needs to have directions repeated to him frequently, the babysitter must know this. She must also understand that the child is not intentionally trying to make her job more difficult.

For your child's safety you must be able to explain AD/HD in a straightforward and concise way, without frightening the babysitter and while stressing the need for supervision. (Energetic sixteen- and eighteen-year-olds often make great babysitters for children with AD/HD, but an older person may not have the energy or desire to follow your child around from one place to another or one activity to another.)

Never just say, "Sam is hyperactive. Do you know what that means?" Most babysitters will answer yes, not wanting to embarrass themselves by telling you they don't understand.

Always assume that the person you are interviewing to care for your child knows nothing about AD/HD. Give a potential babysitter some information on AD/HD to read during an interview and explain how it relates to your child. Then discuss AD/HD with her.

If you decide to hire her, ask her to arrive early on her first day so she can spend some time with your child before you leave. Before leaving, give her a list of instructions. This list should include your child's trouble areas (he tends to climb the fence and go into the neighbor's yard when not supervised) and emphasize those activities he may or may not engage in (he's not allowed in the garage). As well, include how he is to be disciplined, what types of reactions to expect from him, and how to handle various situations that may arise. Personally, I found that babysitters appreciated this openness and guidance. In thirteen years, my children had a total of three babysitters. Despite the difficulties these sitters experienced, including having to take children to the emergency room when I couldn't be reached, one babysitter stayed for two years, another for three years, and the last for eight years.

## Scout Leaders, Coaches, and Other Activity Leaders

Children with AD/HD can benefit from organized group activities. Groups are great for teaching socialization skills and children with AD/HD certainly need help in this area. Children should be encouraged to participate in scouting, religious, and sport activities. However, parents must be honest with group leaders about their child, especially if these people must administer medication. Group leaders also should be given guidance on how to discipline your child. If your child plays a sport, be sure the coach knows exactly what your child's abilities are. You don't want your child standing in the outfield extremely bored if he's capable of being the catcher, but that's exactly where he could end up if you don't explain AD/HD adequately.

Coaching the team or being the scout leader certainly will allow you to control your child's interactions, but if your schedule does not permit this level of involvement, either mom or dad should try to be present for games and volunteer to help at meetings and on special activity days. Be aware that many children come home hyper after these events. Interacting with a group of children often provides more stimulation than the child can handle, but these activities also help channel excessive energy into a positive experience.

Be honest with these people if your child also has learning disabilities. If a scout troop is putting on a short play, your child may not be able to remember the lines. But maybe he can hold a prop or play an instrument or participate in some other way without embarrassing himself.

## Acquaintances

While I certainly won't advise you to tell every person you meet about your child's disorder, I am convinced that it is beneficial in certain situations. For instance, I regularly shop at the same department stores, grocery stores, etc., and the sales clerks and cashiers know me by name. Because I am often with my oldest son, I have found it helpful that these people understand that he does not act up deliberately and that he has a medical problem. Many times, they have kept an eye on my son while I tried something on in a dressing room. I can hear them asking about school or Cub Scouts or camp. One woman keeps a special treat in a drawer under the cash register. My son is permitted to open the drawer and take a piece of gum or whatever is in there when I'm in the dressing room. Another woman allows him to arrange clothing by sizes, and still another clerk lets him fill out an application for a charge card.

Telling these people has permitted me to get my shopping done without sales clerks glaring at me or reprimanding my son. Because I never want them to think that I am taking advantage of them, I always thank them for their help and often remember them with little tokens of appreciation. As a result, my son and I are always welcome in the stores we shop in and many more people are now aware of AD/HD. Before you explain AD/HD to the salespeople you know, plan to heed this advice: never discuss AD/HD in a way that is embarrassing for your child.

Of course the decision to tell or not to tell is ultimately yours. But I encourage you to tell those closest to your child for your sake and your child's. Secrecy only promotes the notion that you are ashamed of your child. As one mother said, "My son is a good-looking boy and I am proud to be his mother. He has a wonderful personality and a beautiful smile. So he has a disability, so what? No one has a perfect child."

Remember, your child's AD/HD is no one's fault. With proper intervention, support from loving parents and friends, and guidance, your child can grow to be a happy, productive adult.

# Problems That Drive You Wild

**M**ANY CHILDREN with AD/HD present challenging behaviors at home that can make living with the child an overwhelming, frustrating experience on a day-to-day basis. As a parent of a child with AD/HD, you already know that your child is different from other children and that he cannot be parented in the same manner. For instance, discipline techniques used with other children may not work with children who have AD/HD. There are, however, different strategies or techniques that parents can exercise to modify some, if not many, of the problematic challenges their child faces (poor impulse control, poor attention, or hyperactivity). Using specific techniques can influence the child's behavior so that the quality of home life improves both for the parent and the child. In this chapter, you will learn strategies parents have used to successfully handle these often complex, but common, behavior problems.

Please note, however, that not all of the strategies outlined in this chapter will work with every child who has AD/HD. This is because symptoms in children with AD/HD are remarkably different: symptoms may be present in differing degrees, some symptoms may not be present at all, or the symptoms may change from one day to the next. Because of this, what works for one child may not necessarily work with another.

Some of these techniques may work for your child. Others may work with slight variations.

## Handling School Mornings

School mornings with a child who has AD/HD are perhaps one of the most frustrating and annoying daily experiences for many parents. Some parents have children with AD/HD who can't get out of bed in the morning and then move at a snail's pace, with no regard for time schedules, once they're up. Other parents have children who wake up too early on their own (between 5 and 6 a.m.) seven days a week. These children have an overabundance of energy in the morning and little control over their actions. They not only wake up early but make sure everyone else in the home is awake also. However, like the slow movers, early risers also move leisurely on school mornings because they, too, have difficulty staying on task. Early risers are just as likely to miss the school bus as the slow movers. Some children experience no problems in the morning, although many of their parents admit to using exactly the same routine every day.

Craig, a father from Red Wing, Minnesota, says he and his wife use the following approach in the morning, "We wake Jody up at 7:15 a.m. and she has until 7:30 to get dressed, brush her teeth, and make her bed. From 7:30 until 7:45 a.m. she watches television as a reward for getting her first tasks of the day done on time. From 7:45 to 8:00 she eats her breakfast. She then watches television until 8:15 when she leaves for her five-minute walk to school. This schedule is posted in her bedroom, in the bathroom, and in the kitchen. Jody always procrastinated until we put her on a strict schedule, which she follows successfully most days." Craig says they bought a clock for Jody's bedroom *and* use the timer on the stove from 7:30 to 8:15.

If possible, use an alarm clock to wake your child. Some children with AD/HD wake up in a cheerful mood, but others wake up ready for a fight—their arms are swinging and legs kicking as verbal insults flow freely. Better that the alarm clock be the recipient of such abuse than you or your spouse.

"Mornings always seem to be a struggle, especially if there are brothers and sisters," explains Joanie of Sylvania, Ohio. "I found that picking out clothes the night before helps speed things along in the morning. I also used a timer for all functions, such as getting dressed, eating, and brushing teeth. Start the first day allowing extra time, and gradually shorten the time the child has to do each task until you find a comfortable amount of time for everyone. Eventually you may not need the timer."

"My son wakes up to his own voice in the morning," explains Dan from Santa Barbara, California. "We helped him make a tape, which we turn on in the morning, then we leave the room. The tape begins, 'Good morning, Jonathan. It is now 7 a.m. and it's time to get up.' Then one of his favorite songs plays for about two minutes. After the song, the tape reminds him (in his own voice) that at the tone he is to get up and get dressed now. Two more songs play (which gives him about five or six minutes to get dressed), and he then tells himself to go downstairs to eat breakfast." Dan admits that until he and his wife implemented this approach, mornings were a disheartening experience in their home.

"Surviving early mornings is still a problem for us as David [who is six years old] takes his medications between 7:30 a.m. and 8:00 a.m., and occasionally he awakes as early as 5:30 a.m.," explains his mother, Kate, from Carlinville, Illinois. "Making beds, getting dressed can last forever with David bouncing around, getting everyone else off track. David also hates being alone and will purposely wake his brothers.

"Currently David can have two bad mornings a week, [but] the third time is a strike out. David then loses his bedroom, which he shares with his brothers, for two nights. He then must sleep in a sleeping bag in another room. If he's too rowdy getting ready in the morning, then he loses television time, which is a big deal for him. Does it work? Not perfectly, but the situation has improved. As he continues to improve, he will gradually be allowed more privileges, like being able to go to the living room to read upon awakening," explains Kate.

"My husband plays a racing game with our son to see who can get dressed first," says Terri from Moravia, New York. "To concentrate on eating breakfast, we play beat the clock," says Beth from Bow, New Hampshire. "We set the timer on the microwave, and my son must finish eating before the beep."

"We have school chores," says Ellen from Oconomowoc, Wisconsin. "They consist of getting dressed, shoes and socks on, hair combed, breakfast eaten, and teeth brushed. If our son finishes by the designated time (7:00 a.m. in our house), he gets a prize. I make up squares of cloth and vary the contents (crackers, pennies, stickers, etc.) and put several items in each surprise package. No chores, no prize."

"The biggest challenge we faced in the morning was trying to get our son up and out of bed," admits Janelle from Ohio. "He had his own alarm clock, which he had to get out of bed to turn off, but usually he would just crawl back into bed. On several occasions, he had missed the school bus. I used to drive him to school, but now if he misses the bus due to his procrastination, he has to walk.

"When I decided to try this approach, I told him what would happen if he missed the bus in the morning. He just sort of chuckled. A few days later his chuckles turned to tears as he set out to walk a mile to school. I telephoned the school and left a message for his teacher." Janelle admitted that the thought of sending her fourth grader out the door on his own was frightening but says everything had been prearranged. She had friends along the route who called her when her son passed their homes and the school secretary telephoned when Philip finally reached his destination, an hour late for school. "That day was also the first and last time Philip ever missed the school bus," Janelle chuckles.

My own son's behavior in the morning before school was awful for four years. It didn't matter what type of mood Christopher woke up in. Halfway through breakfast (he took his medication while eating breakfast so it had no real effect until after he left for school), he would throw his bowl of cereal up in the air, throw food at his brother, hit his brother, argue, and yell at me. After breakfast, he would run through the house screaming and throwing things. I would follow him around putting him in time-out, trying to get him dressed, and keeping him away from his brother who was also trying to get ready for school. It was a nightmare. When it was time to leave for school, he would go out the front door and run around our property refusing to get into the car with his father and brother. When they finally left, I would break down and cry. On several occasions, his dad left without him because our son refused to get in the car. I would call the school and explain that he would be late. I would then drive him to school (because we were seventeen miles away), take him to his classroom, and make him explain to his teacher why he was late. But even that didn't work.

One Sunday evening, in desperation, I made up a chart for the coming week, listing all the tasks Christopher had to do each morning to get ready for school and noting all the unacceptable behaviors that had to stop. I then sat down and explained the chart to him. Each morning he was to check off his tasks as he completed them. If he did not complete a task by the time he had to leave for school or if he misbehaved (ran through the house, threw things, or hit his brother, for example), he would be given extra chores to do after school. Together we drew up a list of chores and I had Christopher write each chore down on an index card. We then estimated the time each chore would take (some tasks would take five minutes, others up to thirty minutes). I explained that for each uncompleted task (not brushing his teeth, for instance) and for each behavior rule that was broken before school (screaming), he would have to draw a chore card out of the box. Those chores would then have to be completed immediately after school before he could play outside, use his video games, talk with friends on the telephone, or do any fun activity. In other words, he would be grounded until his chores were completed.

I further explained that school mornings were his responsibility. If he chose to be noncompliant, then he also chose to be grounded and have chores to do after school. He seemed surprised, yet pleased, at the whole routine I outlined for him. I had him sign a form stating that he understood the terms of our agreement.

Chores and their estimated completion times were listed separately on index cards. Time estimates were given only as a point of reference. Christopher could complete a task in less time or it could take him longer if he chose to procrastinate. However, when he drew a chore from the stack of index cards, he was taking a chance. He could be lucky and draw a chore that takes only five minutes, but he also could draw a chore or two that together take thirty minutes to one hour to complete.

The first morning he checked off each task as it was completed. Instead of running around upstairs, I heard him telling his father about the new system Mom had started and how he was going to try real hard not to "get into trouble" because he didn't want any additional chores. Just before he left, I put a gold sticker on the word *Monday* and handed him a quarter as an additional reward. He gave me a kiss and hug and left that morning with a big smile on his face. We used this system for almost two months. Each week during that time, we watched Christopher's behavior gradually improve. When he finally had two consecutive weeks without any misbehavior, I asked him why his behavior had changed so drastically in the morning. He told me he was tired of doing so many chores after school. He also said that he was trying very hard to be good in the morning so we could be a "happy family."

## Christopher's Morning Schedule

|  | MON. | TUES. | WED. | THURS. | FRI. |
|---|---|---|---|---|---|
| Take medicine |  |  |  |  |  |
| Eat breakfast |  |  |  |  |  |
| Get dressed |  |  |  |  |  |
| Brush teeth |  |  |  |  |  |
| Comb hair |  |  |  |  |  |
| No running |  |  |  |  |  |
| No screaming |  |  |  |  |  |
| No hitting brother |  |  |  |  |  |
| No arguments |  |  |  |  |  |
| Get backpack |  |  |  |  |  |
| Lunch money |  |  |  |  |  |

However, while Christopher's behavior improved in the morning, his younger brother's behavior began to deteriorate. Blake, age four, had always been the "good" child. He always ate his breakfast quickly and would immediately get dressed, brush his teeth, and then watch television until it was time to leave for school. However, when Christopher's behavior improved, Blake initiated arguments with Christopher at breakfast, then began arguing with us, claiming he could no longer get himself dressed. Suddenly, Christopher was the one who was ready for school on time and Blake wasn't. Once again, we were very frustrated.

The situation that developed here is frustrating for well-meaning parents, but it is actually easy to understand. Blake had been seen as the "good" child and Christopher as the "bad" one. Often, without realizing it, parents promote a sense of competition between their children. In this case, we always praised Blake for his cooperation and admonished Christopher for his misbehavior. As Christopher became cooperative, Blake's place as the "good" boy in the family was threatened, forcing him to change his role to reinstate his position in the family.

It is important to remember that this type of situation can easily develop. It is a normal consequence when parents unknowingly promote competitiveness between their children. (Why can't you be good like your sister?) However, it is generally a temporary development that can be extinguished by doing the following:

- **Encouraging your children's strengths**, rather than criticizing their challenges
- **Expressing confidence in your children**
- **Recognizing their daily efforts** and the improvements they make
- **Showing respect for your children**
- **Giving each child your undivided attention for fifteen to thirty minutes** each day
- **Concentrating on their assets** and abilities and the contributions they make to the family

In other words, frequently show and tell your children how important they are to you and how much you love them. Give them your focused time daily, and show appreciation for the contributions they make to the family. Behavior modification plans will fail if children are not shown love and understanding as you strive to help them develop positive self-esteem and self-control. Competitiveness will decrease as your children recognize they have an important place in the family.

Once rules are established, follow through consistently with the consequences. Immediately administer rewards (positive check mark, sticker, a quarter, etc.) or penalties. Provide the opportunity to receive multiple rewards during the first few weeks and use a variety of rewards since children with AD/HD quickly grow tired of a single reward. You might also want to reward three good days out of five with extra television time, a trip to the park or zoo, or doing something special with your child. Or you may want to let your child choose a reward such as a special activity, a play activity, or a creative activity. When the desired behavior reaches a satisfactory level, begin to gradually decrease the number of rewards given. Follow a behavior management plan for at least two weeks before modifying it. It is impossible to change behavior overnight.
If your plan fails to work, examine the reasons for its failure. Ask yourself the following questions:

1. **Did my daughter clearly understand *what* behaviors were not acceptable** before the management plan was initiated? (Write the behaviors down and post them where your child can review them daily.)
2. **Did she fully understand the consequences** of exhibiting the inappropriate behaviors? (Write consequences down and post as a reminder.)
3. **Were the consequences (both reward and punishment) important enough** for my child?
4. **Was I consistent and immediate in delivering rewards and punishments?**
5. **Did my spouse (or babysitter) fail to follow the management plan** or not follow it consistently?
6. **Were we trying to modify too many behaviors at the same time?** (Children do best when you work on only one or two behaviors at a time.)

Now, alter your plan and start over. If repeated attempts at modifying your plan result in failure, you should seek professional help.

Despite our attempts to compensate with our younger son, he still continued to act up in the morning so we made a chart for him. When

## Blake's Morning Schedule

| | MON. | TUES. | WED. | THURS. | FRI. |
|---|---|---|---|---|---|
| Get dressed | | | | | |
| Eat breakfast | | | | | |
| Brush teeth | | | | | |
| Comb hair | | | | | |
| Wash hands | | | | | |
| Prepare backpack | | | | | |

he completed his tasks, he earned a sticker; for every three stickers, he received fifty cents. We did not add unacceptable behaviors to the chart because we wanted to see if the sticker alone would work for him. It worked successfully.

Older children who awaken too early should not be made to feel guilty for doing so (if they were truly tired they would sleep longer). However, they must learn that although they are ready to start the day before anyone else in the family they are expected to be quiet until other family members have awakened.

"Our son has an alarm clock set for 6:30 a.m.," says Ellen from Oconomowoc, Wisconsin. "He can wake up whenever (who can stop that), but cannot come out [of the bedroom] until the alarm goes off (bathroom breaks are permitted, of course)."

Provide an incentive for your child to play quietly in the morning. Tell your child, "When you are able to wait quietly in your room until it's time for everyone to wake up, you will earn fifteen extra minutes of television time or computer time after school." Or you may want to write a contract with your child. For example,

I, Taylor, will not wake anyone up in the morning. I will play quietly in my room. In return, I will receive an extra fifteen minutes of computer time in the evening.

Signed,  *Taylor*

Your child signs the contract, then it is posted in his room where he can easily see it each morning. For children who need immediate reinforcements, give them a token that they can exchange for some special reward later in the day.

If your child is a preschooler or an older child who is impulsive and can't be trusted when left alone, a parent will simply have to get up with the child each morning. Neither type of child should be left unattended.

One final tip: whether your child is an early riser or a slow mover, follow the same routine seven days a week. Cathy from Los Gatos, California, uses the following routine with her six-year-old daughter:

1. Cuddle in bed and talk about the day
2. Make school snacks
3. Brush teeth and hair
4. Collect school items
5. Look at the newspaper together
6. Get dressed together
7. Eat breakfast

"Keeping a familiar routine builds a secure framework in which she can live," adds Cathy. (See chapter 3 for more information on establishing morning routines.)

## Bath Time and Bedtime

Evening bath time signals the beginning of the end of the day—something most children want to delay. If bath time is a battleground in your household, be sure you have established a routine (for instance, baths are taken each evening or every other evening at 7:00 p.m. with no exceptions). Fifteen minutes before bath time, set a timer (the timer becomes the bad guy, not you) and let your child know he has fifteen minutes left to watch television or finish playing. Remember, children with AD/HD often have great difficulty with transitions, thus the fifteen-minute warning and the use of the timer. As a parent, your goal is to help your child make a smooth transition between ending the day and falling asleep. Therefore bedtime preparations should begin early enough to allow sufficient time for bathing and tucking in while still getting the child into bed at the appointed bedtime hour.

Make bath time interesting and enjoyable for your child, so it is something he will look forward to. Bubble baths and foam sculpturing soaps make an ordinary bath fun. Keep a bag of bath toys in the bathroom (to be played with only in the bathtub). Sing songs together or read to him. Give a five-minute warning before ending the bath and again use a timer. Offer a snack before bedtime (use that timer) if this is part of the routine or take the child directly to his room after his bath. Missy from Bow, New Hampshire, adds, "Our son goes to the bathroom, brushes his teeth, and drinks any water he needs. Drinking water before he goes to bed put a stop to the 'I'm thirsty' after he's been tucked in for the night." End the day by reading to your child or giving him a back rub. (Children enjoy having mom or dad read to them, even ten-year-olds.)

All children benefit from spending extra time alone with their parents to talk about the day's events, including any stressful situations they may have encountered or difficulties they may be experiencing in school or with their peers (children may need your help choosing words to identify their feelings). Helping your child find solutions to problems often increases his ability to fall asleep more easily. Allocating special time for this at bedtime often reduces conflicts between parent and child. When children know they will receive special attention they are less apt to argue in an attempt to gain attention at bedtime.

After tucking in your child, remind him how much you love him before leaving the room. A simple "I love you" is worth a thousand words, especially to a child who experiences difficulties every day. "I love you" tells your child you still value, appreciate, and love him for the person he is despite a demanding day. These three words are important for all children to hear, but especially for those who may feel they are too old for bedtime kisses and hugs.

Whether you say, "I love you" "See you in the morning," or "Goodnight," before leaving your child's bedroom, use the same words each night. This is your final signal to him that the day has ended and that you will not see him again until morning. Be assured that by the time most children reach second or third grade they have adapted well to their bedtime routine and often require little or no assistance settling down for the night. For elementary school–age children who have never had a bedtime routine, establish one immediately if bedtime is a stressful event in your home.

Some younger children have great difficulty falling asleep. Says one mom from Montana, "I found that my son (from ages three to five) fell asleep within minutes if I lay down next to him." It may seem simplistic, but tell your child how to fall asleep. My son would jump out of bed minutes after I had tucked him in, complaining that he couldn't fall asleep. One evening I said to him, "Of course you can't fall asleep, Christopher, you aren't even in bed. You must get into bed and close your eyes. Then you will fall asleep." He was asleep within minutes.

You might take another approach, as Marie from Columbus, Ohio, explains. "Let your child know that she must be in bed by a certain time, but don't expect her to fall asleep immediately. Always praise her when she's in bed on time."

Future problems also may be avoided by alternating bedtime duty with your spouse. "Let your spouse put your child to bed every other night, so neither parent becomes the only one who can tuck your child in," advises Jen from Scottsdale, Arizona. "Both parents must follow the same routine though."

Debra from Crown Point, Indiana, the mother of two children (her oldest child, Denny, has AD/HD), both of whom she keeps on the same schedule, shared her evening schedule, which begins as soon as her children get home from school:

1. Do homework
2. Playtime
3. Dinner
4. Bath time

5. Twenty minutes of reading time with each child (I read with one child while the other is taking a bath)
6. One television show
7. Bedtime

Another mother suggests giving baths immediately after school or before dinner. She found that waiting until bedtime created a tense situation in her household.

## Mealtime

Many children with AD/HD have great difficulty sitting still long enough to even eat a simple meal. They would rather eat standing up or with their feet anywhere but on the floor. They prefer to start an argument with a sibling instead of participating in a family conversation. As a parent, you may wonder if your child will ever learn what the purpose of a napkin is or what utensils are for because he always eats with his fingers.

You basically have three or four choices when it comes to mealtimes. First, you can follow the example outlined in chapter 3, whereby you dictate table rules. At the first infraction, your child is excused from the table whether his meal is finished or not. A variation of this would be to tell him to leave the table and then permit him to finish eating alone in another room. On days he abides by the rules he is, of course, rewarded for his appropriate behavior. This approach is often used when parents find mealtimes to be extremely upsetting and agree this is a behavior problem that needs to be worked on and corrected.

As with any behavior you find inappropriate, you must decide how relevant it is. Parents who worry about their child's table manners or the clothes he wears, for example, need to evaluate their motives for changing that behavior. If you're worried that he'll be eating with his fingers, with his feet propped up on the table and wearing the same clothes every day when he's an adult, you are looking into the future instead of concentrating on the present. Let go of the future and work on problems that are more relevant in your child's life today.

Your second choice concerning chaos during mealtimes is to adjust to your child. If he can sit quietly to eat part of his meal, then as parents, accept these few minutes together and plan time together later in the evening for conversing. Active toddlers can sit still about ten minutes as long as they are eating and sometimes much longer if they have something interesting to play with; preschoolers can sit about ten to fifteen minutes; and elementary school–age children can sit about twenty minutes, depending on how long it takes them to eat.

Terri from Moravia, New York, says that to keep their son Ryan seated at mealtime they "use a timer set for a predetermined time." Once a child is able to sit through meals using a timer set for five minutes, for instance, gradually increase the time until the child is able to sit through the entire meal. However, be patient; this won't happen in a week.

The third choice is to occasionally feed your children separately so you and your spouse can enjoy a quiet meal together. Rent a special video for the children to watch while you eat or encourage them to watch something special on television. Try to make this time unique for them also.

The fourth choice is to forget about family mealtimes and concentrate on other issues. "At age eight or nine," advises Heather from Raleigh, North Carolina, "loosen the structure of mealtimes and have some peace. Instead of making our child join us for dinner at a certain time, he comes when he is ready, which is usually when he is really hungry. This gives my husband and me five to thirty minutes of adult quiet time and everyone is happy!"

"Most of what I read and had been told was that Ritalin decreases the appetite, so I would let my son's dose run out then serve food," Patrice from Aurora, Illinois, explains. "The problem then was that he couldn't attend at the table. We have found that by medicating him about forty-five minutes before meals he will actually eat better. I'm sure each child is different, but I did learn to at least try different approaches to find one that works best for him. I also found that if he goes to bed about an hour before his last dose runs out, he falls asleep easier."

Don't engage in battles over food with your child. Children who take stimulant medication are usually very hungry in the morning, eat little for lunch (sometimes not much for dinner also if they take medication after school), and are hungry by bedtime. Serve a nutritious breakfast daily and provide a healthy evening snack. For lunch and dinner, serve at least one food your child particularly enjoys (maybe he'll be tempted to try a few bites), but don't force him to clean his plate. Rest assured that your child will not starve to death. Children do eat when they are hungry!

# Chores

Chores are a necessary part of living in a family. Everyone in the family should have assigned daily and weekly chores. I know it's easier to just complete the tasks yourself rather than involve your child, but you'll be doing your child a great disservice if he isn't assigned household chores. Household chores teach responsibility and self-discipline, provide needed skills for independent living, and make the child a contributing member of the family by sharing in the workload. When assigning chores consider the age of the child, his interests, and his ability to perform the chore.

All children learn to do chores in small steps. Parents can help by first assisting the child with the chore (teaching the task; but first be sure he's old enough to handle the task and has the needed ability). Let's say you want your eldest child to take responsibility for setting the dinner table. Together count out the number of plates needed. Then help him put the plates in the proper locations. Older children may only need verbal instructions, rather than verbal and visual directions. Then count out the number of forks, knives, and spoons needed. Put the utensils in their correct places, then the napkins and glassware. Before you know it, your child will have learned the basics of setting a table. However, learning the basics does not mean he is ready or willing to take full responsibility for the job. He will still need reminders and some supervision before he is able to complete the task completely on his own. Be sure to offer encouragement and praise for all attempts (even if it doesn't quite measure up to your expectations).

Establish a time frame (Chad, I want the table set by 5:30). For younger children who can't tell time, set a timer and let them know that when the buzzer goes off it's time for them to help set the table, pick up toys, or feed the dog. Remember to clarify the task to be completed in detail, step by step. A picture reference showing the steps of a task, if needed, can be posted on his wall and used as a constant reference until the chore becomes routine.

"Chores actually are a great help to David," says Kate, David's mother. "It's a physical way for him to help us. He enjoys helping and even though he complains at times, he does enjoy vacuuming, preparing snacks, and helping sort laundry. Taking the time to teach him the job and monitoring him has now paid off big for us. His vacuuming is passable and his laundry sense is great."

"We try to show Ryan that a family works together," explains his mother, Terri, from New York. "For example, if Ryan does his chores we will have extra time to play or be with him. If [he does] not, we will spend that time doing [his] chores."

Another mom says, "In our home, chores are on a 'paid-for' rather than an 'allowance' basis. Each chore is worth so much. Even [when he was] at an early age, we felt our son must learn that you have to work for what you want."

Above all, remember that the child with AD/HD needs to feel he is an important member of your family. Because he may experience more disappointments, failures, and frustrations than the average child, it is imperative that he knows he is needed in his home. Always choose chores for him that you know he can complete successfully. This will help to build self-esteem.

## Riding in the Car

I vividly recall picking up my first-grader son from school one day. It was obvious from the look on his face as he approached the car that he was angry. Something told me he was about to have a temper tantrum. Bracing myself for his explosive temper, I flashed a big smile and said, "How are you, sweetheart?" As I pulled out into the center lane of a four-lane highway, he began yelling that today was "show and tell" and I had forgotten to remind him to take something blue in color. Calmly, I reminded him that I had told him several times to pick out one of his blue toys and put it in his backpack. "You should have done it for me," he screamed. "I always forget. It's all your fault and I'm really angry at you." With that remark, he unlocked the passenger door, opened it, and swung his legs around preparing to jump out of the car, which by then was moving at forty-five miles an hour. Fortunately he had his seat belt on, and the automobile next to us did not hit our open car door. Trembling, I managed to convince him to close the door, and as soon as I was able I pulled into a nearby parking lot. (Please note that most children with AD/HD do not have symptoms as severe as this.)

I learned a valuable lesson that day. As a parent of an impulsive and hyperactive child, I learned that I had to be on guard at all times, even in our car, a place that I had always regarded as a relatively safe, confined space—a space I felt I had control over. The incident forced my husband and me to establish the following car rules:

1. **Seat belts** are to be put on before the car will be started and must always be worn for the safety of all family members.
2. **The driver decides** which windows, if any, are to be open while the car is moving. Doors are to be locked at all times and no one is to open a door while the car is moving.
3. **Hands, arms, head, and legs are to be kept in the car.**
4. **Items are not to be thrown** inside the car or from the car.
5. **Passengers have assigned seats** and they are expected to remain in those seats at all times.
6. **Children will be separated in the car** if they cannot sit next to each other without arguing and fighting (an adult sits between them or one child is moved to the front seat).
7. **All children will be rewarded** for following car rules.

Discuss the rules with each of your children, and review them frequently as well as the consequences of breaking those rules. Be sure they understand the relationship between their behavior and the consequences (for example, throwing a toy in the car will result in no toys being permitted in the car, or fighting with your sibling will mean you will be moved to the front seat and will no longer be able to play with each other). For children who can read, write the rules down and give them a copy. Remind your children of the rules every time you get into the car. Remember to always reward appropriate car behavior. As in any other situation, catch them being good and give positive feedback.

## When Company Comes to Visit

All children get excited when they learn friends or relatives will be stopping by for an informal visit or a family gathering. Excitement mounts as they watch you prepare food and clean the house. They'll ask you a thousand times how long before grandma and grandpa arrive. If parents are especially anxious, children will pick up on those concerns and tensions and, as a result, may misbehave. Children with AD/HD, especially those with hyperactivity, often become inordinately excited when visitors are expected. Parents should acknowledge their building excitement:

"When I was your age I remember how excited I used to feel waiting for my cousins, but we all need to remain calm so we get everything done before they arrive."

Provide your child with soothing activities to occupy him while he waits such as putting a puzzle together, listening to music, reading, or playing a board game or cards with a sibling. If your child wants to help with the preparations, supervise carefully. If you sense that he is starting to lose control, have him engage in another activity (away from other family members) until he regains control of himself. For instance, suggest that he check the bathrooms for clean towels, soap, and toilet paper.

Clearly state the house rules concerning visitors to your home and the behavior you expect from him several times shortly before guests arrive. Be sure he understands the relationship between his actions and the consequences (time-out for inappropriate behavior, for example). Also, verbally rehearse alternative activities he may choose during the day when he gets bored or overexcited. Make sure he knows his choices before he gets himself into trouble.

"Whether it's one visitor or ten coming to our home, Jamie gets extremely excited. When company enters the house, he practically bounces off the walls," explains Cindy from Brooklyn, New York. "Last Christmas Eve we put him in time-out several times immediately after our guests arrived. Each time he would rejoin the group, he'd lose control again and be sent back to his room. My sister-in-law followed him upstairs the fourth time he went to time-out. She gave him her undivided attention for ten minutes. When he came back downstairs, he was completely under control. Now when we know company is coming, I always ask someone beforehand to spend a few minutes with Jamie when they first arrive. I then tell Jamie, 'Aunt Sue is looking forward to seeing your rock collection (or whatever) when she arrives.' This never fails to work for us."

## Visiting Friends or Relatives

"I talk with my daughter before we visit family and friends and explain the type of behavior I expect," says Cathy from Los Gatos, California. "For example, when we go to her grandparents' house, I remind her that their dog is just a puppy and very excitable and that I know it's very tempting to run around the living room with the dog, but that the ruckus upsets grandma and the puppy. I ask her how I can help her remember not to get wild with the dog. She usually says I can hold her hand.

"When she forgets and starts to get wild, I take her hand immediately and pull her close to me, remind her with a whisper, and give her a hug. I catch her right away because if I let [her behavior] go, even for a minute, she will reach the point where it will be difficult for her to regain control.

"Visiting new friends is always a problem because it's a new situation with different people," adds Annie of Sylvania, Ohio. "If I forget to tell [my son] what type of behavior I expect ahead of time, he'll lose total control when we arrive. If this happens, I put him in isolated time-out until he settles down. If he comes out of time-out and loses control again, we leave and try it again another day."

## Playing with Other Children

AD/HD affects all aspects of the child's life, including playing with other children. Children who are impulsive in school and in the home may also be reckless and rash on the playground, with neighborhood children, and with siblings. When it comes to playing with other children, many children with AD/HD do not respond to normal social cues (tone of voice, body language, facial expressions) that are clear to their peers, which makes it very difficult for them to maintain friendships. "We allow Colin to play with friends only when he is well rested. If he's tired, there are usually arguments with the other children and Colin ends up crying and gets very emotional over everything," Missy from Bow, New Hampshire, explains sadly. "Quiet play is usually achieved when we invite only one friend over at a time. Colin usually does better with children who are easygoing and not real energetic. It seems every time he has a friend over who is also very active they accelerate each other to higher levels of hyper and it usually ends up with someone getting hurt, something broken, or the house destroyed! We have also found limiting playtime to a few hours rather than a whole afternoon or day helps to keep down trouble too. Colin is now almost eight and in school all day, so he is allowed one friend for one and a half hours once a week after school and one friend for three hours on the weekend. We continue to remind Colin of the rules before any activity and repeat, 'Think before you do things.' He is also allowed one sport per season."

"I schedule a visit with another child on a day when I have lots of time," explains Mary from Troy, New York. "What seems to work best is scheduled activities with other children. For example, we work on a project together, play a simple game, or go outdoors. I've also found that going to a playground with the other children seems to cause fewer problems (my son can be as active as he wants and he fits right in with the other screaming active children)."

"Limit the number of children at one time," suggests Terri from Moravia, New York. "We also teach Ryan's friends to share their feelings with Ryan [if Ryan does something they dislike]." Just as parents should teach their child to express feelings verbally rather than physically, it is helpful if playmates are taught to share feelings rather than become hostile or aggressive with the child with AD/HD.

"Ryan has trouble keeping his hands to himself," continued Terri. "We place a © symbol on his hands as a reminder. He likes this." Parents can have rubber stamps like this or one of a hand with a line drawn through it made at most print shops and office supply stores.

Peter from Colorado Springs, Colorado, offers, "Our daughter has the most difficulty on the playground at recess. She would complain that she had no friends, that no one ever wanted to play with her. We talked with her teacher who suggested that Stephanie look for another child who was also alone on the playground and ask that child if he or she wanted to play a game. The next day Stephanie's teacher spotted a child standing alone and encouraged Stephanie to approach her. The two children now play together at recess."

My son had this same problem, so I encouraged him to find a friend on the playground. The friend he found, on his own, was a boy a year younger. Christopher came home from school and elatedly told me about him. I was thrilled until he added, "He's hyperactive, but his parents won't let him take medicine." My heart sank, but with a smile I said, "I'm glad you made a friend, but when you are with your friend you must remember the school rules and follow them at all times." Three days later, I received a call from the school. Christopher and his new friend had spent the past two recesses in the school office and that particular day his friend had talked him into turning off the electricity to the entire school. His homebase teacher then spent the next two weeks keeping the children apart while I worked to convince Christopher that his friend was not a good choice on the playground. Be sure you talk with your child about appropriate playmates and peer pressure. (I must admit that I'm not sure who the real culprit was in the electricity escapade because a year later when we were visiting friends who lived in an apartment—yup, you guessed it—he turned off the electricity to the entire apartment building.)

Julie, from Newark, Ohio, encourages her son "to play with children who are younger than he and who even look up to him. This builds his self-esteem and allows him to practice getting along with other kids without being made fun of by older kids. My husband and I playact behavior that is particularly difficult to modify in our son with AD/HD. Usually, this allows him to see what he is doing wrong. Then we playact other ways to handle a situation." Through role playing, a parent can teach a child to make introductions, to express feelings rather than act out against playmates, how to share a toy and when to do it, what not to do when a playmate is using a toy they want to play with, and how to take turns.

"I try to make sure that my fifth-grader son fits in with the crowd as much as possible," continues Julie. "He is usually made fun of by other children for his behavior and any other little thing that kids can pick on. So I try to make sure that his clothing or haircut or even his lunch isn't another thing that will cause him taunting by friends or classmates. I don't tell him I am doing this, of course.

"I avoid team sports for my son. Swimming, golf, and karate are sports in which he seems to be able to excel. I find that he is about two years behind the other boys his age when it comes to his ability to play sports. Putting him on a team with his peers just causes trouble.

"When my son is having difficulty with socialization, I arrange social contacts for him without his knowledge. My son gets along better with one playmate and I try to arrange the playtime in our home so that I can supervise and correct a situation if it should get out of hand. I have even used bribery in the form of movies, swimming, or special trips or activities to get a reluctant playmate to come over and play."

"I have found that my daughter does fairly well in group situations," Tracy from Indianapolis, Indiana, comments. "She seems to have a good handle on how to behave with her friends, but I have also noticed that she cannot play indefinitely with them. Group situations are very stimulating for her so eventually she becomes bothersome. Currently, she can stay in control for about one hour and fifteen minutes (she used to lose it after fifteen or twenty minutes, so she's making progress). I always give her a specific time frame for playing with friends. When time is up, she's to come inside and find something quiet to do, such as reading or watching an educational program on television. I always make a point of telling her how well she played with her friends (sharing, taking turns, etc.)."

Dan from Santa Barbara, California, advises parents to "establish clear rules for social behavior and then to discuss the rules with your child. Role play. Write the rules down and review them with your child before playtime whenever possible." Also when the child is old enough, around the second grade, he suggests that parents begin teaching how to avoid violating another's personal space, especially when the child gets angry. "Tell your child that when he begins to feel angry or is angry that he is always to keep his hands within his own personal space—that he is not to let his hands reach into another space."

They rarely pick up the importance of personal space on their own. I demonstrated personal space to my sons using a Hula Hoop. One day I heard Christopher say to his brother, "Blake, move out of my personal space." Blake moved, but not before he grabbed the toy he had his eye on!

"Having a family playtime has taught our son how to play with others," says Robin from Warren, New Jersey. "We've taught him how to take turns, to talk politely, to accept that his turn is over for a few minutes, to wait his turn—but practice and patience is needed if you want to be an effective teacher to your child."

"My son wanted to play a team sport," explains Ann from Boston. "Instead of discouraging him, we told him to decide what sport he truly wanted to play. He chose baseball. We then taught him everything he needed to know about the sport. And we practiced with him every chance we got until he could hit and catch the ball very well. We told him if he really wanted to play then he had to become an expert at the game so the kids wouldn't tease him. Although he made some mistakes last year, he was considered a valuable player and he got the respect he deserved. But it took a lot of practice to get where he is."

For information on teaching social skills, read *If Your Child Is Hyperactive, Inattentive, Impulsive, Distractible . . . Helping the ADD (Attention Deficit Disorder)-Hyperactive Child*, by Stephen W. Garber, PhD, Marianne Daniels Garber, PhD, and Robyn Freedman Spizman (New York: Villard, 1990). This book also provides examples on how to help your child learn impulse control, beat distractions, control activity levels and aggression, follow rules, and lengthen attention span. Another book, *Hyperactivity: Why Won't My Child Pay Attention?* by Dr. Sam Goldstein and Dr. Michael Goldstein (New York: John Wiley and Sons, 1992), identifies the social skills children must develop and explains in detail how parents can teach these skills to their children.

Another very informative and useful book is *Helping the Child Who Doesn't Fit In*, by Marshall Duke and Stephen Nowicki Jr. (Atlanta: Peachtree, 1991). In their book, the authors refer to their area of research using the term *dyssemia*, which means a difficulty in using and understanding nonverbal signs and signals. Parents will discover many tips and suggestions that can be used to help teach their children how to fit in.

## Siblings

In families with one or more children who have AD/HD, the scales are often tipped in favor of the child or children with AD/HD, or so it appears to the non-AD/HD sibling. Put yourself in the place of your non-AD/HD child. What do you see? You probably aren't surprised to see a sibling who receives a great deal of attention for everything he does, whether it's appropriate or not—a child who monopolizes mom's and dad's time. You may also see a sibling who never walks by without slugging you, who interrupts and pesters you constantly, a brother who never knocks before coming into your bedroom, or a sister who "borrows" your belongings and never returns them because she cannot find them.

As the non-AD/HD sibling, assess how this makes you feel. You no doubt will discover feelings of resentment, anger, and jealousy. After all, the child with AD/HD does receive a great deal more involvement, support, and focused time from his parents, even when mom and dad strive to strike a balance between their children. Even when the sibling is mature enough to understand AD/HD and the time commitment parents must make to the child, feelings of animosity, indignation, and envy can, and often do, exist. Because of this, it's imperative that parents make a special effort from the start to spend more time with their non-AD/HD children, who need extra assistance and nurturing also.

Be sure your non-AD/HD child is aware that you know that his sibling violates household rules and as a result appears to get away with many things that are off-limits to them. Assure them that their sibling's behavior is often inappropriate but that you are working diligently to help change the troublesome behavior. Children are less apt to harbor hostile feelings if they understand that you are trying to help their sibling maintain control. Empathize with their feelings and concerns; they are legitimate. Enlist their aid. Teach them to recognize appropriate behavior and praise their sibling, or work with them on strategies to alert their sibling in nonhumiliating ways when they are losing control.

## Sibling Rivalry

Debra from Crown Point, Indiana, notes, "At age ten, Denny cannot walk by his sister without tripping her. He constantly walks in on her when she's in the bathroom or her bedroom. He is also always saying or doing things that aggravate her."

Sibling rivalry usually develops when children feel the need to compete for their parent's time and attention. One way to decrease the competition between your children is to spend quality time with each child. You can do this daily by spending fifteen to thirty minutes or so with each child, playing a game of their choice or reading a story to them. Your child will look forward to this special time. Consider making a weekly date with your child. Once a week, on a certain day, spend a few hours of uninterrupted quality time together, perhaps seeing a movie or going bowling.

"We leave the child with AD/HD at home or have him away from the home for a time," explains Ellen from Oconomowoc, Wisconsin. "We then spend that time doing something with our other two children that we couldn't normally do."

Most parents have extremely tight schedules so you may wonder how you can find the time to make a date with your child. Maybe it won't be quite as difficult as you suspect. Take a good look at your week. Is there something you do with your child once a week anyway that could be extended into a date?

For instance, my son had counseling every Thursday at 4:00 p.m. After the counseling session I would take him out to eat at his favorite restaurant. This restaurant has been around forever and still has the old-fashioned jukeboxes at each booth. We played song after song and ate lots of pizza and genuinely enjoyed each other's company. Afterward, we would stop and play a game of miniature golf, visit a video game arcade, or have ice cream. While we were out enjoying ourselves, my husband was eating dinner out with our other son. We gave up one family meal a week to spend individual time with each of our children.

Unfortunately, competing for parent's time and attention cannot be eliminated entirely, so children must also be taught to get along with each other. Children should be encouraged to play together cooperatively, as a team. You can help your children learn cooperative play by offering rewards or incentives that promote choices. Consider setting up a system whereby each of your children receives a penny or a marble to add to a jar every time they play together without arguing and fighting (stickers and a chart can also be used). After they collect twenty marbles, for example, they earn a meal at their favorite restaurant or they can choose a family outing of their choice. If, however, they choose not to cooperate and an argument or fight erupts, they are both sent to time-out or suffer another consequence. The choice is theirs. Before implementing this system, talk with your children about the rules of fair play and how they can earn special privileges for playing together harmoniously.

Take the opportunity to praise your children when they are playing together cooperatively. Positive reinforcement will reduce sibling fights far more quickly than will punishing your children. Encourage your children to come up with their own solutions to problems. ("You both want to play with the same toy at the same time. How can the two of you work this out?")

For children who fight and argue over toys, consider putting the toys in time-out for the rest of the day. Naturally, your children spend the next five minutes (more or less time, depending on their ages) in time-out also. For children whose fighting over a television program gets out of hand, simply turn the television off. Then tell them they can turn the television on in thirty minutes, but it will be turned off again if they can't agree on a program without arguing. This approach encourages children to settle their differences among themselves without involving a parent.

"Encourage your children to express their angry feelings verbally to their siblings rather than striking out at a sibling," offers Suzanne from Houston, Texas. "Even young children can be taught to label feelings if you help them identify how they feel. Attach a name to a feeling such as anger, then the next time a sibling hits them they can say, 'I get so angry when you hit me. Don't hit me again.' Like everything else though, this takes time for parents to teach, but it's worth it in the long run."

Children can be taught to hit a punching bag or pillow or to express their anger on paper through drawing or in a diary. It is the parent's responsibility to teach their children to find creative outlets for anger. Hitting, kicking, biting, pulling hair, or calling a sibling names should not be tolerated. Teach your child how to confront in a controlled manner a sibling who hits, bites, kicks, destroys a treasured toy, or borrows items without asking first. Don't hesitate to give them specific words to use in such situations. For example, "It makes me so angry when you borrow my clothes without asking me. Please don't go into my room again."

Don't be afraid to share stories with your children about the hassles you had with your siblings. Children will be amazed to learn that you and Uncle Tim used to argue over toys or over what television show to watch, especially when they see how well you and Uncle Tim get along now. A good book to review is *Siblings without Rivalry: How to Help Your Children Live Together so You Can Live Too* by Adele Faber and Elaine Mazlish (New York: Avon, 1998).

## When with a Babysitter

Heidi is a twenty-one-year-old college student from Swanton, Ohio. AD/HD runs on both sides of her family. Heidi admits that she also has mild AD/HD and often uses medication to study. Heidi has had four years' experience babysitting two children with AD/HD (on both a full- and part-time basis). She offers the following advice to babysitters:

- **Find things to do with the children**. Don't let them go off on their own or they'll find things to do that will be unacceptable. Include them in what you are doing. If you're fixing dinner for them, let them help. That way you can keep an eye on them.
- **Don't spank or yell when they do something wrong**. Use time-out and use it consistently, otherwise the children will end up controlling you.
- **Investigate even if the situation looks normal**. You may be surprised by what you find.
- **Try to never let them out of your sight**. They can get into trouble in a matter of minutes.
- **Always get instructions from the parents** as to what the child can or cannot do. If you are unsure if the child is able to do something, tell him no, but let him know that you will ask his parents when they telephone home.

- **Be sure you know when to give medications** and how much. Write everything down. Set a timer if you think you might need a reminder for giving medications. Once you've been around the child enough, a timer may not be necessary. You will be able to tell when medication has worn off.

Remember, it's important that the behavior reward-and-punishment system you establish be used consistently, even when your children are with a babysitter. To help the sitter maintain your system, give him or her a written schedule of what to do and when to do it, including exact guidelines for behavior and rewards and punishments.

## Running Errands

Many parents of younger children with AD/HD would rather not take their children with them to run errands. Some parents handle this by scheduling errands, such as grocery shopping, banking, going to the post office and the cleaners, for the same day each week and hire a babysitter to stay with the children. Unfortunately, this is not an option for some parents, either because they can't afford to hire a sitter just for this purpose or they can't find a sitter for just one day a week. If you feel you have no choice but to include your child in errand running, here are some other options to consider:

- **Run errands on your lunch hour or plan one stop on your way home from work each day**. Nancy from Chicago encourages parents to "follow a routine such as the library on Monday, the drugstore on Tuesday, the cleaners on Wednesday, the grocery store on Thursday, the bank on Friday. Even if you must pick up your child on the way home, he or she can usually handle an excursion of less than fifteen minutes, especially once a routine is established."
- "**Consider one-stop shopping** whenever possible," advises Dan from Tampa, Florida. "Always use the drive-in window for banking if the children are with you." Some of this may cost extra pennies, compared with shopping for bargains, but it's worth it for the efficiency.
- "**Negotiate how the errands will be shared with your spouse**," says Greg, a father of two hyperactive children, from Grand

Rapids, Michigan. "Every Saturday morning I do the grocery shopping for the week. This way my wife never has to take the children to the grocery store. If we run out of something during the week, I stop at the store on my way home from work."

- **Ask a neighbor to watch the children** a few hours a week. If you can't afford to pay for the service or the neighbor won't accept payment, offer to care for her children during the week in exchange or offer to pick up items she needs while you are out.

## Shopping with Your Child

Learning to shop is an educational experience and a task that children need to learn to prepare themselves for independent living. On those days when you decide to include your child, consider the following advice:

- **Take your child along when he or she is well rested and in a cooperative mood**. Take along nutritional snacks from home and toys for her to play with when boredom sets in. Remember to keep those hands busy so they are not tempted to reach out inappropriately. Hand-held video games work well for children over age five.
- **Use a stroller or a shopping cart** for younger children. A stroller will keep your child safe and secure and save you from needlessly chasing after him. Even toddlers who are hyperactive will often stay in a stroller (and preschoolers in a cart) as long as you provide them with something to do (toys or snacks) and you keep the stroller moving. But don't expect them to remain seated for hours at a time and remember that, once you let them out for even a few minutes, chances are they won't want to get back in, so plan your time accordingly.
- **Plan short trips**, not major marathons.
- **Establish the rules before entering the store**. Says Brenda from Little Rock, Arkansas, "Our rules are (1) you must stay with mom or dad and you are not to be walking alone, (2) you are not to touch anything without first asking permission to do so, and (3) we buy only items on our list. If a rule is broken, our son is placed in time-out immediately."
- **Praise your child's appropriate behavior frequently**. For example, "You're staying right next to Mom, good for you" or "Thank

you for not touching the Halloween display." Make physical contact with your child often by touching him on the shoulder, holding his hand, or giving him a hug.

- **"Know in advance what you must buy.** Make a list and take it with you," suggests Peter from Colorado Springs, Colorado. "Then involve your child in the actual shopping process as much as possible. Let your child place items in the cart or tell her what items to select from the shelf. Keep her busy and out of trouble."

- **Use time-out if needed**. (See chapter 3 for more hints on using time-out effectively.)

- **Provide a reward**. "After a good shopping experience, I reward my son with an ice-cream cone or take him to the park on the way home," explains Annie from Atlanta, Georgia. "I want him to know that I appreciate his cooperation and that he did a good job controlling himself."

- **Shop as a family**, suggests Terri from Moravia, New York. "That way," she says, "if our son's behavior becomes inappropriate he is taken from the store to the car while the other person completes the shopping."

- **Write your grocery list "according to where the food is in the store**," adds Jody, "then dash through the aisles, and look for the checkout with the shortest line. Use a drive-through to get milk, bread, or other needed items. If possible, send someone else to the store for you."

- **Avoid taking your child to places where he will experience extreme difficulty**. "If there's a place I know he'll misbehave, I avoid it," admits Diane, "but we need groceries and clothing. At first I let him push the cart. That worked for a while. Then I gave him coupons of items to look for, but he became frustrated because he couldn't find the items. Now he gets to pick out one special food item on each trip to the store. This has been working great in combination with the coupons and pushing the cart."

## Taking Your Child to Restaurants

No time to prepare a meal, but recoil at the thought of taking your son or daughter out to a restaurant? While there is no sure way to prevent your child from creating a scene in a restaurant, you can improve the odds by choosing the right restaurant at the right time of the day and following some of the suggestions other parents offer.

"Take your child to a restaurant that is child-friendly," recommends Nancy from Rockville, Maryland. "A child-friendly restaurant dispenses children's menus, place mats for coloring, and provides crayons. They often have a play area with slides and rides. You know when you are in a child-friendly restaurant—there are always lots of highchairs."

Child-friendly restaurants are not always fast-food restaurants. They are often casual family restaurants that serve the type of food adults and child alike enjoy. They provide bibs for babies and toddlers as well as coloring place mats and crayons for preschoolers, and their prices fit a family budget. Sometimes these establishments also have video arcades for older children.

Other suggestions from parents include the following:

- **"Eat at restaurants that have salad, fruit, and soup bars.** Children can begin eating almost immediately. The same holds true for cafeterias. Children can select their own food, which usually means they'll eat what they choose," said David from Snyder, New York.
- **"Don't choose an intimate restaurant for a family meal,"** offers Sharon from Indianapolis, Indiana. "If your child has a temper tantrum or raises her voice, you can bet that everyone in the restaurant will be looking unhappily your way. Choose a restaurant where the noise level is high because of other families. That way when she acts up, no one will notice or care."
- **"Take something along from home to entertain your child** (like a travel-size board game) or read a book to him while you are waiting for your food," advises Mary Jo from Livonia, Michigan. "It's hard for all children to sit quietly and wait for something but doubly hard for hyperactive children. If necessary, one parent can walk the child around the restaurant or take a walk outside for ten or fifteen minutes until the food arrives. When the meal is finished, don't linger drinking two cups of coffee. You're only asking for trouble. Pay your bill and leave."
- **"We always take a favorite babysitter along** with us for special occasions," explains Diane from Northport, Alabama. "She helps our son order his food, amuses him until his meal arrives, and

entertains him until it's time to leave. He's happy because he's receiving her undivided attention when we, his parents, are otherwise engaged."

- **"Don't go to a restaurant during peak dining hours**. Waiters are very busy and service is often slower. We have found dining out to be easiest on all of us if we get to a restaurant around five o'clock in the evening. A nearly empty restaurant seems to have a calming effect on our son," advises George from Wheaton, Illinois.

- **Use time-out**. "When our first grader acts up in a restaurant, we remove him from the table and put him in time-out," explains Debra from Boston, Massachusetts. "Depending on the restaurant, this might be in the foyer, the restroom, or in the car. We always bring him back to the table after five minutes of time-out, as we don't want him to think that if he acts up the whole family leaves the restaurant. Like any other child, he must learn to act appropriately when out in public."

- **Rarely go to restaurants**. "We go to restaurants only when Grandma and Grandpa insist," laughs Jody. "They stay at the table and place our orders. I take the children and walk, run, and crawl around until the food comes."

## Keeping Bedrooms Tidy

"Clean up your room" may mean one thing to you and another to your child. For instance, when I say, "Clean up your room," to my nine-year-old son, I mean make the bed, hang up the clean clothes, pick up the toys, put dirty clothes in the laundry room, clean off the top of the desk, and empty the wastepaper basket. However, if I don't clarify this each time, my son will focus on one thing only and believe his work is completed once that one thing has been done.

Most children do best with a chart that clearly defines and organizes the tasks. We use one that is displayed in our son's room. I supervise from a distance to help him remain on target. He checks off each task as it is completed. For children who can't read, use pictures from magazines or draw your own.

Decide ahead of time what the consequence will be if your child does not clean his room. Noncompliance may mean having to withdraw a privilege (no playing with the neighborhood children tonight). Be certain your child understands this before you start any charting system.

For young children, provide plastic baskets for toys. Label baskets with pictures. Cars and trucks go in one basket, dolls in another, stuffed animals in an additional one. Place a small laundry basket in the child's room where she can place dirty clothes. Provide a footstool so children can reach hangers in the closet. Use a small floor bookcase for books. For teaching a young child how to make a bed, start the process at the end rather than the beginning. In other words, teach the child first to pull up the bedspread or comforter. When that is mastered, have him pull up the blanket first, then the comforter, and so on, until he has mastered making the bed.

Many parents have children who refuse to pick up their toys. Terri, from Moravia, New York, is one such mom. "If toys are not picked up when requested, our son loses the toys for one day." One father says, "We hold everything hostage that we pick up in the bedroom after our daughter has been issued a warning. She then has to earn everything back, including clothes, cassette tapes, magazines, hair ribbons, etc." Another mother uses what she calls the end-of-the-week box. Everything she picks up during the week the children were supposed to pick up but didn't goes into the box and stays there until week's end. Occasionally, she admits, she's willing to negotiate for an item's release before the end of the week.

"Keeping bedrooms tidy was and still is a lost cause," acknowledges one mom. "Part of this is being a boy and part of it is AD/HD. Once I accepted that, my life and my son's became a lot easier. Once a week he has to clean his room. He receives payment for this chore. Clothes that are not turned right side out go through the laundry inside out and are hung up inside out. At age twelve, getting ready in the morning is his responsibility. It's to his advantage to turn his clothes right side out before throwing them down the chute."

"We limit the amount of toys available to play with at one time," explains Missy from Bow, New Hampshire. "We also store some toys and rotate them with toys with which Colin has become bored. We got rid of the messy toy box and have found that shelves (closet or wall variety) work better. Carefully selected toys are within easy view for selecting and have a specific place on the shelf, which helps in picking up. Buckets are great for small toys, cars, and blocks."

## Social Gatherings

Your favorite cousin is getting married and your children are invited to the church wedding and the reception, but you don't feel comfortable including Jimmy in the festivities because of his temper tantrums and wild behavior. Although Jimmy takes medication, you're certain that the change in the daily routine, coupled with the excitement of being with so many friends and relatives, will be too much for him to handle. Yet you don't feel right taking one child and not the other. What can you do to include Jimmy in the celebration gaieties, yet keep his behavior in check (at least most of the time)?

First, take an inventory of your child's strengths and challenges. If he usually attends religious services and is able to sit through much or all of them, then he probably can attend the wedding without being disruptive. But even if your child is used to attending religious services, try to have a backup plan in case he has difficulty sitting through the ceremony. Is there a babysitter you can hire to take along with you? Is there someone who wouldn't mind taking him outside for a few moments during the wedding, such as an older brother, sister, cousin, or favorite relative? Whatever route you choose, be sure to discuss your plan ahead of time with your child and whoever will assist if needed.

Consider the reception. How many other children will be attending? Is it being held indoors or outside? If inside, is it a formal reception at a country club or luxury hotel, or at a Knights of Columbus hall? Obviously, the formal reception may be more difficult for your child to handle. Will cocktails and hors d'oeuvres be served first? If only drinks will be available, how long before the meal is served? What will your child do during cocktail hour? How long can he wait to eat? Would it be more appropriate to take your child home or to a sitter's house after the wedding? Is it feasible to take a babysitter with you to the reception, preferably one who can then drive your child home when he has reached his limit? Does it make sense for you and your spouse to drive separately and then plan for one of you to leave early with your child? Clearly, there are many options for any type of social gathering, so consider your child's temperament and behavior in certain situations and then devise your plan of action. As one mom from Randolph, New Jersey, advises, "Set reasonable expectations."

## Preparing Your Child for a Social Occasion

Before the social event (whether it's a family reunion, wedding, birthday party, picnic, or baptism) talk about it with your child ahead of time, but not weeks in advance since this tends to have a snowball effect with some children. The more you talk about it, the more excited they become, to the point where they can't sleep for several nights before the event because they are so intoxicated with anticipation. Not only can't they sleep but their daytime behavior suffers also. So break the news a few days before, or even the day before, the actual event.

"Make sure you talk with your child about the event so he knows what type of day it will be and what is expected of him," offers Janet from Seattle, Washington. "Tell him what the rules are for that day. Explain the rules again before you leave the house and again while you are en route. Have him repeat the rules to you so you are sure he understands them fully. Be sure your child gets enough sleep the night before and has been fed before you leave your house. [For small children, take along a snack and a few small toys.] Always remind him of the consequences of unacceptable behavior (he'll be sent to time-out, sent home with a babysitter or with dad, while the rest of the family enjoys themselves). If he's older, you may want to emphasize that he will also lose the privilege of having a friend spend the night or going fishing with dad the next evening. Emphasize the benefits of acceptable behavior."

Remember to give praise constantly for good behavior either verbally or with a physical gesture, such as patting his shoulder or his hair, touching his shoulder, giving him a hug, or by giving him tokens, such as stickers, play money, or whatever you use in your home for positive reinforcement.

"Express confidence in your child," suggests Barbara from Mississippi, "and let him know that you appreciate his willingness to be cooperative. If he should fail, don't criticize. Instead, tell him you know he will try to do better the next time."

## Birthday Parties

"I have never let my son with AD/HD have the kind of birthday party where children are invited to our home, simply because I was afraid that no children would come," laments Julie from Newark, Ohio. "Our son, like many children with AD/HD, has been a social outcast throughout most of his school career. So I always have an in-school party because the partygoers will always show up! I make sure the treat I take in is extra 'cool' so that my son has at least some time when his peers think he is also 'cool.'

"If my son is invited to another child's birthday party, I always ask the parent of the birthday child if she could use a little help and then I stay for the party, too. That way I can keep an eye on my son and intercede if he starts to get out of hand."

Kate from Carlinville, Illinois, commented that her son David used to always rain on others' birthday parades. "He grabbed things, tried to be the star, blew out candles, and ultimately pouted or threw a temper tantrum. Oddly enough, seeing his ugly behavior on videotape seemed to shock him a bit and his behavior has improved."

## When You Are Trying to Talk on the Phone

Establish age-appropriate rules and explain those rules to your child. "I remind Ryan of the phone rules and if he does not comply, he waits in his room until my conversation has ended," says Terri from Moravia, New York. Jackie from Monroe, Michigan, explains, "Tell your child, 'You are not to interrupt me when I am on the telephone. If you need something, please stand next to me quietly until I notice you.' Never make your child wait longer than a minute and always reward him for following the rules."

"Older children can be encouraged to write a note," offers Mary Squire, PhD, "if it's something that just can't wait. A parent can then write the answer to the child." But do not let children use this method as a means to avoid talking with the parent.

"Teach your child to say 'excuse me' and then to wait for you to acknowledge him," advises Lynn. "Never allow him to say 'excuse me' and begin to talk with you immediately. He must realize that you are having a conversation with someone else and that you must also say 'excuse me' to the person with whom you are speaking before you can speak with him."

"I tell my children that I need to make a phone call and if they have anything important to discuss with me or ask me they should do it now, before I place the call," shares Joanne from Iowa. "They do know that it is okay to interrupt me if there is an emergency. In an emergency, they are to say, 'Excuse me, this is an emergency.' Be sure you explain to them what *you* consider an emergency."

"Teach your children by example," offers Ann from Boston. "Never interrupt them when they are talking, and tell them you expect the same courtesy from them when you are talking. Be consistent. Never let them interrupt you one time and punish them for interrupting the next time."

"When I talk on the phone we make it into a contest," says Mary from Troy, New York. "Every time I got on the phone I would inform [my son] beforehand and then set the timer. Each time he would try to break his record from the previous call (for example, one minute of not interrupting the first call; one minute ten seconds the second call). When he broke his record he received a star (on a chart) and then would receive a special treat."

## Bad Manners

"Always use good manners in the home," advises Hanna from Richmond, Virginia. "Children with AD/HD seem to have a problem learning appropriate manners. I think if you consistently say 'please' and 'thank you' to your child, eventually she'll learn to say 'please' and 'thank you' to you and to others. We also always use formal table manners at home. We've established the rules for good manners that we expect to be followed at all times. We've written them down for our son and daughter and we remind them to use good manners when they are out with us. For instance, 'When I introduce you to a friend of mine, I expect you to say hello with a smile on your face' or 'Always say excuse me when you must step in front of someone.' Always compliment your child when she displays good manners." Etiquette and manners classes are often available in the community. (You might inquire at the local YMCA or other community centers.)

You may want to write down the appropriate way to answer the phone on an index card and place the card next to the phone. Remind your child to use the card every time he answers the phone. With practice, he will soon be answering the phone in the proper manner on his own.

## Temper Tantrums

Many children experience temper tantrums, but children with AD/HD experience tantrums that are often more frequent and intense. Parents report these tantrums to be severe, very explosive, long in length (sometimes as long as an hour), and not age-appropriate. As one mom said, "You expect two-year-olds to have temper tantrums, but not seven-, eight-, or ten-year-olds." Some reported their child's tantrums as violent. "My son has had several tantrums that were so severe that he literally tore his room apart in a matter of a few minutes," one mom sadly admitted. "He was totally out of control." One dad reported that it took him an hour to patch all the holes in his son's bedroom walls. (Remember, many children with AD/HD will not experience such extreme temper tantrums.)

Tantrums usually happen because the child has lost his ability to cope—the result is usually an angry or frustrated child. As parents, you can help your child by looking for the cause of the tantrum. What has upset him? Has he been required to sit still too long? Did you fail to give sufficient notice before changing activities? Is he frustrated by a homework assignment? Were your expectations too high? Is he overstimulated by the day's activities? Was he surprised to find visitors in his home when he came home from school? Slow-to-adapt children may have difficulty with changes in routines.

Every time your child experiences a temper tantrum, record the details: time of day, where it happened, and the perceived cause. Eventually a pattern will develop and you will then have something to work with. For instance, my son generally experiences tantrums after school. He either loses it in the car on the way home or as soon as we get home. He rarely has difficulties with his behavior at school and I believe this is because he works very hard to keep himself under control during school hours. Once he feels he is on safe turf, he loses total control because he's been pressured for hours beyond his ability to cope. Once I recognized the pattern, I was able to formulate a plan. He loves classical music; he finds it very soothing and relaxing, so one of his favorite CDs is always playing now when he gets in the car. On warm or hot days, I always have a cold bottle of fruit juice waiting for him. On cold days, I offer him a snack. Because we have a long drive home (30 minutes), I let him set the pace. Some days he wants to talk, but most days he just sits quietly, sipping his drink and listening to the music. Nine out of ten times this approach works very well.

With a little effort on your part, you too can often help your child prevent tantrums that occur at specific times or under certain conditions by tuning in to your child's temperament, recording your findings, and devising a plan. The important thing to remember is that these types of tantrums are not premeditated nor is the child trying to manipulate you. Your child needs you to help him find a way to prevent the tantrum or to help him stop one that has started. The good news is that eventually the temper tantrums decrease in intensity and finally dissipate.

## Ways You Can Help

You can help your child deal with these types of tantrums. Not all of the following suggestions will work with every child, so you may need to try a few before you find one that works.

"We've tried holding our daughter when she has a temper tantrum, but she only pushes us away and seems to get angrier," recalls one mother from Baton Rouge, Louisiana. "Now, we stay in the same room, wait a few minutes, then start talking to her in a calm, firm voice. We'll say something like, 'I know you are disappointed (or angry), but now it is time to stop. You must stop. Now take a deep breath. Now take another deep breath.' This usually works for her."

"When Ryan's tantrum escalates, we usually hold him until he calms down," says Terri, his mother. "When he's really upset, we stay with him and do holding therapy. We use a one-minute cool-down time (the child must remain still and breathe deeply) after the tantrum to make sure the tantrum is really over. If Ryan destroys his room in anger, money is taken from his bank to help with the [cost of] repairs or Ryan is expected to [physically] help repair his room." For detailed information on the holding technique, consult *Holding Time* by Martha G. Welch, MD (New York: Simon and Schuster / Fireside, 1988).

"Baths are a great way to calm down a child," says Janie from Scranton, Pennsylvania. "Whenever my daughter lost control when she was younger (under age six), I'd immediately put her in the bathtub. The water always had a calming effect on her within minutes. I must admit though that getting her into the bathtub was sometimes a real hassle."

"Temper tantrums were a big problem for David before Ritalin," remembers Kate. "Nothing worked really well, but things always went poorly if he managed to draw us in emotionally. We found it necessary to remove him physically from the room, put him in his room, shut the door, and walk away. (David rarely tore up anything so this worked.) He would scream and scream but eventually tire out. To avoid going nuts, we would turn up the television and try our best to ignore him. David hated that! No audience, no fun."

Some children can be sent to their rooms, but most children are safer (and feel safer) if you remain nearby. If your child experiences violent temper tantrums, it is imperative that you stay with him. Don't give him the opportunity to destroy his room or hit you or anyone else. Set household rules for children who react violently and be sure they understand the consequences. In our home our children may not hit, spit, swear, or throw anything. They can, however, beat on a pillow, jump up and down, throw themselves down on the floor or their bed, or ask for someone to hold them. Should one of them break the rule and throw something, I ask if he is choosing to give up a favorite activity that evening. Sometimes that is enough to halt the behavior. If the throwing continues, I then stop it by gently putting my arm across his arms and speaking calmly to him until the tantrum subsides. Once he has calmed down we talk about what happened (we identify the cause of the tantrum) and discuss other ways that he might have dealt with his feelings.

Children who continue to have temper tantrums often do so because, unlike adults, they lack the necessary vocabulary to adequately express the anger or frustration they feel. Talking to your child about his feelings and labeling those feelings is the first step you can take to begin teaching your child to express his feelings in words rather than in actions. So, listen carefully when your child talks about those feelings. The next time you witness the beginning of a tantrum, intervene. Remove him from the activity and then help him verbally label those feelings. If you remain calm, your child will calm down much faster.

"Show your child how you handle frustrations and disappointments," offers Hanna from Richmond, Virginia. "If you burn dinner, point this out to your child. Say something like, 'Look what I did. Well, I'll just have to microwave last night's leftovers for dinner tonight. We'll have meatloaf tomorrow night instead.' This teaches your child other ways to handle frustrations." Parents who encountered mishaps like Hanna's might want to ask their child if they can think of other ways to handle the problem. Let your child help brainstorm solutions to problems with you.

Unfortunately, for some parents it's easy to get caught up in their child's temper tantrum. You may find yourself striking back at your child if he hits or kicks you. If he's screaming, you may find yourself screaming back. Please realize that this is a high-risk situation. It is during times of stress that parents are at risk of physically or verbally abusing their children. If you find yourself getting caught up in the moment, take a giant step or two away from your child, take a deep breath, and count to ten. If necessary, leave the room and ask someone else to step in.

## Nonstop Talking

"My son will ask the same question over and over again. I answer his question, then ask him to repeat the answer," explains Kristin from Flint, Michigan. "Once I'm assured he has processed the information, I refuse to answer the same question again."

"We understand our daughter's need to talk about her day and we are willing to spend time listening and discussing it with her," acknowledges Jim from Norfolk, Virginia. "But given the opportunity she'd talk nonstop until bedtime. We now give her scheduled time after school (thirty minutes), after dinner (ten minutes), and just before bedtime (fifteen minutes). She may talk about whatever she wants and we listen carefully, but when the timer goes off the conversation must end shortly after (usually one minute). This generally controls the excessive talking."

"We use *1-2-3 Magic*," offers Missy from Bow, New Hampshire. "For example, 'Please be quiet.' Child continues to talk. 'One!' Child continues talking. 'Two!' Child does not stop talking. 'Three! Take five in your room. When the five minutes are up, you can come out if you are quiet.'" For more information on this technique, refer to *1-2-3 Magic: Training Your Preschoolers and Preteens to Do What You Want* by Thomas Phelan, MD (Glen Ellyn, IL: Child Management Press, 1985).

## Summertime

Some parents look forward to summer because they no longer have to handle phone calls from teachers, school conferences, hassles with homework, lost school books, torn clothes, broken eyeglasses, and school mornings. Other parents dread the thought of summer because their children behave appropriately at school and have few problems with schoolwork. The major difficulties they experience with their children take place at home, so the end of the school year signals distress for these parents. How will I find someone who understands that Jessica is impulsive and needs constant supervision even when she's on medication? Whom can I trust to handle Matthew's behavior problems in an appropriate manner? How will I manage the stress of being with my impulsive, overactive child twenty-four hours a day? How will I keep him occupied and out of mischief long enough to straighten the house in the morning and get my errands done? I can't trust him to play at the neighbor's house or go off bike riding with his friends, yet I don't want to babysit all of the neighborhood children every day either. What will I do with her all day every day for the whole summer? These are real concerns for parents of elementary school–age children who can't be trusted because they are impulsive and hyperactive.

"Even during the summertime, my son needs to be on medication," confesses Jennifer from Cleveland, Ohio. "He's very difficult. At nine years of age, I can't trust him to go off on his own. I worry about his safety, and I worry because he's always getting into things he shouldn't. The first week after school let out he and his younger brother started a small fire in our shed, spray painted brown spots on our white garage doors, went into the neighbor's pond uninvited and unsupervised, and dumped a bucket of paint on the garage floor. Although my youngest son does not have AD/HD, he'll go along with anything my oldest son suggests. After that week, the children were not allowed outside together all summer unless I was with them. So I made a schedule. One child stayed inside for an hour while the other played outside, then they changed places. I did this for the whole summer. It was exhausting, but it kept them out of trouble."

"We put our son in summer day camp. Last summer he went to one camp for six weeks and when that ended I sent him to Boy Scout camp for two weeks," says Linda from Louisiana. "I wish it didn't have to be this way, but at least with camp he stays on a schedule that is not much different than the one we use during the school year. He enjoys camp and it keeps him busy. Be honest though with the camp staff about your child. Make certain they understand your concerns and know what time to administer medications."

Always remind camp staff that medicine *must* be given when indicated. If they inadvertently give a medication later than scheduled, they must let you know so you don't give the next dosage at the usual time. Be sure they understand the necessity of sharing this with you. (My son once received forty milligrams of Ritalin in a two-hour period because the staff failed to inform me that the medication they were to give at noon wasn't administered until two o'clock.) Be sure camp staff understands AD/HD. If your child is hyperactive-impulsive and is a risk taker, make sure camp staff knows he must be monitored closely during unstructured activities, such as swimming or horseback riding. Accidents do happen. In an endeavor to fit in by showing off, my son once attempted to dive off the high platform at a community pool. Unfortunately, at that time, he did not know how to dive. His "dive" not only knocked the wind out of him but he hit the water face first, resulting in a badly bruised forehead and two black eyes. A former teacher witnessed the entire incident and later said she forgot that he needed to be supervised constantly.

"Keep your child on a schedule," advises one mom from Kentucky. "When my daughter wakes up, she eats breakfast, gets dressed, makes her bed, and then can play outside until lunchtime. Lunch and dinner are served at the same time every day. Establish a routine for the summertime, just like you do for the school year. On the first day of vacation, post the schedule and go over it with your child."

If you work and wonder what you should do when summer camp ends, consider Debbie's recommendation: "Hire a babysitter to come into your home. I found it's easier and less problematic if your child is allowed to stay in her own home."

"When boredom sets in, children misbehave," observes Darlene from Kansas City, Kansas. "The trick is to keep your child busy outdoors with a friend, preferably a friend who does not have AD/HD. Structured activities work better than just sending kids outdoors on their own to find something to do. My daughter loves to play dress-up with her friend (a structured activity). I help them create a special area and use a clothesline to hang clothes on. They play for hours. I also keep a list of activities tacked on the bulletin board that she can consult when she gets bored and is looking for something fun to do. Another fun structured activity is "painting" our deck. I give them each a bucket of water and a paint brush and let them paint away. We visit the park once a day, and the library once a week, where she participates in the summer reading program. We have a community neighborhood pool we visit regularly. She plays with the children while I watch from the sidelines and talk with the other mothers. It's a nice break for me.

"We run errands early in the morning because she's usually in a better mood and more cooperative than she is in the afternoon after playing all day. Once the fun starts, she doesn't want to miss anything. But if something does come up and I have to leave, I always invite a friend of hers to come along. Every evening before bedtime I tell her what tomorrow's day will be like. This seems to help a lot."

"I work in my home so taking care of my son myself every day is not an option," Liz from Minneapolis, Minnesota, explains. "But I do want him in the home, so I hire a babysitter four days a week. It works out well for all of us. She entertains my son, but when he needs something only a mom can provide, I'm available. I take more breaks during the summer because I want to be there when he needs me. I plan my summer work schedule months in advance, so the bulk of my work load is completed during the school year.

"Each summer we rent a cottage for two weeks or take the children camping. Before we leave we all get together and make a schedule outlining our day. It's imperative that we maintain a routine so the children, especially our daughter who has AD/HD, know what to expect each day, and we try to maintain that schedule."

Parents not employed outside the home, who face most summer days alone with their child or children, can make weekly charts such as the one shown in table 5.1 that include educational goals for the child to reach as well as time for fun activities and the usual household chores. Set realistic but challenging goals. Be sure educational goals and household chores are age appropriate so they give your child a sense of accomplishment.

Use stickers freely for all completed activities as a means of giving immediate positive feedback. Set a weekly goal that your child can work for and collect on the weekend (sleeping outside in a tent, seeing a movie of her choice on Saturday afternoon, going fishing with grandpa, baking cookies with mom, horseback riding, a day at the beach, bowling, bicycle riding with dad, etc.) after earning a specific number of stickers. Charts can be revised on weekends for the following week and new goals established. If your child is older, be sure to let her choose the weekend activity with your approval.

"I find that if we have someplace to go almost every day, we seem to do better," notes Patrice from Aurora, Illinois. "This past summer I had a notebook of places to go, people to see, and activities to choose from. Having the notebook cut down on [having to make] big decisions out of the blue. I tend to lose my ability to brainstorm and think clearly when my son has especially noisy, active days. Car rides seem to be easier for

Table 5.1. **Weekly Chart**

| Week 1 | Mon. | Tues. | Wed. | Thurs. | Fri. |
|---|---|---|---|---|---|
| Make bed each morning | | | | | |
| Pick up clothes every day | | | | | |
| Begin a collection of something (colored stones, shells, stamps, baseball cards, or postcards) | | | | | |
| Do assigned chores | | | | | |
| Begin to learn to type (15 minutes a day; computer programs are especially helpful because they give immediate feedback) | | | | | |
| Help parent with one meal daily | | | | | |
| Spend time with family playing board games, etc. | | | | | |
| Put toys away before bed | | | | | |
| Get ready for bed | | | | | |

Note: Week 1's chart can be *slightly* altered for week 2.

me than a lot of physical chasing. I do, however, have to separate the kids; one in the front seat and the other in the back seat. I always carry an activity box and lots of snacks."

Other suggestions for summer activities include beginning a garden, taking swimming or golf lessons, playing miniature golf, horseback riding, taking weekly field trips to such places as a firehouse, a farm, the airport, the train station, a boat marina, historical sites, the zoo, the art museum, a computer store, a video arcade, a bicycle shop, a dairy, the veterinarian's office, or an amusement park. Before weekly field trips, visit the library and choose books on the subject of your upcoming visit.

## Transitions

Shifting from one activity to another is often very difficult for the child with AD/HD. "Drew usually doesn't have problems with transitions if it's something he wants to do. If it isn't, you'll pay for it," says Debra from Crown Point, Indiana. "I try to always tell him ahead of time if there's a change in routine. The other day, though, I scheduled a hair appointment for him after school. Of course, I couldn't forewarn him because I made the appointment that morning. He ended up throwing a temper tantrum in the car. I have to admit it really aggravates me sometimes that I have to schedule appointments around his temperament. My advice is to make appointments the day before, then you can warn about changes in routine in advance."

Making transitions from one activity to another or from one place to another may be extremely difficult for certain children with AD/HD. All children, not just children with AD/HD, accept changes in routine and act more cooperatively when they are forewarned. As parents, attempt to provide your child with a smooth transition whenever possible. With small children, a ten-minute warning may be sufficient. With some children warnings about changes in schedules may need to be given hours before or even days before, so they can process the information and prepare themselves mentally for a doctor's appointment, a shopping venture, or a visit to grandma's after school. Other children will think about it and work themselves into a tizzy if you tell them too soon. Children with AD/HD are not trying to make life difficult for you as they truly have trouble making transitions, so discover what method works best for your child and use it consistently.

Parents should also be aware that major transition times (meals and bedtime) are especially difficult for children with AD/HD. Because of this, it's important that parents—not an alternate caregiver—try to be present during these times.

When giving warnings that changes are about to occur, make eye contact and speak clearly and positively to your child. For example, "In ten minutes, when the buzzer goes off, it will be time for all of us to leave for church. I know changing activities is difficult for you. That's why I'm giving you a ten-minute warning."

## Watching Too Much Television

Like many other children, children with AD/HD enjoy watching television. However, some parents report that their children with AD/HD (those displaying hyperactivity) did not watch television until the early elementary school years, possibly because they couldn't sit still until they reached school age or they simply found other activities more stimulating.

My son was one of those children who never watched television or videos until he reached second grade. Instead, he was a whirlwind of activity from morning until bedtime. When I heard other parents complain that their children watched too much television, I was envious. I would have given anything just to have him sit down and watch television for a half hour so I could let my guard down for a few minutes. When he was finally able to sit through a program, I rejoiced. For the first time in seven years I was able to use the television as an electronic babysitter, and I must admit it felt good. However, I did find that I had to closely monitor the types of programs he watched.

One day my husband innocently purchased the movie *Home Alone*. The three of us sat down that evening to watch the movie together. Within fifteen minutes I knew the movie was a big mistake when my son excitedly exclaimed, "He's hyperactive, just like me." After that movie, jumping on the beds became the sport of the day. A can of hair spray and a lighter made a torch. Broken Christmas tree ornaments were scattered on the garage floor. A goose-down pillow and a fan (taken from the garage without my knowledge) covered his room in feathers and made a mess that I wouldn't wish on my worst enemy. The rule in our house changed: no movie was to be seen by my son until one of us had previewed it.

Certain cartoons were prohibited, as were programs that emphasized violence of any kind. (I received enough karate chops during temper tantrums to last a lifetime.) The problem with certain types of television programs and movies and some children with AD/HD is that the children don't know where to draw the line. They can't just watch Superman; they *become* Superman, Batman, the Karate Kid, or in our case, a very dangerous Kevin McCallister.

But many parents of AD/HD children do use television as a reward, and they use it quite successfully. If watching television keeps your child quiet and out of trouble long enough to fix dinner or get dressed, use it, but use it cautiously and monitor all programs closely. If your child is addicted to television, you may want to limit its use. "We started very early in life limiting television time," says Ellen, from Oconomowoc, Wisconsin. "To break our son away, I often need to start a project that he can help with. He soon forgets the television and seldom asks to go back and watch."

Parents whose children enjoy television should take advantage of it and use it as a reward for appropriate behavior, such as completing chores, finishing homework, or getting ready for school on time. Television time can be used as a reward or sold. You may tell your child, "When you earn ten dollars in play money, you may purchase television time. However, your limit is one hour per day."

## Traveling

Traveling with your AD/HD child is not as frightening a prospect as you might believe. Actually, it can be handled quite successfully with proper preparation even with the most difficult children. Before we had children, my husband and I traveled frequently. When our first child arrived we never gave much thought to not taking him. We just packed and went. By the time he was a year and a half old, we knew we had a hyperactive child on our hands. Our choices were to decrease the number of trips we took, eliminate them completely, or take our son along. We opted to take our son with us. We were fortunate in that our son always slept whether we were traveling by car or airplane.

When our second child arrived, we faced the same choices. Again, we opted to take the children with us. We took our first trip with both children when the youngest was three months old. We flew from Ohio to California with a baby who cried nonstop from 5:00 a.m. to 4:00 p.m. Our return trip was the same. So much for babies who are soothed by the sound and movement of an airplane. Blake didn't sleep one minute either way. Two months later we flew to New Orleans with both children and this time Blake slept about one hour.

Our friends often ask us how we manage to travel with our children. My answer has always been the same: "We think out each trip very carefully." We make our plans and try to stick to as many routines and schedules as we can, just as we do at home. We have now been traveling many years with both of our children and we've all become seasoned travelers.

That's not to say that we never have problems. Actually, it's usually the opposite. We have all kinds of problems, but we have found ways to handle them.

We have taken our children on all sorts of trips, and we've traveled by airplane, boat (cruise ship), and car. We've found our children prefer flying simply because it's faster. Car trips of more than two hours are just too long for them and they fight constantly (physically and verbally), but some children do better. We all prefer staying in the same hotel for the entire vacation because we have found it easier to stay on a schedule and keep a routine. When we move from one spot to another, the children have difficulty settling down in a new place day after day.

Here are some tips for traveling with difficult children we and other parents have found helpful:

- **Share travel plans with your child**, along with each day's schedule on the appropriate day. Keep to routines as much as possible. Meals and bedtime should be at the same time they are at home if possible (often impossible on days spent reaching a destination).
- **Travel on the day of the holiday**, "when traveling by air, . . . instead of the day before or after, [when] the plane is less crowded, which is always easier on a family with a child with AD/HD," suggests Julie from Newark, Ohio.
- **Put your baby or toddler to bed in a sweat suit** or other wrinkle-free outfit when you are traveling by air and departing very early in the morning. Wait until the last minute to wake him, change his diaper, and out the door you go. For older children, lay out clothes the night before. Wake them an hour before you leave. Dress them and feed them something light, even if they will get breakfast on the plane. They may still be tired, but at least they won't be hungry.
- **"My motto is 'Be prepared'** when traveling by air," says Julie. "I try to be prepared for anything, especially lost luggage. So I pack a special carry-on bag with enough medication to get us through the entire vacation (in case our luggage is really lost). I pack enough clothes for one day for everyone. I figure that most of the things in our suitcases can easily be purchased at our destination, but trying to replace lost medication (which is a controlled substance in the United States and some countries) is impossible.

And I always carry snacks in my purse for easy access during the flight."

- **Time medication dosages carefully.** Even if the flight isn't terribly long, the day will probably be much longer than usual.

- **Pack another carry-on bag with snacks, small toys and books, bottles**, diapers, baby wipes, a stuffed animal, and a change of clothes. If you're lucky, your little darling will sleep most of the trip. Older children should be encouraged to carry a small bag of items that they have chosen to occupy themselves. Do check the bag to be sure they've put the right types of toys in (especially with the new flight regulations) and make sure it isn't too heavy, or you'll end up carrying it along with your own carry-on.

- **"Try to book the bulkhead seats** because they have the most room and there is no seat in front of those seats for children to kick," advises Julie. "If those seats are taken, with four of us traveling, I reserve the window and aisle seats in two rows. With three seats in coach, the chances are that the middle one will not be booked and you get extra room, which is always a bonus with a child with AD/HD." The disadvantage of bulkhead seats is that carry-ons with toys and snacks cannot be stored under the seat in front, which means a parent or flight attendant must get bags out from the overhead storage compartments.

- **Don't board the plane until the final boarding call.** The earlier you board, the longer your child has to sit on the plane. For children who don't fall asleep, be prepared to keep them entertained. Hand-held electronic games will keep most older kids busy for a few hours. Carry back-up games just in case, along with coloring books, travel games, snacks, and gum for children who may experience ear pain from increased cabin pressure. A CD player is useful also.

- **Be prepared to make trips to the restroom.** Some children with AD/HD can't make it the whole trip without getting up and moving around. If there's an empty seat near you, let them move to that seat for a while. Window seats are great because you have better control over your child's movements (I keep my tray down so they can't move past me), but if your child needs to use the restroom it means she has to crawl over two other people unless you are flying in the first-class section. An aisle seat is convenient, but extremely tempting to children who can't sit still. My son once took off running down the aisle, bumping into flight attendants as they were attempting to serve beverages, then threw a temper tantrum when I tried to pick him up. What those people had to say about my abilities to parent!

- **Obtain pillows or blankets** as soon as you get on the plane if you will need them, especially on long flights. Also ask for playing cards, children's magazines, and a set of wings once you've settled in. After takeoff, flight attendants are very busy and you may have to wait for these items. Remember, difficult and strong-willed children usually can't wait in silence.
- **Have the flight attendant bring your child's meal before yours** so you are able to get her started without worrying about your tray accidentally tipping over. A five-minute delay will also guarantee that your food will be hot when you are ready to eat.
- **Get off the plane as quickly as possible** when you reach your destination. If children have been particularly difficult, most people will gladly step aside so you can exit, especially if your child is still screaming.
- "**When traveling by car, we find that making frequent stops** at rest areas and letting our son with AD/HD run around (under close supervision) helps him during the trip," offers Julie. "What worked best for us on our car trips was to keep the length of the driving days short, even if that meant taking an extra day to get where we were going. When we stopped, we tried to make it no later than 4 p.m., and we always stayed at a motel with a swimming pool. We immediately try to get our son in the pool to swim and play off his excess energy before dinner. Dinner then becomes a more pleasant experience."
- **When driving, separate children in the back seat** with a small suitcase to define boundaries. Define the car rules. Mom or dad should plan to spend part of the trip in the back seat (one child moves up front with the driver).
- **Try to give five-minute warnings before stopping** for a stretch break or a meal (admittedly, this is not always feasible). If you are driving through several states and taking back roads, take sandwiches along and stop at rest stops or parks for picnics along the way. Carry a thermos of water or juice, cups with lids, and lots of straws to prevent spills.

- **Consider leaving early in the morning** (after 2 or 3 a.m.) so children can sleep part of the way in the car, although some hyperactive children will not go back to sleep once awake. You know your child better than anyone.

- **Consider taking a babysitter with you**. A sitter who regularly cares for your child is an excellent choice. Take her along as a mother's helper rather than as a babysitter. Be sure she understands exactly what her responsibilities will be. Mother's helpers can assist with unpacking, share a room with one or two of the children, get up with children who wake up early, walk children around while you are waiting for food to arrive, help with daytime excursions or just babysit them around the pool or on the beach, and stay with them if you want a night out.

- **Divide responsibilities**. For instance, if you have two children, you take responsibility for bathing and dressing one child; she takes responsibility for the other. Or take turns watching children who need daytime naps. Be sure your sitter has time for herself each day, plus time for showering and dressing. Don't dump the workload entirely on her shoulders or she'll never want to travel with you again. The trip has to be enjoyable and fun for her also.

- **Make use of sitters who are available through hotels** if your budget will not accommodate a full-time helper. If you find someone who works in housekeeping that you particularly like, don't be afraid to ask if she is available for babysitting in the evening. Many women who work in housekeeping babysit for guests as a way of supplementing their income. We have found some excellent sitters this way.

- **Be realistic**. Your AD/HD child will be very excited for the first day or two and will try your patience. Once they become familiar with surroundings and schedules, most will settle down. If you're staying in a hotel or motel with a pool, the possible loss of swimming privileges for an hour, or half a day, usually is the only incentive a child needs to cooperate. In fact if you want a totally relaxing trip, choose a hotel with a pool or beach access. The water will entertain and wear out most children day after day.

- **If you find a place you all enjoy, consider returning to it again and again.** Children settle in easier and much faster when they are vacationing in a spot they have visited before.

- **Take night-lights**, a first-aid kit, a potty seat for younger children, acetaminophen, a thermometer, syrup of ipecac, medical insurance card, and prescription medication.
- **Take a variety of toys** (travel-size board games, cassette player, Legos, dolls, small cars and trucks, paint sets, cards, etc.). If you are driving, keep some of the toys in the trunk and rotate them. Bring along story cassette tapes children can listen to as they follow the book (check your library). On longer vacations we've taken a CD player and several movies for rainy days and evenings with a sitter in the room. Disposable cameras also are great for small children.

One mom who has traveled to Disney World gives the advice "not to give up medication at this overstimulating place. We found that if we could have a day at the park, a day at the beach, a day at the park, etc., we did a little better. We also discovered that our daughter always has a huge sleep deficit and increasingly higher activity levels as a result. Even the medication helps very minimally at this point. We just put up with the situation. A purse-pack on my waist or a backpack frees my hands for her when we reach this point."

## Problems with Inattention

Children and adolescents with AD/HD have difficulty concentrating and sustaining attention in different situations. Their ability to concentrate and pay attention is particularly challenged when they are faced with boring, redundant tasks and activities, such as chores. Consequently, they have difficulty hanging on to a thought long enough to get a task completed. However, when a child with AD/HD is occupied with something she chooses to do, like playing a video game or watching a movie, she has little or no difficulty sustaining attention. Because of this inconsistency, people often label children and youth with AD/HD as lazy, disorganized, flaky, or even stupid, maintaining they could concentrate and pay attention if they really wanted to or if they really tried.

The following are some of the symptoms that fall under the heading of inattention and some ways that parents help their children with attention difficulties in the home.

## Easily Distracted

"I have found that my daughter gets distracted whenever she has to do something she's not fond of," says Jolene from Chapel Hill, North Carolina. "When it's time to do homework, for instance, I have to take her to her desk and help her get started. If it's a chore, I have to help her begin it. I then reward her for completing the task using a chart system."

"You can't ever tell my son to do something later," explains AnnaMarie from Evanston, Illinois, "or it will never get done. If it's something that has to be done, he's to do it now while it's fresh on his mind, like getting his Boy Scout uniform out for tomorrow or putting clean gym clothes in his backpack. If I say don't forget to do . . . , he'll forget."

"We try to provide an atmosphere free of distractions when Brittany is told to do something like homework or a chore," comments Chrissy. "No television, no radio, no friends, no phone calls. This helps keep her on task."

"We list everything that our daughter needs to do on a chart, including the time that she must start the task," offers Michelle from Deer Park, New York. "We also use a timer. She has the same chores each day—ones we know she can do successfully. We help her stay on task by reminding her of the time, setting the stove timer, helping her get started and reminding her daily of the rules and her schedule."

"My daughter, Holly, always loses track of time," says Megan from Irving, California. "I'm constantly reminding her to check her watch. This is a big problem for her at school as she is always late for her classes. One of her friends is in the same classes as my daughter, so I asked her friend to keep reminding Holly of the time. This has helped immensely."

## Fails to Listen

"Vikki's biggest problem is with listening," acknowledges her mother, Marsha, from Montreal, Quebec. "As a result, she does things but not correctly because she doesn't listen to the directions. She's capable of cooking an easy dinner for the family as long as she has written directions to follow. So I write down each step for her."

"Always give directions to your child [while] making eye contact," suggests Paul from Princeton, Wisconsin. "Keep directions simple—no more than one or two steps. You're asking for trouble if you give a long list of things to be done without writing each task down. Once you give the directions, ask your child to repeat them back to you so you're sure he understands. If the directions are written down, make sure your son or daughter checks off each step as it is completed."

"Don't try to tell your child how to do something with the television on, the baby screaming, and your other child practicing the piano," advises Kelly from Phoenix, Arizona. "Take him to a room where it's quiet so he's not distracted and can concentrate on listening."

## Difficulty Following Verbal Directions

"If something is really important and your child must follow the directions carefully then tell him just that," offers Jolene from Chapel Hill, North Carolina. "I say, 'Katie, it's important that you listen carefully. Please take your blouse out of the dryer right now and hang it up so you don't have to iron it later.' We have found this usually works with our daughter. Sometimes she still doesn't follow through, so she's had to iron a blouse or two, which is the consequence of not listening."

"Verbally give directions, but also write them down or have your children write them down," advises Janey from St. Paul, Minnesota.

## Other Behavior That May Confuse or Frustrate You

My sons, and some other children with AD/HD I know, have experienced other baffling traits that appear to be AD/HD related. For instance, some children are what I call "hot" children. Even if it's ten degrees outside, they are hot. Not warm, but hot. Their faces get flushed and they sweat profusely, but often the face and head are the only places where perspiration is noticeable.

Many children with AD/HD complain about labels in their clothing or that their clothes are itchy. I know several adults with AD/HD who still cut labels out of their clothing. It appears that their sense of touch (sensory defensiveness) is so acute that the slightest raised edge is extremely uncomfortable for them. If your child says she can't wear a garment, don't force the issue. Let her wear clothing that she finds comfortable. In many cases, this means she'll have to go shopping with you so she can choose clothes with fabrics that feel good to her.

Another unusual behavior I've noticed regarding touch is that some children with AD/HD hate to have anyone touch their face or head. I first noticed this when my son was about fifteen months old. Getting a hair-cut is a very trying experience for him, the stylist, and me. I've also noticed that he even hates to touch his own face. When he washes or puts lotion on his face, he does so very reluctantly using only one finger. Other parents have noticed the same type of behavior with their children.

Certain children with AD/HD also appear to be sensitive to smells, sounds, and sights. Children will complain about smells or sounds that you cannot smell or hear. We've had to leave all sorts of places because of a smell or sound that only my son found very unpleasant.

While some children became more excited or hyper when they are someplace with an abundance of stimulation, other children will with-draw. The stimulation is just too much for them to handle. One parent recalled the time she threw a birthday party for her daughter at a popu-lar pizza restaurant that has all sorts of video games and play activities for children. "After the children had eaten pizza and cake and played some games, it was time to open the birthday presents," recalls Becky. "I looked around for my daughter and found her sitting in a booth with her grandparents. I said, 'Come on, sweetheart, it's time to open your presents.' She shook her head no that she didn't want to open them. So my husband and I opened the presents and thanked all of the children, while my daughter remained sitting quietly. When we got home she went up to her room and listened to music. She finally looked at her presents the next day. I believe all of the stimulation was just too much for her to handle and she knew it. That's why she withdrew from her friends. Our doctor told us that's a great quality for her to have—to be able to with-draw quietly when things get to be too much for her."

When some children with AD/HD become ill they may not need their medication for AD/HD. My son, who is extremely overactive, does not require medication when he's sick. He's affectionate, sweet, even tem-pered, and a pleasure to be with. I hate it when he's sick, but I have to admit I enjoy seeing this wonderful side of him. He's also never spent a sick day in bed. However, other children seem to need their medication even when they are ill.

As is common with all aspects of AD/HD, your child may display some of these unusual behaviors, other unique ones, or none at all.

C H A P T E R 6

# Becoming a Proactive Parent

E EACH HAVE our own parenting style (often based on the way we were raised), temperament, past experiences, and ability to deal with child-related stress. Research shows that there are basically four types of parents:

- Dominant parent
- Neglectful parent
- Lenient parent
- Firm and loving parent

The type of parent we are influences our child's behavior.

## The Dominant Parent

Dominating parents have high expectations and expect rules to be followed with little or no explanation. They usually want complete control over the child. A dominant parent often believes children are to be seen and not heard, and children are not permitted to question the whys of anything. Freedom of expression is not usually permitted. Obedience is often the parent's goal. Dominating parents may not offer enthusiastic, loving support to the child. As a result, dominant parents may have an aggressive, angry child—a child who may be disrespectful, rebellious, and demanding, with little regard for rules and authority.

## The Neglectful Parent

Neglectful parents also do not give tender, loving support to the child nor do they have any control over the child. Neglectful parents get irritated easily and often lash out at the child when pushed to make time for him. They have plenty of time to pursue their own personal interests but little or no time for their child. Babysitters often spend the most time with the child. As a result, the child may be insecure, be rebellious, have low self-esteem, and have little motivation to excel.

## The Lenient Parent

Lenient parents are usually warm and supportive, but they fail to establish rules and consequences. Lenient parents react strongly against authority figures, believing they are too inflexible and uncompromising. When their child misbehaves, they rarely discipline him or her because they don't want to be seen as rigid parents. Lenient parents believe that children, through choice and experience, will learn how to live within society. They encourage individuality. Children of lenient parents are often manipulative, insecure, have low self-esteem, believe they are in control, and have difficulty abiding by group rules.

## The Firm and Loving Parent

Firm and loving parents establish clearly defined rules and consequences and freely give love, support, and focused time to their child. Children of firm and loving parents typically feel more secure, have higher self-esteem, and know they are loved unconditionally.

Firm and loving parents attain a delicate balance between domineering and permissive parenting to create effective parenting. The following are suggestions for creating an effective parenting style in your home:

- **Accept the fact that your child has AD/HD.** Trying to hide the fact, or refusing to talk about it, only tells your child that you are uncomfortable and embarrassed by him. Never forget that this is a genuine medical problem that just happens to affect such things as your child's attention span, self-control, schoolwork, social relationships, ability to organize, etc. The earlier you accept his disability, the sooner you can effectively advocate in his behalf.

- **Think AD/HD.** Do not expect your child to display normal age-appropriate behavior regularly. Have realistic expectations.

- **Establish house rules, routines, and schedules.** Be consistent every day whether you feel like it or not. Do not nag, negotiate, or make exceptions to the rules unless you are ready to revise the rules or change the routines. Be sure others caring for your child follow your rules, routines, and schedules at all times. Realize that house rules, routines, and schedules will change as your child grows and matures. Include elementary school–age children and teenagers in discussions when establishing house rules.

- **Be clear about unacceptable behaviors** and the consequences for your child. In other words, be specific when talking to your child, maintain eye contact, and have the child repeat what you say concerning rules. Deliver all consequences, both rewards and punishments, immediately and consistently. When you correct or discipline your child, be sure to establish which type of behavior is expected in that particular situation. Write it down if necessary.

- **Be prepared.** If you know a specific situation will cause problems for your child, either prepare the child ahead of time or avoid the situation if at all possible.

- **Make a lifetime commitment to your child.** This is one of the most important steps in effective parenting. Your child must know that no matter what happens, even if you don't approve of his actions, that you will be there with unconditional love. Children of parents who only show love and approval when their child cooperates, is dressed neatly, or gets good grades will never feel unconditional love.

- **Plan for and schedule time with your child.** One of the most important gifts we can give our children is our focused time—fifteen to thirty minutes each day doing something they want to do. While this is important for all children, those with AD/HD especially need this time because it boosts their self-esteem and shows they are loved. In our home we spend a half hour of quality time with each child every evening. During this focused time, each child can choose an activity of his choice and we spend that half hour doing what he chooses according to his rules. Some evenings we read together, play a couple of games of pool, take a walk, play a board game, hit golf balls, or just talk. It's very important that the child chooses the activity and the parent respects that decision.

- **Unscheduled time is also important**. How many times can you remember your child asking for time with you and you've told him, "Not now, I'm busy. Maybe later," but later never came? Whether you were truly too busy at that moment or had just sat down to read the newspaper, what you were doing is irrelevant. What matters is the message you sent your child. In this case, the only thing the child heard was, "She's too busy for *me*. What she's doing is more important than me." Unscheduled time is also beneficial because children with AD/HD are constantly told what to do, how to act, etc. by well-meaning others every day. They need the opportunity to feel they are in control at some point. Be prepared for unscheduled time demands—requests come frequently—so you can handle the situation in a loving and supportive way.

- **Make frequent eye contact** when talking with or listening to your child. If your child is young, get down to his level so you can establish eye contact. Many children with AD/HD have trouble maintaining eye contact, so you may have to turn his face toward you or remind him to look at you while you are talking with him. He's less apt to be distracted if you insist on, and maintain, eye contact.

- **Treat your child with tenderness and respect**. Screaming or yelling, ridiculing, nagging, and sarcasm only tell children that they are of little value to us, which reduces their self-esteem and often causes behavior to deteriorate. Nagging, lecturing, and arguing can lead to various types of problems for all children but can be particularly destructive for the adolescent with AD/HD, so learn to control such responses now while your children are young. If your child insists on arguing with you or won't drop the subject, walk away from him. Make sure if you walk away that it is not seen as a sign of giving up. Do not argue. Do not acknowledge their statements. This is a no-win situation. I know this is extremely difficult at times. I have found that when I do lose control, a sincere apology followed by a hug works wonders. I see it in my children's eyes and posture. Remember that the apology is for losing control, not for correcting their misbehavior.

- **Be patient**! Remember that your child may have little self-control and is not intentionally trying to displease you. Patience is another wonderful gift you can give your child.

- **Show love for your child**. A pat on the head or the shoulder, holding the child's hand, or offering a hug or kiss assures your child that he is loved. Tell your child you love him at least once a day. A truly wonderful book to read to preschoolers and young school-age children is *Love You Forever* by Robert Munsch (Willowdale, Ontario, Canada: Firefly, 1986). It's a warm, sensitive story about a caring mother and her child. I highly recommend it to all families but particularly for families that struggle with a difficult child.

- **Praise your child** whenever you catch him in appropriate behavior. Praise can be verbal (I'm pleased to see you set the table) or nonverbal (a smile, pat on the head, a wink, etc.).

- **Identify feelings with your child**. Reminding your child that you too have felt frustration when faced with a challenging homework assignment, that you have trouble paying attention at times, or that you sometimes say things you regret tells your child that you understand what he is going through because you have experienced the same types of feelings, disappointments, failures, and hurt.

- **Don't expect perfection from your child** or imply that he must be perfect. Be sure your child understands that everyone makes mistakes, including you.

- **Show faith and confidence in your child**. Believe in your child, so he can believe in himself. Acknowledge all improvements.

- **Concentrate on strengths and abilities** of your child. Acknowledge your child's strengths and assets. Suggest ways he can use his assets to help others or to make a contribution to the family or school.

- **No negative labels**, please. The child who is constantly told that he is stupid, bad, lazy, dumb, stubborn, or unable to do something will eventually believe just that. Not only will he believe it, but you'll witness it in his behavior and see it in his eyes. Remember, egos are fragile and often difficult to repair.

- **Pick your battles carefully**. If you insist on getting your own way all the time, you are setting yourself up for constant power struggles. Choose your battles carefully.

Parents should examine their particular parenting style to see what effect it might be having on their children. The style of parenting used can make a situation with a child with AD/HD much worse than it needs to be. I encourage you to explore this with a professional, particularly if you suspect that you might be (unintentionally) a contributing factor to aggressive or noncompliant behavior. The way you respond to misbehavior, what you anticipate from your child and whether she is capable of meeting those expectations, your child's temperament, and how she reacts to your parenting style are all factors that should be examined.

## Smart Discipline Strategies That Work

While many different types of discipline strategies are presented here, you must remember that *not all of the strategies will work with each child.* Try different techniques until you find the ones your child responds to. Remember, your objectives are to *increase* the time your child behaves appropriately, *decrease* the unacceptable behavior, and *teach* your child how to control himself.

### Use Time-Out

Explain time-out to your child before using it and make sure he understands that this is not a punishment but rather an opportunity to get himself under control (some parents, however, use time-out exclusively as a punishment). Time-out can be used when your child is

- in the process of breaking or has broken the rules
- acting foolishly or is irritating
- screaming or fighting
- talking back

The advantage of using time-out is that it is an immediate, but brief, consequence to an undesired behavior. Time-out is a very kind way of stopping an inappropriate behavior and allowing the child to calm down without feeling embarrassed. Time-out can be used on the spot, no matter where you are. (See chapter 3 for more information on using this technique.)

## Ignore the Behavior

The approach of ignoring the behavior is best used when your child is displaying behavior you find marginally upsetting yet tolerable—often it is a behavior that is used to get a parent's attention, such as whining, swearing, or name calling. Let's say you've told your child to go to time-out immediately and on the way he calls you a butt-head or something worse. Ignore it. Consider it nothing but noise. He's trying to irritate you. If you respond, he knows he has gotten your attention and thus you have rewarded the misbehavior. Usually the name calling, whining, or swearing will escalate when you ignore it before it dissipates, so don't give up. Without an audience, the behavior eventually stops.

## Give a Prearranged Signal

If you are leaving for religious services or a movie and know your child often talks out loudly, arrange a special signal between the two of you that will notify him that his behavior is unacceptable in this place (touch his shoulder or make a time-out sign with your hands). Prearranged signals usually do not work if your child is losing control while with a group of friends who are playing a stimulating game or visiting an amusement park, but there is a time and place for this discipline strategy. Prearranged signals often work well in the classroom when the teacher and the child agree on a special signal that notifies the child that he is not paying attention or is disturbing the child seated next to him.

## Offer a Choice

Rather than telling your child what to do, offer a choice: "Would you like to cut the grass or wash the car?" "Would you like to hold my hand in the mall or should we get the stroller out of the trunk?" Give your child the opportunity to make his own decision, but be sure he understands that if he doesn't make a choice you will assign one. Offering minor choices also directs the debate away from the important nonnegotiable rule. For example, "Would you like to do your homework in the dining room or your bedroom?"

## Use Grandmother's Rule

Grandmother's rule is basically a simple arrangement that says, "When you have done what you are supposed to do, then you may do what you want to do." For example, "When you make your bed, then you may go outside." "When your homework is finished, then you may use the computer." "When you wash the car, then you may drive it." Grandmother's rule is appropriate for all ages and is extremely easy to use. However, be careful to never substitute the word "if" for "when." To do so will only invite your child to ask, "If I don't do it, what happens?" Grandmother's rule works because it is always phrased positively. "You may go to the play, and when (or after) you do . . ." You are never saying, "No, you can't."

## Use Positive Reinforcements

Positive reinforcements motivate children to try harder and encourage good behavior. This is an effective way for parents to reward behaviors they want continued. By rewarding good behavior, the child learns to identify the desired behaviors and receives the much-needed attention he desires. Remember, these children see *all* interaction as positive attention, even negative attention.

Verbal praise and tangible rewards (stickers, play money, hair ribbons, baseball cards, etc.) are positive reinforcements that most children enjoy receiving. However, always be sure you focus any form of praise on the behavior and not the child.

Never give rewards or privileges before the desired behavior is achieved. If you pay your child before he starts his chores, there's a good chance that the chores will never get completed. Once he has his reward he has nothing to work for. Again, remember to always use rewards for positive behaviors. Do not use rewards in an attempt to get a child to stop an undesired behavior (don't pay your child to stop hitting his sister).

## Make a Promise

Some children with AD/HD respond positively to promises. Promises made by a parent, teacher, or caretaker encourage a child to behave for a defined time, to do a particular chore, or to resume an existing behavior for a longer time.

Promises are like using rewards for appropriate behaviors. However, I have found that if promises are not used too frequently you will usually get superior results. For instance, let's say you just arrived home with your children and there is a message on your answering machine regarding a job you've applied for. You're elated and you want to return the call immediately, but it's imperative that your children, who are fighting with each other at the moment, are quiet during your conversation. What can you do? Promise that in return for their silence for ten minutes you will give them something they want as soon as you get off the telephone. At a time like this, you're more apt to promise them just about anything in return for their cooperation. So what you promise will be more than a sticker on their chart, and if you've used this method before and have always shown that you keep your promises, your children will respond positively to another promise. Because they have learned from past experiences that promises mean something a bit more special, they are more likely to cooperate. To use this strategy effectively, it's important that promises are *always* kept.

## Token System

With the token system, your child receives stickers, check marks, play money, or some other type of token for following the rules or completing tasks outlined on a chart designed by the parent and discussed with the child. The tokens earned can then be used to buy privileges, such as a trip to the park or zoo or having a friend spend the night. Or the tokens may be saved and exchanged for money to buy a desired item. Many families use a chart in the morning listing the tasks that must be completed before the child leaves for school (see the charts in chapter 5). When the child successfully completes the tasks, he receives a sticker or other token for a job well done.

## Withdraw Privileges

Removing privileges (activities a child considers enjoyable and would not want to lose) is an effective discipline technique for parents of elementary school–age children and teenagers. This can involve taking away such things as the use of the telephone, car, computer or video games, television, favorite toys, or bicycles. It's important that the withdrawal be directly proportional to the inappropriate behavior (don't remove a meaningful privilege for a minor violation), and be delivered as quickly as possible after the infraction.

## Grounding

A child who breaks a major household rule, such as not calling home when he decides to take off from school to visit a friend or taking the car without permission, needs to learn the consequences of inappropriate behavior. Grounding the child, that is, removing all privileges for a defined time, is one strategy that can have a positive effect on children. Grounding is the equivalent to jail time. (See chapter 8 for information on using grounding effectively.)

In the book *Why Johnny Can't Concentrate*, by Robert A. Moss, MD, with Helen Huff Dunlap, the authors recommend grounding in conjunction with completing household chores. Depending on the severity of the violation, the child is assigned a certain number of household chores. Until the chores are completed, the child is grounded (all privileges are removed). Other than attending school, working, or eating, the child will be isolated in his bedroom. In this case, the child is the one who actually determines the length of time spent being grounded. If the child can complete the chores satisfactorily in a few hours, then the child is no longer grounded. If, however, it takes the child an unusually long time (days) to complete the chores, the authors suggest that you reassess the arrangement. It just may be that life isn't quite dull enough for him yet.

## Natural Consequences

Children can also learn desired behaviors by allowing natural consequences to occur. Let's say you have a rule in your house prohibiting wearing shorts and short-sleeved shirts to school unless the temperature is expected to exceed seventy-five degrees. One morning your child comes to breakfast dressed in summer clothes but it's not expected to reach sixty degrees that day. As a parent you have two choices: you can insist that he change his clothes, or you can mention that he is dressed inappropriately for the weather but allow him to wear the clothes and hope that he feels the discomfort (natural consequence) of choosing the wrong clothing. If you choose the latter, you are permitting him to learn that wearing summer clothing on a chilly day is unwise (some children with AD/HD may need to experience this several times before it truly sinks in). Missing the school bus is a consequence of not getting out of bed on time. Having to walk to school is a consequence of missing the school bus. Of course, if the natural consequence poses a risk to the child, a parent must not back down from enforcing the household rule.

## More Is Not Always Better

When I was teaching school years ago, I had a little boy in my class whom I'll call Matthew. Matthew was a good-looking and intelligent child, with blond hair and blue eyes. Although he had been diagnosed with AD/HD, he was not a difficult child. He usually sat when required and basically did well in school. I liked Matthew, but he had an annoying behavior problem that occasionally surfaced and I was determined to put an end to it: Matthew liked to spit.

For the first three months of the school year, I tried everything to stop the behavior. One day when he was in time-out, he turned around and spit at one of the children seated at her desk. And suddenly I knew what I could do to stop that behavior. I called Matthew to my desk and together we drew a picture of a little boy's face. When it was completed, I tacked it on the wall. I then placed Matthew in front of the picture and told him that for the next five minutes he could spit at that little boy's picture as much as he wanted. Well, Matthew got the biggest smile on his face and said, "You mean I can just stand here and spit and no one will get mad at me?" "That's right," I said. "You can spit and spit for a whole five minutes, and no one will get angry with you. In fact, anytime you want to spit just let me know and I'll hang this picture up for you. Is it a deal?" Matthew readily agreed.

Matthew began spitting, but wanted to stop after a short time. I encouraged him to continue and reminded him of our deal. When time was up, I had to tell Matthew only once. What started out to be a whole lot of fun for Matthew soon lost its appeal. Matthew never had a problem with spitting after that. More is not always better.

## Write a Note

Notes are a great way to urge a child to do something that he is supposed to do but occasionally forgets, such as putting his bike away, feeding the dog, etc. An example of this sort of note might read like the following:

> Dear Jason,
>
> I had a horrible day today. First, your mother backed out of the garage and almost ran me over. Then some guy came to fix the washer and almost hit me. To top it off, it rained all afternoon and now I'm soaking wet. I'm waiting for you to put me away and dry me off.
>
> Your Bicycle

Notes also work well when you have something important to say to your teenager. Since teens often tune out when parents are trying to tune in, notes can be an effective way to make a point.

## Write a Behavior Contract

Writing a contract to encourage good behavior or to eliminate annoying behavior is easy and effective. Sit down with your child and define the problem (for example, putting a bike in the garage). Then decide on a reward (a friend can spend the night when five points are earned) together. Your contract might read like the following:

> I, Jason, agree to put my bike away each day.
>
> Every day that I put my bike away without a reminder, I will earn one point.
>
> When I earn five points, my friend Daniel can spend the night.
>
> Signed, *Jason*

Contracts can be used with young children, but they work best with older children and teenagers.

## Use a Timer

Make a game of eating, getting dressed, picking up toys, and other tasks by setting a timer and playing Beat the Clock with your child. This strategy works best with younger children. Be sure to give abundant praise and a small token when your child successfully beats the clock. Remember that not all children respond favorably to Beat the Clock. (See chapter 7.)

## Be Explicit When Making Requests or Giving Commands

Clearly and simply state your request or give your command. Telling your child "stop" or "behave" is usually meaningless. Be clear: "Shelly, stop running now," or "Jake, hitting your brother is not acceptable. Go to time-out for five minutes." Remember, one minute per year of the child's age. A child who is age six spends six minutes in time-out; a three-year-old, three minutes.

## Use Praise with a Hidden Message

Praise that includes a message permits you to compliment desired behavior while mentioning unacceptable behavior at the same time: "Thanks for putting your clothes in the hamper, instead of throwing them on the bedroom floor." Make sure you sound upbeat and encouraging, not sarcastic, when using this method.

## Think Ahead

Many times, parents can prevent certain problems if they plan ahead. If you are going out to eat, take toys or books to entertain your child while you wait for food to arrive—prevent misbehavior by keeping the child occupied. The more proactive you can be in problem solving, the less reactive you have to be. Reactive disciplining is much more stressful.

## Use "I" Statements

Use "I" statements whenever the consequence of a behavior interferes with your needs: "When you throw your clothes on the bedroom floor at bedtime (behavior), I feel frightened (feeling) because I trip over them during the night when I check on you (consequence)." Or "When you don't come home on time or call to say you'll be late (behavior), I feel scared (feeling) because I don't know if something bad as happened to you (consequence)."

## Avoid Arguments

Remember that it takes two people to have an argument, so don't grab the bait. My son used to argue with me whenever he needed stimulation. I would calmly tell him that I had no intention of arguing with him and walk away. If he followed me through the house, I would ignore him until he had settled down. Eventually he got the message: I was not going to be his audience.

# A Plan for Change

Examine your style of parenting and make any necessary changes. While your parenting style will not cause the primary symptoms of AD/HD, you may find that specific ways of handling your child may actually cause or escalate the problems you experience in your home. On the other hand, parents who are firm and loving may reduce the number of behavior problems because their child responds favorably to such child-rearing practices. Developing effective parenting skills and remaining committed to those skills is not easy. However, those who practice effective parenting will find that the rewards for the child and parents over the years arc far too numerous to count.

**7**

# Working with Your Child's Teacher and School

W HEN IT COMES to your child's education it would be a great injustice if you did not take the time to meet with your child's teacher or teachers. Appropriate interventions are compulsory for children with AD/HD to succeed in school. Always remember you are your child's best advocate and that together with teachers you can make a tremendous difference in your child's education.

## Start the School Year Off Right

"I always find out in August who my son's teacher will be. Then I ask the principal to help me arrange a short meeting of introduction to discuss my son's AD/HD with the teacher," explains Julie, a former high school teacher, from Newark, Ohio. "Having the principal relay this information to the teacher is important because I have found I get better cooperation from a teacher if she feels the principal is involved. At this meeting I introduce myself, tell the teacher my son has AD/HD, and listen carefully to see if she knows anything about this disorder. I give her written information about AD/HD and my phone number. I tell her I am available to help her in any way and not to hesitate to call me if there are any problems or questions. I discuss medication with her and tell her how important it is for my son to be able to take his medication quietly on his way to lunch so that the other children will not make fun of him."

I approach a new school year in much the same way. When school begins, I make an appointment with each of my sons' homebase teachers. Before the meetings, I put together a packet of information on AD/HD that I plan to leave behind with the teachers. I come to this meeting well prepared: I know what I want to discuss, the points I need to stress, and what questions I need answered. The teachers are left with valuable information about my sons' disorder and knowing that I am a strong advocate for them.

Fortunately, my sons' school is family oriented so it is easy to meet other parents. About midyear, I start talking with parents whose children are in the grade my sons will be in the following year. I try to determine what they like or dislike about their child's homebase teacher. In particular, I am interested in the teachers' teaching style so I can determine which will be best for my children. I also ask my oldest son what teacher he likes best because I think it's imperative that he have a teacher he likes and who likes him. At the last school conference of the year, I ask my sons' homebase teachers which teacher they feel will be best for the next year. Once I've reached a decision, I then speak with the director of the lower school and ask for his or her input.

If recent surveys are accurate, teachers voice a great deal of frustration about the lack of parental assistance. Most teachers are enthused and delighted to have parents work with them in assisting and teaching their child. What most teachers want is a partnership with the parents—an alliance based on openness, trust, and support.

Don't be afraid to speak up at parent-teacher conferences. Ask questions. For example: "How have you handled Andrea's daydreaming? Has it worked?" "Do you recall, at the last meeting I suggested that you initiate a system whereby you would put your hand on Jonathan's shoulder when he starts to lose control? Have you tried this approach? Why not?"

## To Tell or Not to Tell

Several years ago, when my son was just beginning preschool at age four, I asked his doctor if it was better to tell teachers he had AD/HD or to not say anything. The physician answered, "Would you rather the school knew he had AD/HD, which would explain any inappropriate behaviors and school difficulties, or would you rather have him known as a troublemaker who has problems in school?" I decided I would rather not have my son labeled as a troublemaker or a school failure because of his AD/HD (some parents disagree with this approach). I concluded it would be better for him to be labeled as a child with AD/HD—at least there would be a medical reason for any behavior problems or difficulties in school. This decision was based on the following considerations:

- **Time with child.** A child spends nearly seven hours a day at school; more time than he spends awake at home on weekdays. During school hours, parents rely on teachers to meet their child's needs. To fulfill those needs and for your child's success, the teacher must know the child has AD/HD and understand the disorder.
- **Medication.** Approximately one-third of children with AD/HD take medication. If a child takes medication and must receive an afternoon dose, someone at school must be there to administer it. Schools require a parent's and doctor's signature and the name of the medication before they can give prescription drugs to students. (Fortunately, the longer lasting medications available now have reduced the number of students who must take a medication at school.)
- **Medication's effects.** Because a teacher spends so much time with the child, parents must rely on the teacher's observations for feedback on the medication's effects. Is it working effectively in the morning and afternoon? Has he or she noticed any side effects, such as sadness, irritability, or headaches?
- **Team member.** If support services are needed in school, parents are most likely to turn to their child's teacher. He or she can enlist the help of other school personnel, such as the school psychologist or a speech therapist. If a support team of professionals is needed to work with the child, the child's teacher will be part of this team.
- **Child's best interests.** If a child's AD/HD was not shared with the teacher, who would be hurt the most? If telling means swallowing one's pride and admitting that your child is not perfect, then so be it.

## Before School Starts

Prepare your child for the beginning of the school year. Some schools hold an open house a day or two before the first day of school. At the open house, children can meet with their teachers, see a list of their classmates, locate their desks or lockers, walk around their classrooms, and visit a short time with other schoolmates. If your child's school does not have an open house, ask if the two of you can visit the classroom before school starts. For first-timers, visit the classroom and tour the inside of the building. Afterward, take a walk around the outside of the building, visit the playground area, and show your child where the buses will be parked after school. You also might want to visit your local library and pick up some books about the first day of school. This will give your child some idea of what to expect. For younger children returning to the same school, be sure you inform them that some of the children (maybe even some of their friends) from the previous year may have moved and will not be in class this year.

If your child is a slow mover in the morning, initiate practice runs a week or two before school starts so he can begin adjusting. (Some parents of elementary school–age children keep their children on the same morning schedule the entire year.)

Check out extracurricular activities before school begins. Sit down with your child and determine which activities, if any, he might be interested in. If you do this before school starts, you won't have an angry child two months into the school year demanding to know why all his friends are involved in soccer and he isn't. Check on Girl or Boy Scout activities, which are great for improving socialization skills in children with AD/HD. Look for activities that match your child's abilities. Avoid competitive activities before second grade (you may need to avoid competitive activities even longer for some children with AD/HD).

Restrict the number of after-school activities. Children with AD/HD often burn out quickly. Because of this, they do much better with a balance of structured and unstructured activities. Free time, time for climbing a tree, is important for all children, and unstructured activities teach children to play independently. Set ground rules for free time or you may find your child spends this time doing the same thing, like watching television or playing video games. Together, you can make a list of things he can do during unstructured play time, and then rotate the activities.

When planning after-school activities, remember that most activities require commitment on your part, even if it's only picking up your child at 5:00 rather than having him take the school bus home.

## The First Day of School

Let your child choose the clothes he wants to wear the night before school starts. Many of us grew up when the first day of school signaled the time to wear a brand-new outfit, complete with new school shoes. Times have changed. If an older child insists on wearing something that wouldn't be your choice, remember that peer pressure is high. Your child's concern is fitting in with the group; he wants to wear what his friends will be wearing.

Set your alarm for an earlier wake-up time. All family members must adjust to the new routine. It may take a week or two to get back into the swing of things, especially for the slow-to-adapt child. If you use a charting system in the morning, be sure it is hanging up with a pencil nearby. Make certain you have stickers, or whatever reward you offer, available. If your child buys his lunch at school and you often forget to give him lunch money, include this on a chart system. Make it the child's responsibility to ask for lunch money. Even first-graders can be given this responsibility.

If your child will be riding on the school bus, write down the bus number so he knows which bus to look for when school is dismissed. This number can be written on a luggage tag that is attached to his backpack or pinned inside a jacket, sweater, shirt, or blouse for younger children. If he is younger, try to find another child in his class who rides the same bus.

## The First Few Weeks of School

All children feel more comfortable when they arrive at school on time. If you drive your child to school, leave the house in plenty of time so that he gets to school five or ten minutes early. Some teachers use the first few minutes of each morning to tell children the day's agenda. If there will be changes in the routine, teachers will point them out at this time. Because children with AD/HD need routines and have difficulty with schedule changes, it's imperative that your child gets to school on time.

Beginning the first day of school, tell your child where she is to put all notices the teacher sends home. Returning responses to the teacher is also a problem for most children with AD/HD. Always put responses in the same place each time so a child knows where to find them. One mother reports that her daughter hand delivers notes to her teacher and has been taught to give the note to her teacher as soon as she gets to school. This mom says nine times out of ten the note reaches its destination using this method.

Check with your child's teacher about field trips ahead of time and write them down on your calendar. If you are able and willing to assist a teacher on a field trip, volunteer your services. Your child will enjoy having you along and you will be able to observe his behavior firsthand. The same holds true for volunteering in the classroom whenever possible. "Volunteering in the classroom helps us to see Colin's performance in the classroom setting," says Missy of Bow, New Hampshire, "and if he is falling behind in specific academic or social areas." Volunteering also gives you the opportunity to meet your child's classmates and discover who his friends are. Consider arranging play dates for your child with his friends—one friend at a time as previously discussed usually works best.

Attend all parent-teacher conferences. Also try to attend parent-teacher association meetings, school concerts, etc. If you are unable to attend some events, be sure to telephone the school and let them know you are aware of the event but unable to attend (this shows that you are interested, just not able to be present). Don't feel like you can't attend certain events because you have small children at home and can't find (or afford) a babysitter. Most parents take their young children to school activities. After all, schools are designed to accommodate children. Some schools even provide child care while parents attend conferences with teachers.

## The Teacher as an Ally

How you view your child's teacher will have a great effect on your relationship with him or her. If you view the teacher as an adversary, you are setting yourself up for a frustrating relationship during the school year. But if you see him or her as an ally—someone with whom you want to form a partnership—the chances are good that you can work together in your child's best interest.

"This year we are blessed with a wonderful teacher," says Diane, whose son has AD/HD. "She admits she does not know much about AD/HD. I have been supplying her with articles and ideas to help him in school."

Every parent hopes to find a teacher who is sensitive to the issues facing the child with AD/HD. When this is not the case, don't lose hope. With some effort on your part, you usually can form a working relationship with your child's teacher. The following strategies will help you earn the teacher's respect and ensure your child's chances of having a successful school year:

- **Meet with your child's teacher** either before school starts or within the first few weeks. Call and make an appointment, rather than just showing up after school one day. An appointment tells the teacher that you respect his or her schedule and it emphasizes that what you want to discuss is important enough to warrant a pre-arranged meeting.

- **Think of the teacher as an ally**, even if you have heard things about him or her you don't particularly like. Be sincere, friendly, and cheerful. The first few minutes of a meeting often set the tone for the entire discussion time.

- **Come to the meeting prepared**. Know what issues you want to address (for example, which seating arrangements have worked best for your child in previous years—what didn't work and why) and write them down. Ask for the teacher's cooperation in meeting your child's needs.

- **"Take along a one-page summary of AD/HD** and how it affects your child," advises Mary Squire, PhD.

- **Take notes during the meeting** and date them. Keep all notes together in a file folder so you can quickly access them if you need to at a later date.

- **Request that specific tests be handled differently** for your child if necessary. If your child has difficulty with writing, and as a result cannot write fast enough to keep up with the class, then asking that weekly spelling tests be given orally is not unreasonable. Never hesitate to ask a teacher to write down nightly homework assignments for your child or to at least check to see if your child has written them down accurately. Also ask if he or she is willing to accept your child's call at home if there is confusion regarding an assignment. Some teachers now place homework assignments online at their school's website. This has relieved a lot of stress in my family at homework time.

- **Be empathetic.** You *know* how frustrating dealing with your child can be. Now imagine having your child plus twenty-five others to handle. Make a point of letting the teacher know that you appreciate the fact that he or she has many students to work with and that some require extra assistance. You'll be surprised how much compassion you'll receive when you need it the most just because you have shown you empathize with him or her.
- **Accept that your child has limitations** and is not perfect. Do not become defensive when talking with the teacher. It will only create a hostile atmosphere.
- **Be honest, open, and offer your support.** Speak with the teacher about your child's strengths and limitations, disciplinary methods that work, and effective instructional techniques. This is one of the first steps parents need to take to ensure that their child's needs are met academically, emotionally, and socially in the school setting. Talk with him or her about the ways you work with your child at home and the difficulties you have in certain areas. Share what works for you and what works best for your child. Make the teacher your confidant.
- **Ask for the teacher's feedback** on specific behaviors (being disruptive in class or not paying attention, for example) or certain subjects if you would like to have it. Be sure he or she understands that you will provide support and suggestions (for consideration) on how to deal with challenges your child may present. Let the teacher know that you will monitor schoolwork and homework and will inform him or her of anything at home that may affect your child's schoolwork and behavior. (If grandpa is in the hospital and you are under a great deal of stress, this may affect your child in school in ways you may not even be aware of.) Above all, encourage the teacher to contact you concerning any problems. A simple statement, like "Please don't ever hesitate to call me. You won't be telling me anything I haven't heard or seen before," assures the teacher that you are a person who is approachable and open to discussion about your child.
- **Arrange for regular communication** with the teacher if you want to have it. Decide if you want to meet with him or her monthly, talk by phone every other week, exchange e-mails, or send notes through the assignment pad. Be sure to pass along any favorable

comments that your child has made about him or her, or school in general, at these times.

- **Ask for information about homework assignments** (how often, what subjects, how much time your child should spend on homework) and suggestions for helping with homework. Find out whether homework assignments are posted online.

- **Volunteer to help** in the classroom or with a class project. This is an effective way to observe the teacher's classroom teaching style and your child's response to it.

- **Express appreciation for the time he or she gave you** for the conference. You may want to summarize the main points of the meeting in your thank-you letter. Then if there is a discrepancy between your and the teacher's understanding of what was agreed, the teacher will undoubtedly notify you immediately. (Many teachers will also follow through by sending a letter to you that summarizes the points discussed and his or her plans to help in specific areas.)

- **Share magazine and newspaper articles on AD/HD** with your child's teacher during the school year. Most teachers will be pleased to receive additional information on AD/HD but especially pleased to know that you have thought of them.

Teenagers may feel embarrassed by having their parents contact their teacher directly. If this is a problem in your home, you may want to use a letter that he can hand deliver to his teacher. Consider the following letter, which was written by Mary Squire, PhD, to her son's teachers:

---

Dear _____

_____ has attention-deficit hyperactivity disorder (AD/HD). AD/HD is a physical/neurological disorder characterized by age-inappropriate levels of inattention, hyperactivity, or impulsivity or a combination of these. The primary manifestations for _____ are difficulties with attention and concentration, organizational skills, and difficulty staying on task. In a classroom, he may disturb other children at times by talking but he is not disruptive. His attention difficulties are most evident in math, due to the degree of concentration required for accurate calculation.

We will be changing _____'s medication in early October due to motor tics that result when he takes Ritalin. He will be taking Ritalin until that time, but his current dosage may be a bit low. Therefore, feedback from teachers will be especially important during the first quarter to help us monitor dosage.

Accommodations that improve _____'s classroom functioning and academic performance include the following:

_____ should be seated in the front of the classroom surrounded by the attentive students.

_____ will likely require more time on tests and other assignments than the majority of students in the class. He should be encouraged to check his work, especially in math.

If _____ fails to turn in assignments or comes to class without his homework done, it is important to notify me before his grade is adversely affected.

_____ is capable of doing honors-level work. Superior work should be expected of him, and he should not be placed in lower levels simply because of his attention difficulties. He has very high aspirations, and together we can help him achieve them. If his quarter grade average falls below a B (or A in science or English), please call me immediately. I can be reached at home at _____ or work at

_____.

Thanks very much for your help.

*Mary Squire*

Mary Squire

You may wish to use a similar letter; however, it must be tailored to meet the needs of your individual child and be sure to provide the following information:

- **The current medication** being administered
- **Specific difficulties** your child experiences in the classroom
- **Accommodations** that will improve academic performance. (The school district can develop a 504 plan—similar to the individualized education program (IEP)—which incorporates these accommodations and is legally binding. Parents may have to request it. (The 504 plan and the IEP are discussed later in this chapter.)

"My teenage son has never been able to talk with his teachers, so I draft a letter to each teacher every year, about the third week of school," says Janet Robinson, RN, PhD, who is the mother of an eighteen-year-old. "In the letter I begin by listing his strengths and abilities, then list the specific problems he has (like disorganization). I make only one request, and that is if he misses more than two assignments, that I'm notified. Most of the teachers, when you are real concrete, are supportive. I've seen them write in their roll book, 'misses two assignments, call mother.' They don't have to speak with me necessarily. I give them my voice-mail number and e-mail address. Whenever I see my son going into a self-destructive pattern, I send the teachers a note that says I'm concerned about how he's doing. I put in a self-addressed postcard and all they have to do is make a check mark or fill in a blank." Dr. Robinson's postcard is similar to this:

---

_____ He's doing fine
_____ No changes
_____ Not doing as well
_____ Missing _____ assignment(s)


_____
Teacher's signature

---

"Anything we can do to make the teacher's life easier is usually very appreciated," explains Dr. Robinson. "Most high school teachers are surprised that parents don't want to be involved in their kid's lives. I think it's essential every parent of an AD/HD student gets to every parent-teacher conference. Teachers have to know we are interested. It's easy to assume that because our kids don't hand in assignments that we don't care either. Stay involved with the school, even when there are problems. I know it's hard to go to conferences and have to sit and hear the negatives, but parents must become involved."

Parents should always assess the teacher's knowledge of AD/HD before sending a letter. "Some teachers only think of AD/HD as a severe behavior disorder," explains Bruce Pasch, MD. "One high school teacher thought one of our students was mentally ill and advised other students not to associate with him."

## Problems with Teachers

Sometimes, despite your best efforts, problems do develop with a teacher. Your child may complain of being treated unfairly, of never having enough time to finish in-class assignments, or regularly losing recess or physical education as a form of punishment. Any complaint your child voices should be investigated thoroughly before you meet with the teacher. First, try to find out exactly what has happened, or is happening, from your child.

My youngest son once told me that he was caught talking during class. When I asked what his teacher said, he answered, "She didn't say anything. She just put tape on my mouth so I couldn't talk again." My first instinct was to immediately telephone the teacher, but I decided to hold off until I learned more. That evening I asked my son to tell his father what had happened in school. My son told the same story. In fact, he relayed the same story after two additional days of questioning. On the third day he said, "Mom, I was only kidding about the tape on my mouth. My teacher really didn't do that. I was playing a joke on you."

Had I reacted hastily, I might have caused a great deal of unnecessary stress for an excellent teacher, so it's wise to find out what you can from your child first. Had my son not revealed the truth, I would have cautiously asked other parents how the teacher handled children who talked during class. Or I would have dropped by school unannounced and observed the teacher firsthand.

If you discover there is (or appears to be) a problem, request a parent-teacher conference. When you meet with the teacher, express your concern in a relaxed, nonconfrontational manner. Discuss what your child needs, rather than focusing on what the teacher is doing incorrectly. This is where your knowledge of AD/HD can be greatly beneficial.

Ideally, you should present specific concerns: "Evan seems to be having a problem finishing his math tests. I've noticed the last two rows of problems are rarely answered on the timed tests. This is having an effect on the grades he's receiving and I'm very concerned. As you know, Evan has AD/HD and we've found that timed tests are difficult for him because he tends to work slower than the average child. It takes him longer to get started, to process the information, and write it down. I know the children are expected to complete one hundred addition problems in five minutes before they can move on to subtraction, but this may be impossible for Evan to achieve."

Together you can work toward finding a solution to the problem, one that is acceptable to both the teacher and you. A parent might say, "It's my hope that together we can help Evan move on to subtraction. He's becoming very discouraged because he is the last child on addition and many of his classmates are already on multiplication and division. We work with Evan nightly and know he can answer these problems. Do you have any suggestions?" Be sure to give the teacher the opportunity to offer his or her suggestions before offering any of your own. In a case like this, suggestions a parent might make include the following:

- **Reduce the number of problems** to fifty, thereby reducing the amount, not the quality of work.
- **Give the test untimed** (it's his knowledge that is being tested, not his attention span or how fast he can complete the test).
- **Give the test orally**.
- **Alter the grade scale**.

If you use a constructive approach, you will find that the teacher will be more receptive to any suggestions (for consideration) you have to offer and less apt to react negatively to you or your child. Remember that many adaptations or interventions can be implemented in the regular classroom to meet the needs of most children with AD/HD. Parents who are interested in learning about various interventions and strategies that work with children who have AD/HD should refer to the book *How to Reach and Teach ADD/AD/HD Children* by Sandra F. Rief (West Nyack, New York: The Center for Applied Research in Education, 1993).

If, despite your best efforts, you are unable to reach a satisfactory solution to a problem, then, and only then, should you take your concern to the principal. Approach the school principal using the guidelines presented previously.

What should parents do if their child is experiencing academic failure despite interventions in the regular classroom? If you have been working together with the teacher, he or she may suggest that your child be evaluated to determine if he has a learning disability and the nature and extent of the special education and related services that the child needs. If a teacher does not suggest this, you have the right to ask that your child be evaluated. If a teacher does not feel this is necessary, your next step is to request a conference with the principal. If the school refuses to evaluate your child, then ask the principal for the name of the special education contact person for your area or the name of the director of special education, and request a conference.

"If you suspect that your child's teacher is not capable of handling a child with AD/HD [after parent-teacher conferences have failed to produce results], then talk with the principal and see if there is a more suitable teacher for your child in the school," says Joanie from Sylvania, Ohio.

"With ongoing problems, I find that daily communication with the teacher helps," says Julie, a former teacher from Newark, Ohio. "You can do this two ways. Either briefly ask the teacher how things went that day when you pick your child up or use a message envelope for a daily report. Teachers who will not take the time to write a daily note will answer you if you appear in person." If a teacher is not willing to write a daily note, give him or her a supply of daily checklist forms (noting your child's specific problem areas) that can be filled out within a few minutes and sent home with your child.

Unfortunately, not all teachers are willing to accommodate a child who presents challenges. "My son was switched from a public school to a private school after one quarter in first grade. The problem was both his ADD and his teacher's response to it," explains one mother. "Rather than accept a different child in her class, she made him feel as though he was an outcast and, thus, he became one. Phone calls came at least three times a week. She offered no solutions, nor, in my opinion, did she even try to understand . . . she just complained. Conferences with the principal were to no avail. Eventually, we all benefited . . . she got her wish and, ultimately, we got ours (which was a better education for our son). We transferred him to a private school. At the private school, difficulties were discussed with individual teachers and allowances were made for motor-skill problems and speech difficulties. He was required to do at least half of the work (half full rather than half empty principle) that the other children were expected to do. With time, these allowances were decreased and now, in seventh grade, he is operating fully with his class. Were changes dramatic when he transferred schools that first year? No. But it was certainly a [positive] start. He was treated as an individual and not as a clone."

"In our experience we have found that young teachers are usually wonderful with children with AD/HD," says Dewey from Santa Fe, New Mexico. "Because they are younger, they are energetic, have more patience, are willing to spend extra time reaching the child with AD/HD, and are eager to learn more about this disorder. In our opinion they are more open to suggestions from the parents." (Remember, many older teachers are also young at heart and enjoy working with children who have challenges.)

## What Type of School Is Best for the Child with AD/HD?

Most experts agree that children with AD/HD do better in a more structured setting (where prescribed work patterns are the norm) rather than in a school that promotes open-ended choices, yet some parents I interviewed felt differently. Their children attend schools that are less structured (open-classroom concept) and are doing considerably well.

When my husband and I decided to send our oldest child to the school he now attends (an independent, open-concept school), we did not know that the professionals recommend that children with AD/HD be schooled in a structured setting. We looked at the schools in our area and decided this particular school would be best for a child with AD/HD because it was the least restrictive. Our son would not be required to sit at a desk all day nor would he have the same teacher all day long. After we enrolled him that summer, we mentioned this to his psychologist, who was disheartened to learn of our choice. He told us this school would not work for our son, but time has proved otherwise. Parents who have their children in small private and independent schools say that many of these schools offer the following:

- **Small classes,** in which children receive more focused time from teachers and teachers are able to immediately respond to appropriate and inappropriate behavior because of the smaller student-teacher ratio
- **Many one-on-one learning experiences,** which are wonderful for children who have AD/HD and experience difficulty staying on task in group situations
- **A hands-on approach to learning,** allowing children to learn through touch along with sight and sound
- **The use of computers for in-class work,** providing instant feedback and reinforcement
- **The choice to use computers for homework assignments,** even in primary grades, making it much easier for children with fine-motor-skill deficits
- **A variety of teachers throughout the day,** which lessens the chance of one teacher being drained by the challenges of the child with AD/HD. Also, children learn how to change classes at an early age rather than having to learn this skill and adapt at the junior high or high school level
- **Morning meetings,** where students find out what they will be studying that particular day and are told of schedule changes ahead of time is great for the slow-to-adapt child
- **A weekly check of schoolwork,** which requires a parent's signature and is an automatic home-school feedback system
- **An organized-notebook approach,** which often includes color-coded folders for homework and various subjects, a folder for notices sent home, a pencil holder, and most important, an assignment-pad folder, helps children improve their organizational skills
- **The choice of educational activities during free time** in the school day, teaches children to make choices and to entertain themselves while developing some skills independently (interests and talents often become evident with this type of learning approach)
- **Freedom to get up and move around** quietly (within limits), which encourages recognizing children as individuals with vary-

ing needs (*not* as problem children) who won't be punished if they can't sit still for long periods
- **Less concentration required in the last hour** of the school day because it is reserved for classes such as music, art, and physical education, which is advantageous for children whose medication may be wearing off or has worn off

Says Heather, a former teacher who lives in Raleigh, North Carolina, "Traditional structured classrooms are not required for all kids with AD/HD. I taught in an open classroom and the students went off medication in my class because of the flexibility. There were fewer conflicts yet there was structure (for example, reading first, then math, then playtime, etc.) Each child had an individualized assignment, but some talking and moving around was allowed." Structure is always needed, but it must allow for flexibility.

For information on how to evaluate curriculum and staff and public and private schools, you may want to take a look at *Your Child's First School: A Handbook for Parents,* by Diana Townsend-Butterworth (New York: Walker, 1992).

## Home Schooling

"If school has become a horrid experience and your child's self-esteem is slipping away, consider home schooling," suggests Kate from Carlinville, Illinois. "We home school all of our children. Since David is AD/HD/gifted, it affords him the opportunity to study his current interests in depth. He doesn't compete with thirty others for attention. A four-to-one ratio in a class is great. . . . He doesn't have a bad 'rep' at this school. And he can't con this teacher. And no one loves or understands him like I do, so I get the best results. He gets plenty of socialization through neighborhood friends, church, and sports. For David, school socialization would take over academics to negative extremes in both areas."

A growing number of parents teach their children at home. Many school districts permit this and some districts even cooperate with parents by permitting them to use school resources. Home schooling involves a significant commitment, but parents who make that commitment can effectively teach their children at home. For more information on home schooling consult *The Home School Manual,* 5th edition, by Theodore E.

Wade Jr. and others (Auburn, California: Gazelle Publications, 1993). Curriculum guides are available through your school system, a local library, or may be ordered through bookstores.

## Gifted Children with AD/HD

More than three million children in the United States have an IQ of 125 or higher. But having a high IQ is not the only criterion involved in evaluating a gifted child. Often, a child is regarded as gifted when he or she shows exceptional abilities in one or more areas, including mathematics, music, leadership, language, computer science, creative thinking, or special talent in the performing or visual arts.

In her book *The Gifted and Talented*, Gilda Berger describes gifted children as those who do things earlier, faster, better, and a little differently than other children. But what about gifted children with AD/HD? What difficulties will they experience in school and what is their prognosis for the future? Unfortunately, there is little information available on this particular group of children, but it is known that when gifted learning-disabled children receive appropriate intervention they can have a successful, rewarding future.

Appropriate intervention includes many strategies because multiple areas of the child's life are affected. First, psychological counseling may be essential for the child and family. Educational therapy is imperative. Second, intellectual deficits must be identified (the deficits are often masked by the giftedness) and adjustments made that will enable the child to take control and learn to adapt to his unique situation. Third, the child must be taught to deal with anger and stress (often caused by frustration) using distinct behavioral techniques. Finally, the child's teachers and school administrators must be involved in all aspects of the child's educational program.

The following are some hints for parents with gifted children who have AD/HD:

- **Most gifted children show an early interest in books**. Read to your child and discuss the stories with him. Talk about the characters, ideas, actions, and meanings. Have age-appropriate interesting books in your home for young children who are reading on their own.

- **Provide access to a computer**. It's challenging for even the brightest child, and it provides immediate feedback.
- **Help your child develop interests and hobbies**. Provide space, time, materials, and encouragement for activities he enjoys.
- **Buy toys that help to develop mental and physical abilities**. Toys that involve problem-solving or decision-making skills are best.
- **Provide reference books** (encyclopedias, dictionaries, etc.) for young children. Some gifted youngsters intuitively know how to use reference manuals.
- **Say what you mean and mean what you say**. These children are smart—they'll catch you every time if you don't.

For more information on gifted children contact The Association for the Gifted, Council for Gifted Children, 1920 Association Drive, Reston, VA 22902, or the National Association for Gifted Children, 1155 15th Street NW, Suite 1002, Washington, DC 20005. You may also be interested in the book *The Survival Guide for Parents of Gifted Kids: How to Understand, Live with, and Stick Up for Your Gifted Child* by Sally Yahnke Walker (Minneapolis, MN: Free Spirit, 2002).

# Homework without Hassles

No matter what type of school your child attends, one thing is certain: your child will have homework. If you are fortunate, your child's teacher will check his assignment pad every day to make certain your child knows what his homework is. Because some teachers are unwilling to do this, believing that the child needs to learn responsibility for taking accurate notes on his own, you may find that your child is not sure what his homework is. Some children take notes but then can't read their writing or they don't have the appropriate books with them to complete the assignments. Without a doubt, homework can be a very frustrating experience both for the child and for the parents.

## Homework Patterns

Homework for younger school-age children may follow a pattern or schedule. For instance, every Monday they have a spelling test and on Tuesday evenings they are expected to write ten sentences using as many of their spelling words as possible. Ask your child's teacher whether he or she follows such a schedule. If you know what to expect from week to week it will help you and your child tremendously and prevent many nightly battles.

## Daily Assignment Pads

Whether or not a homework pattern exists, the daily assignment pad is still the most beneficial tool available. Your child records his assignments during the day and then his teacher checks the assignment pad and signs it before he leaves for home. You, in turn, sign the sheet after the homework is completed and it is taken back to school the next morning. For assignment pads to work parents, teachers, and students must work together to establish some kind of monitoring plan. "Teachers may need to write down the assignment for some kids with AD/HD," says Mary Squire, PhD, "This may be necessary for even some of the older children."

Says Annie from Sylvania, Ohio, "My son writes his assignments down and has a friend check it for accuracy. The friend then signs the assignment sheet. Chase enjoys collecting coins, so every day that he brings home his signed assignment sheet and the right textbooks he receives $2.00 to use for coin shopping on Saturdays with his dad. If he misses a day, he loses a coin from his collection because he's in the negative (down $2.00). The next day if he brings the assignment sheet home signed, he's now $2.00 up and he gets the coin back. The following day if he brings home the assignment sheet signed, he gets $2.00." This is a great idea for children who collect something they value because children with AD/HD often respond better when they must work to keep something they already have.

## Assignment Sheet for Elementary School Children

Encourage your child to use an assignment sheet as soon as he starts receiving homework assignments. If the school does not provide an assignment sheet (or book), design one of your own and make enough copies to last the entire school year. All sheets should be kept in a loose-leaf notebook that your child carries to and from school every day.

## Unclear Assignments or No Books

There may still be times when your child is unclear about an assignment. It's helpful if the teacher accepts calls at home, but if this is not possible, be sure your child has the phone numbers of a few classmates he can call. If a phone call is necessary, your child must be the one to make it no matter his age. You may have to get on the line to help write the assignment down if he's forgotten his spelling book, for example, but the call must be made by your child because homework is his responsibility, not yours.

If your child consistently forgets to bring home his books or brings home the wrong textbooks, you may want to purchase a second set of books that remain in the house. "This also allows for highlighting and writing notes in the margins, which is necessary for many AD/HD children," says Mary Squire, PhD. This is, of course, costly and many teachers discourage it. If you prefer not to buy extra textbooks, you might insist that your child bring home every textbook every night, whether he has homework or not (reward him daily for remembering his books until it is no longer necessary), or make photocopies of chapters to keep at home.

## Your Homework Responsibilities

Homework should be a part of your child's daily schedule and listed on his chart. This means it should be done at the same time each day whenever possible. It is your responsibility to see that your child has a proper area for studying and completing homework, whether that spot is the desk in his bedroom or the dining room or kitchen table. This area should have sufficient lighting and be as free of distractions as possible. (Siblings are distractions so it is your responsibility to keep them out of the study area.) If you find that your child is unable to concentrate in a quiet room, it may be because he needs background sound. The hum of a small fan or a tape playing softly, with the tranquil sound of summer rainfall, may be just what is needed to help him concentrate. And remember to turn off the television set.

Provide your child with a box of school supplies that are to be used only during homework time. This saves you and your child from the nightly hunt to find those items needed to complete homework. When homework is finished, the box should be put away in the same place.

Encourage your child to do his homework on his own. Encouraging independent work does not mean that you are not available to assist. It means that you are available to help get him started by making sure he understands what the assignment is and assisting him with the first problem. It also means helping your child break larger projects into smaller steps. "Set mini-goals for assignments," advises Dr. Squire. A book report can be overwhelming to some children, but if you break it into smaller parts (title, author, illustrator, the setting, list of characters, main idea in two or three sentences, etc.), the assignment will be much easier to complete. Twenty-five math problems can be broken down into five-problem sections. "Or children can do every other problem," offers Dr. Squire. "But always talk with a teacher about this ahead of time. Reward your child after completing each mini-goal." Rather than having your child study an entire list of twenty spelling words the night before a test, have him learn to spell five words a night for four nights. Many assignments can be broken down into smaller parts or divided over several days so the task becomes manageable. "Children then can see the progress they are making," adds Dr. Squire.

While doing homework, offer your child the opportunity to take short breaks every ten to fifteen minutes. Encourage him to get up and move around, stretch, take a drink of water, or use the bathroom. Use a timer to signal when he must return to his homework. If your child is having difficulty in a certain subject, help him budget his time so he can spend a short time reviewing work in that area. "If there is a subject area in which my son is having difficulty, I try to teach him the next lesson just before the teacher presents it in the classroom," says Julie from Newark, Ohio. "Then he will not miss the point of the lesson because of his short attention span and get frustrated. As well, my son is able to answer the in-class questions the teacher asks and this increases my son's self-esteem."

When homework is completed, praise your child for starting his homework on time, sitting quietly and working, writing legibly, and finishing it in an appropriate amount of time. "An after-school dose of medicine may help children who have difficulty working on homework," suggests Dr. Squire. (Be sure to check with your physician rather than adding another dose of medication on your own.)

## Slowpokes

For children who take forever to do their homework, play Beat the Clock. Together, you and your child determine how much time he will need to complete his homework, including break time. Tell your child how much time he has to do his homework, then set the timer. Reward your child for completing his homework within the time frame, using the chart system (he gets a sticker or another reward). After three or five days of successfully completing homework, your child earns a special privilege, such as a trip to his favorite restaurant. For older children, you may wish to increase the number of successful days to ten (or whatever you feel is appropriate) before your child earns a privilege. As your child develops the ability to stay on task and completes his homework within the time frame, you can increase the number of successful days it takes to earn a privilege. Always praise your child once homework is completed. Compliment him for staying on task, neatness, controlling frustrations, and finishing the assignment. Ideally, praise for completing the assignment correctly should come from the teacher, but since this does not always happen, parents should praise their child for a job well done.

"If you use Beat the Clock, watch your child carefully," suggests Bruce Pasch, MD. "Some impulsive children will rush through their homework making careless errors. Or Beat the Clock may encourage impulsivity in slowpokes who are slow because they are checking themselves."

## The Rejectors

For children who refuse to do their homework, remove all privileges. This means no television, telephone calls, visiting friends, using the computer, etc. until homework is completed. If he intentionally forgets assignments or his textbooks and is not able to do his homework, he still loses all privileges for the evening. If this continues for a week, take away all privileges on the weekend also. It's important that the child realize he always has a choice. He can do his homework and the privileges are automatically reinstated, or he can refuse to do the work and lose all privileges. This is a frustrating situation, but it's important to control yourself. Don't argue with your child. Don't make idle threats. Don't yell or scream. State the rules in a firm, but positive, voice and be consistent every night. For example, "You may watch television after your homework is completed," not "You can't watch television because your homework isn't done." When homework is completed, immediately follow through with rewards and remember to praise your child for completing homework during the scheduled time frame.

## The Speeders, Forgetters, and Insisters

My nine-year-old used to complete his homework in a matter of minutes. He could do twenty math problems and study twenty spelling words in five minutes. Sounds impressive, doesn't it? The problem is that most of the math answers were wrong and he couldn't have passed the spelling test if his life had depended on it. Maybe you have a child who's a speeder. Speeders often sit down to do their homework without being told (this pleases mom and dad greatly and speeders know it), but then always have something more important to do and rush through their assignments. Speeders almost always have to redo their homework because of wrong answers or sloppiness.

Some children are forgetters. They often forget their assignments or books and then say they can't do their homework. Speeders and forgetters can be handled the same way. At the usual scheduled homework time, children must still sit down and do schoolwork no matter what. No time-off is given for short assignments, no assignments, or forgotten books. Speeders must work on homework for a predetermined length of time. Forgetters work on math, or language arts, or write a book report assigned by the parents. Parents can base assignments on subjects and skills the child is studying or is expected to study in upcoming days or weeks. Assignments should be created in advance and kept on file, so parents always have work prepared—even when schedules are hectic. Parents should always find more to do than the teacher assigns, providing the student the incentive to bring home assignments. Eventually, speeders learn to slow down and do it right the first time and forgetters remember their assignments and textbooks.

The insisters are the children who maintain they completed their homework at school or that they didn't have any homework. "If you hear this too often," advises Jenny from Seattle, Washington, "then call the teacher and find out for yourself."

## Falling Behind on Homework

If your child has trouble with his homework for an extended period (two weeks), make an appointment with his teacher. Is he having the same problems in school with class assignments? Are other children struggling with homework assignments? Maybe your child has missed some basic points days or weeks earlier that may account for his difficulties. Or if other children are having trouble with homework, maybe the homework is not grade appropriate. Just as you want to know what's happening in school, the teacher wants to know what is going on with homework assignments, so keep in touch. School failure may contribute to, or worsen, a student's low self-esteem, depression, or anxiety.

For further tips and hints on motivating children to complete homework, you may want to read the books *Homework without Tears: A Parent's Guide for Motivating Children to do Homework and Succeed in School*, by Lee Canter (New York: HarperPerennial, 1988), and *The Homework Solution: Getting Kids to do Their Homework* by Linda Agler Sonna (Charlotte, VT: Williamson Publishing, 1990). For hints on improving your child's schoolwork, refer to *1,001 Ways to Improve Your Child's Schoolwork: An Easy-to-Use Reference Book of Common School Problems and Practical Solutions* by Lawrence J. Greene (New York: Dell, 1991).

## When Homework Isn't Turned In

Discovering that completed homework is not being turned in to the teacher is incredibly frustrating and commonly occurs with children who have AD/HD. If this is a problem for your child, schedule a three-way meeting involving you, your child, and his teacher. It's imperative that your child participate in this meeting—his contribution is crucial. Together develop a turn-in-homework plan. Then arrange to meet again in two weeks to see if the system is working.

If problems continue with homework (forgetting books or assignments, not turning in homework) ask the teacher if your child can complete his homework at school sometime during the day or ask if there is a place at school where he can do homework after school. At one point, we made arrangements for my youngest son to do his homework after school in the office of the director of the middle school. He hated it, but his homework was completed every night. Since all of his teachers were aware of this, when he said he didn't have his homework they knew he had completed it but had forgotten where he put it. Very, very AD/HD! Another semester, he was so behind in his homework that the principal actually went with him to his locker where they discovered together all his misplaced assignments. My son, who had forgotten that he had completed all the work, was shocked, but most important, he was relieved to find all his missing assignments. In his case, once he completed his homework he completely dismissed it from his mind. According to him he had "more important things to do." This led to brief and repeated conversations with him that getting an education was his "job" in the family, with a reminder that if Mom and Dad did their work but never turned it in, there would be no paychecks (read that, sweetie, as "no money to buy you the things you want and need") and Mom's books would never get published. Fortunately, his teachers are now aware of the problem, and when he doesn't turn in an assignment, he is sent to his locker to retrieve it.

## Hints for Junior High and High School Students

As your child encounters more demanding school days and homework sessions you may want to share these tips with him.

**Participate during Class**  Pay more attention in class by participating during class. Judy, a former high school teacher and a parent of a child with AD/HD, from Toledo, Ohio, says this is best accomplished by the following:

- **Sitting close to the teacher** in lecture-style classes where students not only hear better but will have fewer distractions
- **Taking notes** in classes and using a tape recorder
- **Partaking in class or group sessions** (this includes asking questions when the student doesn't understand something and offering answers when he does)
- **Coming to class prepared** (homework is done or the student has studied a lesson the night before it is presented in class)
- **Writing a summary of the lecture** after the class. "Always ask a teacher if she has an outline of the lecture," suggests Judy. "If she does, maybe she'll share it"

**Organize Class Materials**  Use a color-coding system to organize class materials. For example, use a blue folder for math papers, blue sticker or blue book cover on math book, red folder for history papers, red sticker on history book or red book cover, and so forth. All folders are then kept in one loose-leaf notebook. On the outside of the notebook is a color-coded listing for each subject. Then when he's on the way to history class, for instance, he can stop by his locker, check the front of his notebook and see that he needs all red-covered or red-stickered books or materials for history class. The notebook also holds other school supplies your child uses frequently. Completed homework is always placed in the appropriate color-coded folder in the loose-leaf notebook.

For older children changing classes, help them draw a map showing the location of their locker and the route they must take to each class. Color-code each classroom according to the color used on books and file folders.

**Use an Assignment Folder**  Using an assignment folder entails creating an assignment sheet to fit the child's schedule, making a copy for each week school is in session, and placing all of the sheets in a folder, which remains in the loose-leaf notebook at all times. The assignment sheet lists the days of the week across the top; the subjects are listed down the left-hand side. A new sheet is started every Monday. Janet Robinson, RN, PhD, suggests that parents use the color-coding system on the assignment sheet also. "My son must enter his assignments next to the proper color. If there is no assignment that particular day, he is to write 'No Assignment' next to that subject. Parents can give points for entries next to each subject."

Older students, with different classes on different days, should buy a daily planning calendar to keep track of classes throughout the school year, noting, for example, where and what time they meet and designated study-period times. In this planner they can write down test dates, essay and term paper due dates, and outline plans to study for tests and write papers.

**Set a Time and Place to Study**  Negotiate a plan that defines a specific time period and place to study and complete homework each day with your older student and put it in writing. Older students can earn such privileges as use of the car or telephone for staying on task during homework time. Likewise, students can lose telephone time or the use of the car for not staying on task.

**Take Notes**  Taking notes, even when reading chapters for homework assignments, helps to reinforce what has just been read: the student is not only reading it but writing it down. Highlighting major points is also very helpful to students as is writing in the margins as Dr. Squire explained earlier, but only if the books are personally owned and not the property of the school system. Highlighting major points is particularly helpful when reviewing for tests.

## Some Study Hints for Students with AD/HD

Because students with AD/HD have difficulty organizing materials, concentrating for extended periods of time, and selecting important information from written and auditory direction, it's imperative that students tackle assignments with a game plan. In this section, we will cover some of the types of assignments that older students may have difficulty with. If a specific type of assignment is not listed here, parents should be able to alter some of the following tips to meet their child's specific needs.

**Reading Chapters in a Textbook** A textbook chapter can appear monumental to a student with AD/HD, but when broken down into sections the task becomes less overwhelming and threatening. When studying chapters in a textbook, students should be taught to use the popular SQ-3R method:

**S—Scan the chapter.**

- Read the title of the chapter.
- Read each subtitle.
- Study any illustrations, graphs, charts, etc.
- Read the study guide questions at the end of the chapter.
- Read the chapter summary.

**Q—Make up questions using the subtitles**. For example, if the subtitle is "Jury," the student should ask himself or herself, "What is a jury?" "How many people sit on a jury?" "When is a jury used?"

Once they have done all of the above, they now turn to the 3Rs.

- Read the text to answer your questions.
- Write the answers down.
- Review everything that you wrote down at the end of the study period.

Keep all notes to review at a later date, when you will be tested on this material.

———————— , ———————— ———————— , ¹⁹——
DAY　　　　　MONTH　　　DATE

| Subject | Assignments | Date Due | Test Day |
|---------|-------------|----------|----------|
| Reading | | | |
| English/ Language Arts | | | |
| Spelling | | | |
| Math | | | |
| Science | | | |
| Social Studies | | | |
| | | | |
| | | | |

### Things To Take Home

1._____

2._____

3._____

4._____

5._____

### Things To Bring To School

1._____

2._____

### Messages

**Studying for Tests**  Before beginning to study for a test, the student must be sure he knows exactly what information he will be tested on. He can clarify this with the instructor or another classmate. Once he has determined exactly what will be covered, he goes through his color-coded folder and pulls notes from classes and homework sessions. If the test covers chapters 5 and 6 and the test will be given in five days, that gives him two days to study each chapter, chapter notes, and old tests and quizzes. The student details this plan in his planner. For example,

> Monday, January 18
> Study half of chapter five.
> Review notes and summaries.
>
> Tuesday, January 19
> Finish studying chapter five.
> Review notes and summaries.
>
> Wednesday, January 20
> Study half of chapter six.
> Review notes and summaries.
>
> Thursday, January 21
> Study remainder of chapter six.
> Review notes and summaries.
> Review all notes and summaries from both chapters. (This review of
> both chapters could be saved for the day of the test.)

**Major Assignments**  A major assignment, such as a twelve-page report on alcoholism due in six weeks, not only has to be broken down into manageable parts but must be worked on during an established time each week. The schedule might be like this:

**Week 1**: The student gathers the resource materials she'll need to write the report. Resource articles are downloaded on the computer or printed out; books are purchased or borrowed from the library. If the books have been borrowed, the student reads through them and takes notes.

**Week 2**: The student decides which main topics to include in the report and lists them on index cards using numbers. For instance,

1. Define alcoholism.
2. Who is at risk?
3. How does alcoholism affect the abuser?
4. How does alcoholism affect the family?
5. What can the abuser do to help himself?
6. What can families do to help the abuser?

**Week 3**: Take notes on each topic, listing them on index cards using the number assigned to each topic. The number should be placed in the top right-hand corner on each index card. All number 1 cards are then banded together, as are number 2 cards, and so forth. Notes should be written in the students' *own* words and in complete sentences. This will make the rough draft relatively simple to write.

**Week 4**: If the instructor requires an outline, this is the next step. With the notes numbered by topics, the student determines the order the facts should be presented in, using a formal or simple outline form.

**Week 5**: The student begins writing the rough draft. The rough draft does not have to be perfect. If the student is not sure of the spelling of certain words, she should not stop to look them up in the dictionary; she should just circle the word. At this stage, she is only trying to get her thoughts down in paragraph form, beginning with the number 1 cards and so on. She should skip lines so words or sentences can be inserted if needed. After the student completes the rough draft, it should be set aside for one day. Then it should be read slowly, one line at a time, while making the needed corrections in spelling, punctuation, etc.

**Week 6**: Before beginning the final draft, the student reviews the points she needs to remember when rewriting. (Did the instructor ask students to write on every line or every other line? Is this to be typed? Double spaced? What are the margins to be? Is there to be a separate title page?) After the student completes her final draft, she sets it aside for one day. Then she carefully rereads it, line by line again. Spelling and punctuation should also be checked (check for spelling errors by reading the paper from the bottom up if handwritten), as well as the overall look of the paper.

A word-processing program on a computer will underline misspelled words and grammatical errors. If your computer program does not, look to see whether this feature is turned on. It will also give suggestions on how to rewrite a sentence so that it is not in the passive voice, for instance. If the sentence she just typed is an incomplete one or a fragment, it will alert her. Students today who are permitted to use a computer for writing essays are very fortunate. Even a not-so-good writer can produce an almost grammatically correct essay with few spelling errors. Unfortunately, the program will not tell you that you should have used *here* instead of *hear* or *than* instead of *then*, so the work will still need to be checked word by word. You may need to tell your children about this feature, as they may not notice it, or if they do notice, they may not understand why certain words or parts of sentences are highlighted.

A final word about major school papers or essays and book reports: it is far easier today than ever before for a student to steal another's work and claim it as his or her own. All they have to do is go online and find what they are looking for. One high school student, I know, found exactly what he needed for his essay and more. The "more" was another article that he found, retyped on his computer as if it were his own work, and then sold to one of his classmates complete with the student's name on the cover sheet. The teacher caught the students! Both essays sounded familiar so she went online and found "their" articles. And, yes, this high school student has AD/HD. He didn't think about the repercussions of being caught, only the fact that this was an easy way out. His impulsivity got in his way and clouded his judgment.

## Computer Use

There is no doubt that the use of computers is a tremendous help to children (and adults) with AD/HD. As stated previously, the features of a good word-processing program allow students to check for spelling and grammatical errors immediately. Most important, the quality of work will be better than if they had written the assignment by hand, especially for children who have great difficulty writing—forming the letters and using appropriate spacing between words and sentences. For those children a short paragraph will take much longer to write than for the average student and will be more difficult for a teacher to read—their handwriting and inability to space words often makes it tricky to determine where a sentence has ended and where the next sentence begins.

Viewing their work on the screen allows them to see what they have actually written rather than what they think they have written. Errors can be easily corrected on screen. Computers can be used not only for homework assignments for the younger student but also for note taking and major writing assignments for the older student. Some high school and college students with AD/HD carry laptop computers to class with them.

Supervise children when they are using the computer and are online. Children can easily play a game instead of doing homework, minimizing the screen when they hear a parent coming to check on them.

## Providing an Appropriate Education to Children with Attention-Deficit Hyperactivity Disorder

(*Source*: ERIC Digests, published by The Council for Exceptional Children.)

Schools must provide appropriate educational services to students who have been identified as having AD/HD. In September 1991, the Department of Education issued a policy clarification on the topic of children with attention deficit disorders. . . . The memorandum was intended to clarify state and local responsibility under federal law for meeting the needs of children with AD/HD in the educational system as a whole. . . . The report recognizes that:

- **Regular classroom teachers are important** in identifying appropriate educational adaptations and interventions for many children with AD/HD.
- **State and local districts should take the necessary steps** to promote coordination between special education and regular education programs.
- **Regular education teachers and other personnel need training** to develop a greater awareness of children with AD/HD and of adaptations that can be implemented in regular education programs to address the instructional needs of these children.

### Federal Laws Affecting Children with AD/HD

(*Source*: ERIC Digests, published by The Council for Exceptional Children.)

Both the Individuals with Disabilities Education Act (IDEA) and Section 504 of the Rehabilitation Act of 1973 provide coverage for children with AD/HD. When the disability adversely affects educational performance, eligibility for special education should be approached through the processes of IDEA. When the disability does not affect educational performance but does substantially limit one or more major life activities, eligibility should be approached through Section 504. The following are highlights of each law as it affects the education of children with AD/HD.

Individuals with Disabilities Education Act, Part B:

- **Requires that state and local districts make a free appropriate public education** (FAPE) available to all eligible children with disabilities [if they qualify by discrepancy criteria].
- **Requires that the rights and protections of Part B of IDEA are extended to children with AD/HD** and their parents.
- **Requires that an evaluation be done,** without undue delay, to determine if the child has one or more of thirteen specified disabling conditions and requires special education and related services.
- **Requires that children with AD/HD be classified as eligible for services** under the "other health impaired" category in instances where AD/HD is a chronic or acute health problem that results in limited alertness that adversely affects a child's educational performance. Children with AD/HD can also be served under the categories of "learning disabilities" or "emotionally disturbed" if the evaluation finds these conditions are also present.
- **Does not allow local districts to refuse to evaluate the possible need for special education** and related services for a child with a prior medical diagnosis of AD/HD solely because of that medical diagnosis. *On the other hand, a medical diagnosis of ADD does not automatically make a child eligible for services under Part B (IDEA).*
- **Requires that a full and individual evaluation of the child's educational needs must be conducted** in accordance with requirements in Part B (IDEA). These requirements include: a multidisciplinary team must perform the evaluation, and at least one teacher or other specialist with knowledge in the area of AD/HD must be on the team.

- **Requires that a due process hearing take place**, at the request of the parents, if there is a disagreement between the local district and the parent over the request for evaluation, or the determinations for services.

Section 504 of the Rehabilitation Act of 1973:

- **Prohibits discrimination** on the basis of disability by recipients of federal funds (i.e., the public school system).
- **Provides appropriate education** for children who do not fall within the disability categories specified in Part B (IDEA). Examples of potential conditions not typically covered under Part B (IDEA) are: communicable diseases (HIV, tuberculosis), medical conditions (asthma, allergies, diabetes, heart disease), temporary medical conditions due to illness or accident, and drug/alcohol addiction.
- **Requires that a free, appropriate public education be provided** for each qualified child who is disabled but does not require special education and related services under Part B (IDEA). A free, appropriate education (FAPE) under Section 504 includes: regular or special education and related aids and services that are designed to meet the individual student's needs and are based on adherence to the regulatory requirements on education setting, evaluation, placement, and procedural safeguards.
- **Guarantees parents the right to contest the outcome of an evaluation** if a local district determines that a child is not disabled under Section 504.
- **Requires the local district to make an individualized determination** of the child's educational needs for regular or special education or related aids and services if the child is found eligible under Section 504.
- **Requires the implementation of an individualized education program** (IEP). One means of meeting the free, appropriate public education requirements of Section 504 is to follow the IEP guidelines as set forth in the regulations for Part B (IDEA).
- **Requires that the child's education must be provided in the regular education classroom** unless it is demonstrated that education in the regular environment with the use of supplementary aids and services cannot be achieved satisfactorily.

- **Requires that necessary adjustments be made in the regular classroom** for children who qualify under Section 504.

Because IDEA and Section 504 can be confusing not only to parents but teachers, what follows is a comparison of these two federal acts.

## A Comparison of IDEA and Section 504

The Individuals with Disabilities Education Act (IDEA) and Section 504 of the Rehabilitation Act of 1973 are two attempts to improve the lives of those with disabilities. (*Source*: NICHCY.)

### Type and Purpose

**IDEA:** An education act to provide federal financial assistance to State and local education agencies to guarantee special education and related services to eligible children with disabilities.

**504:** A civil rights law to prohibit discrimination on the basis of disability in programs and activities, public and private, that receive federal financial assistance.

### Who Is Protected?

**IDEA:** Children ages 3–21 who are determined by a multi-disciplinary team to be eligible within one or more of 13 specific disability categories and who need special education and related services. Categories include autism, deafness, deaf-blindness, hearing impairments, mental retardation, multiple disabilities, orthopedic impairments, other health impairments (note: AD/HD falls under the category of health impairment), serious emotional disturbance, specific learning disabilities, speech or language impairments, traumatic brain injury, and visual impairments.

**504:** Any person who (1) has a physical or mental impairment that substantially limits one or more major life activities, (2) has a record of such an impairment or (3) is regarded as having such an impairment. Major life activities include walking, seeing, hearing, speaking, breathing, learning, working, caring for oneself, and performing manual tasks.

### Provides for a Free, Appropriate Public Education (FAPE)

**IDEA:** Yes. A FAPE is defined to mean special education and related services. Special education means "specially designed instruction at no cost to the parents, to meet the unique needs of the child with a disability . . ." Related services are provided if students require them in order to benefit from specially designed instruction. States are required to ensure the provision of "full educational opportunity" to all children with disabilities. IDEA requires the development of an Individualized Education Program (IEP) document with specific content and a required number of participants at an IEP meeting.

**504:** Yes. An "appropriate" education means an education comparable to that provided to students without disabilities. This may be defined as regular or special education services. Students can receive related services under Section 504 even if they are not provided any special education. Section 504 does require development of a plan, although this written document is not mandated. The Individualized Education Program (IEP) of IDEA may be used for the Section 504 written plan. Many experts recommend that a group of persons knowledgeable about the student convene and specify the agreed-upon services.

### Funding to Implement Services

**IDEA:** Yes. IDEA provides federal funds under Parts B and C to assist states and local education agencies in meeting IDEA requirements to serve infants, toddlers and youth with disabilities.

**504:** No. State and local jurisdictions have responsibility. IDEA funds may not be used to serve children found eligible under Section 504.

### Procedural Safeguards

**IDEA:** IDEA requires written notice to parents regarding identification, evaluation, and/or placement. Further, written notice must be made prior to any changes in placement. The Act delineates the required components of the written notices.

**504:** Section 504 requires notice to parents regarding identification, evaluation and/or placements. Written notice is recommended. Notice must be made only before a "significant change" in placement. Following IDEA procedural safeguards is one way to comply with Section 504 mandates.

### Evaluation and Placement Procedures

**IDEA:** A comprehensive evaluation is required. A multidisciplinary team evaluates the child, and parental consent is required before the evaluation. IDEA requires that reevaluations be conducted at least every three years. For evaluation and placement decisions, IDEA requires that more than one single procedure or information source be used; that information from all sources be documented and carefully considered; that the eligibility decision be made by a group of persons who know about the student, the evaluation data, and placement options; and that the placement decision serves the student in the least restrictive environment. An IEP meeting is required before any change in placement.

**504:** Unlike IDEA, Section 504 requires only notice, not consent, for evaluation. It is recommended, however, that [the] district obtain parental consent. Like IDEA evaluation any placement procedures under Section 504 require that information be obtained from a variety of sources of the area of concern; that all data are documented and considered; and that decisions are made by a group of persons knowledgeable about the student, evaluation data, and placement options. Section 504 requires that students be educated with their non-disabled peers to the maximum extent appropriate. Section 504 does not require a meeting for any change in placement.

### Due Process

**IDEA:** IDEA delineates specific requirements for local education agencies to provide impartial hearings for parents who disagree with the identification, evaluation, or placement of a child.

**504:** Section 504 requires local education agencies to provide hearings for parents who disagree with the identification, evaluation, or placement of a student. It requires that parents have an opportunity to participate in the hearing process and to be represented by counsel. Beyond this, due process details are left to the discretion of the local education agency. It is recommended that districts develop policy guidelines and procedures.

## Establish the Proper Learning Environment

Parents must become advocates for their children and offer concrete suggestions to teachers that will provide the proper learning environment for children and youth with AD/HD. Remember, most teachers want to help students with AD/HD but many may not fully understand this disorder to be truly effective. To achieve a learning environment appropriate for your child, suggest that teachers do the following:

1. **Place students with AD/HD near the teacher's desk**, so the child can be heard, seen, and touched. With his back to the rest of the class, the student with AD/HD can then keep classmates out of view.
2. **Surround students with well-behaved role models**, preferably students whom they view as meaningful others.
3. **Avoid distracting stimuli** by seating AD/HD students away from air conditioners, high-traffic areas, pencil sharpeners, doors, or windows. (But *not* in a hallway or closet!)
4. **Avoid transitions** when possible, physical relocation (monitor them closely on field trips), changes in schedule, and disruptions because students with AD/HD do not handle change well.
5. **Provide a stimuli-reduced area for studying**. All students should have the right to use this area, not just the student with AD/HD (try not to make the student with AD/HD feel different).
6. **Allow students to use headphones or soft-foam earplugs** while working at their desks.
7. **Remind teachers that medication improves but does not cure the symptoms of AD/HD**. The child may still not have skills that equal those of other students and extra assistance may be needed.
8. **Tape a checklist for assignments on the student's desk** so he can check off assignments as they are completed.
9. **Permit students to use learning devices** such as a tape recorder, computer, spell-checker, calculator, or a word processor.
10. **Write a contract with the student** outlining what is to be done and what reward will be earned for staying on task.

Parents should review these guidelines carefully and not hesitate to ask teachers to make adjustments for their child. (*Note*: some suggestions were selected from ERIC Digests, published by The Council for Exceptional Children.)

## Delivering Instructions to Students with AD/HD

When giving instructions, teachers should do the following:

1. **Maintain eye contact during verbal instruction**. Get the child to repeat instructions.
2. **State directions clearly and briefly**. Be consistent. Follow with written instructions on the chalkboard in the same place each day.
3. **Streamline complex directions**. Do not give multiple instructions.
4. **Make sure AD/HD students comprehend instructions** before they begin the task. Break instructions down into steps if necessary, and give next step after completing preceding step.
5. **Repeat directions**, when necessary, in a favorable manner. Have them repeat certain directions to make sure they understand.
6. **Encourage students to seek assistance** from peers or from teachers (most children with AD/HD will not ask for help), explaining to the child when and how he may ask for help.
7. **Circulate among the students and check some of the AD/HD child's work**, while students are working independently. This will increase on-task activity. Provide the student with a prompt if he is off task such as tapping the student's shoulder or addressing the student.
8. **Reduce the amount of the work, not the quality** (one hundred math problems can be reduced to fifty, for instance), when necessary.
9. **Make sure the student's desk is not cluttered** with materials not needed for the current assignment.
10. **Modify the grade scale** if necessary.
11. **Set quotas of productivity and correctness** of work.
12. **Offer the student choices**. For instance, he can choose to write the book report or give it orally.
13. **Gradually decrease the amount of support**, but keep in mind that students with AD/HD may need more help for a longer time than the average child.

14. **Color code classroom subjects** (science is red, math is blue, language arts is green, etc.). This will help all students, not just those with AD/HD.
15. **Use colored chalk that corresponds with the subject's color code** to write assignments on the board.
16. **Assist students with color coding** textbooks and folders.
17. **Require a daily assignment notebook.**
18. **Make sure each student writes down all homework assignments correctly each day** (use colored stickers in assignment notebook). Homework assignments should be written on the chalkboard and left there until the end of the school day. The teacher should assist a child who is not able to do this on his own, writing it out for him.
19. **Teachers should sign the assignment notebook each day** to let parents know that homework assignments have been recorded accurately. Parents should sign the notebook before it's returned to school, indicating assignments have been completed and were put in their child's backpack.
20. **Teachers should use the notebook for daily communication with parents.** Parents can also use the notebook to express concerns or ask questions of the teacher.
21. **Help the student organize** his notebook, desk, and locker.

(*Note*: some suggestions were selected from ERIC Digests, published by The Council for Exceptional Children.)

## Giving Assignments to AD/HD students

When describing assignments, teachers should do the following:

1. **Make sure the class is quiet** before giving directions or assignments.
2. **Be sure they have the attention of the student with AD/HD.** They may need to touch his shoulder or back.
3. **Give only one task at a time.**
4. **Give students (and parents) a copy of an assignment sheet** for predictable homework on a weekly or monthly basis if possible.
5. **Do not give homework assignments at the end of the class** or the end of the school day when children are tired and ready to move on to other activities.

6. **Ask for homework assignments at the beginning of each school day** or each class. Many students with AD/HD need a verbal reminder. Children who continually forget their homework often have it in their locker or backpack but forget they placed it there. Be sure to ask where the homework is if they say they did complete it or if their response is "I don't know."

7. **Monitor AD/HD students frequently in a supportive fashion.**

8. **Modify assignments as needed**—shorten or allow for less written work if child has motor problems (difficulty writing). Confer with special education personnel to identify specific strengths and weaknesses of the child with AD/HD. If necessary, develop a customized education program.

9. **Test knowledge, not attention span.** Decreasing the volumes of expected work may actually improve compliance and accuracy.

10. **Allow additional time for certain types of tasks.** Do not penalize students with AD/HD who need extra time. Some take longer to get started, process information, organize materials, and complete assignments. Remember, you are testing knowledge not how quickly she can complete a task.

11. **Remember that students with AD/HD are easily frustrated.** Stress causes children to tire and decreases their self-control, leading to unacceptable behavior. They need a lot of encouragement.

12. **Remember that some students with AD/HD are unable to judge or use time effectively.**

(*Note*: some suggestions were selected from ERIC Digests, published by The Council for Exceptional Children.)

## Behavior Modification and Self-Esteem Enhancement

When working with students who have AD/HD, teachers should do the following:

1. **Be proactive.** Try to look at activities ahead of time and think of possible problems that might arise. Problem solve before problems appear.

2. **Stay calm**, state the infringement, and avoid arguing with the student—discipline with dignity.

3. **Set consequences for misconduct** (time-out, etc.). Try not to take away recess. Children with AD/HD need this time to release energy and clear their minds.
4. **Deliver consequences immediately.**
5. **Post classroom rules and invoke rules consistently.** Students with AD/HD may need extra reinforcements.
6. **Make sure the consequence fits the crime.**
7. **Avoid ridicule and criticism.** Keep in mind that children with AD/HD have trouble staying in control. If you ridicule or criticize, the child may blow up, making a situation much worse than it needs to be.
8. **State rules for unstructured times,** such as in cafeteria, hallways, library, recess, gym class, a field trips. Children with hyperactivity-impulsivity must be monitored closely in potentially high-risk situations. Accidents can and do happen.
9. **Reward more than you punish**—catch the student being good—to build self-esteem.
10. **Immediately praise all positive behavior and performance,** but make sure you say it sincerely, and keep it short. "Good job, Courtney," or give a high five. Acknowledge improvements, no matter how small.
11. **Replace rewards if they are not stimulating enough** to change behavior.
12. **Look for ways to encourage** the student.
13. **Teach the child to reward himself or herself** through positive self-talk and thinking-aloud skills ("You did very well remaining in your seat today. How do you feel about that?" or STAR: Stop, Think, Act, Review).

## Other Educational Recommendations

(*Source*: ERIC Digests, published by The Council for Exceptional Children.)

1. **[Arrange for] educational, psychological, and/or neurological testing** to determine learning style and cognitive ability and to rule out any learning disabilities.
2. **[Use] a private tutor** and/or peer tutoring at school.
3. **[Enroll the child in] a class that has a low student-teacher ratio.**

4. [Employ] social skills training and organizational skills training.

5. [Administer] training in cognitive restructuring (positive self-talk, such as, "I did that well" or "Whenever, I do that, I always seem to . . .").

6. Use a computer for schoolwork.

7. Use a tape recorder for lecture notes.

8. [Encourage the child to participate in] individualized activities that are mildly competitive or noncompetitive, such as bowling, walking, swimming, jogging, biking, karate. (Note: Certain children with AD/HD with motor skill deficits or social skill deficits may do less well than their peers in team sports).

9. [Encourage the child to become involved] in social activities such as scouting, religious groups, or other youth organizations that help develop social skills and self-esteem.

10. Allow children with AD/HD to play with younger children if that is who they fit in with. Many children with AD/HD have more in common with younger children than with their same-age peers. They still can develop valuable social skills from interacting with younger children (for example, reading to younger children, learning to play cooperatively, sharing).

## Definition of Learning Disabilities

(*Source*: A fact sheet titled "Learning Disabilities" published by NICHCY.)

The regulations for the Individuals with Disabilities Education Act (IDEA), define a learning disability as a "disorder in one or more of the basic psychological processes involved in understanding or in using spoken or written language, which may manifest itself in an imperfect ability to listen, think, speak, read, write, spell or to do mathematical calculations." The federal definition further states that learning disabilities include "such conditions as perceptual handicaps, brain injury, minimal brain dysfunction, dyslexia, and developmental aphasia." Definitions of learning disabilities vary among states.

The label "learning disabilities" is all-embracing; it describes a syndrome, not a specific child with specific problems. The definition assists in classifying children, not teaching them. Parents and teachers need to concentrate on the individual child. They need to observe both how and how well the child performs, to assess strengths and weaknesses and invent ways to help each child learn. It is important to remember that there is a high degree of interrelationship and overlapping among the areas of learning. Therefore, children with learning disabilities may exhibit a combination of characteristics. These problems may mildly, moderately, or severely impair the learning process.

## Characteristics

Learning disabilities are characterized by a significant difference in the child's achievement in some areas, when compared with his overall intelligence. Students who have learning disabilities may exhibit a wide range of traits, including problems with reading comprehension, spoken language, writing, or reasoning ability. Hyperactivity, inattention, and perceptual coordination problems may also be associated with learning disabilities. Other traits that may be present include a variety of symptoms, such as uneven and unpredictable test performance, perceptual impairments, motor disorders, and behaviors such as impulsiveness, low tolerance for frustration, and problems in handling day-to-day social interactions and situations.

Learning disabilities may occur in the following academic areas:

1. **Spoken language**: delays, disorders, or discrepancies in listening and speaking;
2. **Written language**: difficulties with reading, writing, and spelling;
3. **Arithmetic**: difficulty in performing math functions or in comprehending basic concepts;
4. **Reasoning**: difficulty in organizing and integrating thoughts; and
5. **Organization skills**: difficulty in organizing all facets of learning.

## Educational Implications

Because learning disabilities are manifested in a variety of behavior patterns, the individualized education program (IEP) must be designed carefully. A team approach is important for educating the child with a learning disability, beginning with the assessment process and continuing through the development of the IEP.

Some teachers report that the following strategies have been effective with some students who have learning disabilities:

- **Capitalize on student's strengths**
- **[Provide] high structure and clear expectations**
- **Use short sentences and a simple vocabulary**, emphasizing important facts or details so the student understands the importance of the material being presented
- **[Provide] opportunities for success** in a supportive atmosphere to help build self-esteem
- **[Create] flexibility** in classroom procedure (e.g.: allow use of tape recorders for notetaking and test-taking when students have trouble with written language)
- **[Use] self-correcting materials**, which provide immediate feedback without embarrassment
- **Use computers** for drill and practice and teaching word processing
- **[Provide] positive reinforcement** of appropriate social skills at school and home
- **Recognize that students with learning disabilities can greatly benefit from the gift of time** to grow and mature

### Parenting Tips for Coping with the Child Who Has AD/HD and a Learning Disability:

- **Accept the fact that aspects of your child's learning disability are medically determined.** Remember your child does not have an *inability* to learn—he has a *disability* that makes learning more difficult, but definitely not impossible.
- **Read as much as possible about learning disabilities.** The knowledge will empower you. Attend conferences. Join a parent support group.
- **Become an advocate for your child.** Find out what services are available for your child within the school system and your community.
- **Provide tutoring** for your child. Tutoring usually decreases the amount of stress parents often feel from having to help their child with a great amount of schoolwork. However, tutoring does no good if you haven't identified the specific problem.

- **Try not to become overwhelmed by your child's disability**. In two-parent families, parents should take turns helping their child with schoolwork.
- **Keep your academic expectations realistic**. Don't expect A's and B's in areas where your child is unable to achieve anything but C's. If you were an A or B student, remember that a C is considered an average grade. Many learning-disabled children go to college, but some do not.
- **Set realistic behavioral expectations**. Children respond best to behavior modification techniques, such as tangible rewards.
- **Encourage and support your child**. Praise what she does well and do not focus on her failures.
- **Be empathetic**. Be sure your child understands that you realize how frustrating this is for her.
- **Know what your child's true disability is**. Make sure you get an understandable explanation and specific suggestions for how you can help your child at home.

## Commonly Asked Questions about Special Education Services

(*Source*: "Questions Often Asked by Parents about Special Education Services," published by NICHCY.)

### Introduction

**I think my child may need special help in school. What do I do?**
Begin by finding out more about special services and programs for students in your school system. Also find out more about the Individuals with Disabilities Education Act (IDEA). This law gives eligible children with disabilities the right to receive special services and assistance in school. These services are known as special education and related services. They can be important in helping your child at school.

### What is special education?
Special education is instruction that is specially designed to meet the unique needs of children who have disabilities. This is done at

no cost to the parents. Special education can include special instruction in the classroom, at home, in hospitals or institutions, or in other settings.

Over 5 million children ages 6 through 21 receive special education and related services each year in the United States. Each of these children receives instruction that is specially designed:

- **to meet the child's unique needs** (that result from having a disability); and
- **to help the child learn** the information and skills that other children are learning.

This definition of special education comes from the Individuals with Disabilities Education Act (IDEA).

### Who is eligible for special education?
Certain children with disabilities are eligible for special education and related services. The IDEA provides a definition of a "child with a disability." This law lists 13 different disability categories under which a child may be found eligible for special education and related services. These categories are:

- Autism
- Deafness
- Deaf-blindness
- Hearing impairment
- Mental retardation
- Multiple disabilities
- Orthopedic impairment
- Other health impairment
- Emotional disturbance
- Specific learning disability
- Speech or language impairment
- Traumatic brain injury
- Visual impairment, including blindness

According to the IDEA, the disability must affect the child's educational performance. The question of eligibility, then, comes down to a question of whether the child has a disability that fits in one of IDEA's 13 categories and whether that disability affects how the child does in school. That is, the disability must cause the child to need special education and related services. (Note: Most eligible children with AD/HD will fall into the "other health impairment" category.)

## Services to Very Young Children

Infants and toddlers can have disabilities, too. Services to these very young children are also part of the IDEA. These services are called early intervention services (for children birth through two years) and preschool services (for children ages 3–5). These services can be very important in helping the young child develop and learn. For more information about early intervention and preschool programs, contact NICHCY.

## Part I. Your Child's Evaluation

**How do I find out if my child is eligible for special education?**
The first step is to find out if your child has a disability. To do this, ask the school to evaluate your child. Call or write the Director of Special Education or the principal of your child's school. Say that you think your child has a disability and needs special education help. Ask the school to evaluate your child as soon as possible.

The public school may also think your child needs special help, because he or she may have a disability. If so, then the school must evaluate your child at no cost to you.

However, the school does not have to evaluate your child just because you have asked. The school may not think your child has a disability or needs special education. In this case, the school may refuse to evaluate your child. It must let you know this decision in writing, as well as why it has refused.

If the school refuses to evaluate your child, there are two things you can do immediately:

- **Ask the school system for information about its special education policies,** as well as parent rights to disagree with decisions made by the school system. These materials should describe the steps parents can take to challenge a school system's decision.

- **Get in touch with your state's Parent Training and Information (PTI) center.** The PTI is an excellent resource for parents to learn more about special education, their rights and responsibilities, and the law. The PTI can tell you what steps to take next to find help for your child. (Parent Training and Information Centers are listed in the appendix by state.)

### What happens during an evaluation?

Evaluating your child means more than the school just giving your child a test or two. The school must evaluate your child in all the areas where your child may be affected by the possible disability. This may include looking at your child's health, vision, hearing, social and emotional well-being, general intelligence, performance in school, and how well your child communicates with others and uses his or her body. The evaluation must be complete enough (full and individual) to identify all of your child's needs for special education and related services.

Evaluating your child appropriately will give you and the school a lot of information about your child. This information will help you and the school:

- **Decide** if your child has a disability; and
- **Design** instruction for your child.

The evaluation process involves several steps. These are listed below.

Reviewing existing information. A group of people, including you, begins by looking at the information the school already has about your child. You may have information about your child you wish to share as well. The group will look at information such as:

- **Your child's scores on tests** given in the classroom or to all students in your child's grade;
- **The opinions and observations of your child's teachers** and other school staff who know your child; and
- **Your feelings, concerns, and ideas** about how your child is doing in school.

- **Deciding if more information is still needed**. The information collected above will help the group decide:
- If your son or daughter has a particular type of disability;
- How your child is currently doing in school;
- Whether your child needs special education and related services; and
- What your child's educational needs are.

Group members will look at the information they collected above and see if they have enough information to make these decisions. If the group needs more information to make these decisions, the school must collect it.

Collecting more information about your child. If more information about your child is needed, the school will give your child tests or collect the information in other ways. Your informed written permission is required before the school may collect this information. The evaluation group will then have the information it needs to make the types of decisions listed above.

### So the school needs my permission to collect this extra information?

Yes. Before the school can conduct additional assessments of your child to see if he or she has a disability, the school must ask for your informed written permission. It must also describe how it will conduct this evaluation. This includes describing the tests that will be used and the other ways the school will collect information about your child. After you give your informed written permission, the school may evaluate your child.

### How does the school collect this information?

The school collects information about your child from many different people and in many different ways. Tests are an important part of an evaluation, but they are only a part. The evaluation should also include:

- **The observations and opinions of professionals** who have worked with your child;
- **Your child's medical history**, when it relates to his or her performance in school; and

- **Your ideas about your child's school experiences,** abilities, needs, and behavior outside of school, and his or her feelings about school.

The following people will be part of the group evaluating your child:

**You,** as parents;

- **At least one regular education teacher,** if your child is or may be participating in the regular education environment;
- **At least one of your child's special education teachers** or service providers;
- **A school administrator** who knows about policies for special education, about children with disabilities, about the general curriculum (the curriculum used by nondisabled students), and about available resources;
- **Someone who can interpret the evaluation results** and talk about what instruction may be necessary for your child;
- **Individuals (invited by you or the school) who have knowledge or special expertise about your child;**
- **Your child,** if appropriate;
- **Representatives from any other agencies that may be responsible** for paying for or providing transition services (if your child is 16 years or, if appropriate, younger and will be planning for life after high school); and
- **Other qualified professionals.**

These other qualified professionals may be responsible for collecting specific kinds of information about your child. They may include the following:

- School psychologist;
- Occupational therapist;
- Speech and language pathologist (sometimes called a speech therapist);
- Physical therapist and/or adaptive physical education therapist or teacher;
- Medical specialist;

- Educational diagnostician;
- Classroom teacher(s);
- Others.

Professionals will observe your child. They may give your child written tests or talk personally with your child. They are trying to get a picture of the "whole child." For example, they want to understand:

- **How well your child speaks and understands language;**
- **How your child thinks and behaves;**
- **How well your child adapts to changes** in his or her environment;
- **How well your child has done academically;**
- **What your child's potential or aptitude (intelligence) is;**
- **How well your child functions** in a number of areas, such as moving, thinking, learning, seeing, hearing; and
- **What job-related and other post-school interests and abilities your child has.**

The IDEA gives clear directions about how schools must conduct evaluations. For example, tests and interviews must be given in your child's native language (for example, Spanish) or in the way he or she typically communicates (for example, sign language). The tests must also be given in a way that does not discriminate against your child, because he or she has a disability or is from a different racial or cultural background.

The IDEA states that schools may not place children into special education programs based on the results of only one procedure such as a test. More than one procedure is needed to see where your child may be having difficulty and to identify his or her strengths.

In some cases, schools will be able to conduct a child's entire evaluation within the school. In other cases, schools may not have the staff to do all of the evaluation needed. These schools will have to hire outside people or agencies to do some or all of the evaluation. If your child is evaluated outside of the school, the school must make the arrangements. The school will say in writing exactly what type of testing is to be done. All of these evaluation procedures are done at no cost to parents.

In some cases, once the evaluation has begun, the outside specialist may want to do more testing. If the specialist asks you if it is okay to do more testing, make sure you tell the specialist to contact the school. If the testing is going beyond what the school originally asked for, the school needs to agree to pay for the extra testing.

## Part II. Your Child's Eligibility

**What does the school do with these evaluation results?**
The information gathered from the evaluation will be used to make important decisions about your child's education. All of the information about your child will be used:

- **To decide if your child is eligible for special education** and related services; and
- **To help you and the school decide what your child needs educationally**.

**How is a decision made about my child's eligibility for special education?**
As was said earlier, the decision about your child's eligibility for services is based on whether your son or daughter has a disability that fits into one of the IDEA's 13 disability categories (see the list presented in Part I) and whether that disability affects how your child does in school. This decision will be made when the evaluation has been completed, and the results are in.

In the past, parents were not involved under IDEA in making the decision about their child's eligibility for special education and related services. Now, under the newest changes to IDEA (passed in 1997 and amended again in 2004), parents are included in the group that decides a child's eligibility for special education services. This group will look at all of the information gathered during the evaluation and decide if your child meets the definition of a "child with a disability." (This definition will come from the IDEA and from the policies your state or district uses.) If so, your child will be eligible for special education and related services.

Under the IDEA, a child may not be found eligible for services if the determining reason for thinking the child is eligible is that:

- **The child has limited English proficiency,** or
- **The child has a lack of instruction** in math or reading.

If your child is found eligible, you and the school will work together to design an educational program for your child. This process is described in detail in Part III. . . .

As parents, you have the right to receive a copy of the evaluation report on your child and the paperwork about your child's eligibility for special education and related services.

What happens if my child is not eligible for services?

If the group decides that your child is not eligible for special education services, the school system must tell you this in writing and explain why your child has been found "not eligible." Under the IDEA, you must also be given information about what you can do if you disagree with this decision.

Read the information the school system gives you. Make sure it includes information about how to challenge the school system's decision. If that information is not in the materials the school gives you, ask the school for it.

Also get in touch with your state's Parent Training and Information (PTI) center. The PTI can tell you what steps to take next. Your PTI is listed in the appendix.

## Part III. Writing an IEP

### So my child has been found eligible for special education. What next?

The next step is to write what is known as an *individualized education program*—usually called an IEP. After a child is found eligible, a meeting must be held within 30 days to develop the IEP.

### What is an Individualized Education Program?

An individualized education program (IEP) is a written statement of the educational program designed to meet a child's individual needs. Every child who receives special education services must have an IEP.

The IEP has two general purposes: (1) to set reasonable learning goals for your child; and (2) to state the services that the school district will provide for your child.

**What type of information is included in an IEP?**

According to the IDEA, your child's IEP must include specific statements about your child. These are listed below. Take a moment to read over this list. This will be the information included in your child's IEP.

**What information is in your child's IEP?**

Your child's IEP will contain the following statements:

- **Present levels of educational performance**. This statement describes how your child is currently doing in school. This includes how your child's disability affects his or her involvement and progress in the general curriculum.
- **Annual goals.** The IEP must state annual goals for your child, meaning what you and the school team think he or she can reasonably accomplish in a year. This statement of annual goals includes individual steps that make up the goals (often called *short-term objectives*) or major milestones (often called *benchmarks*). The goals must relate to meeting the needs that result from your child's disability. They must also help your son or daughter be involved in and progress in the general curriculum. [Please note that annual goals are not required as of July 2005, however; if parents would like annual goals included in the IEP, they must make that request to the evaluation team.]
- **Special education and related services to be provided**. The IEP must list the special education and related services to be provided to your child. This includes supplementary aids and services (such as a communication device). It also includes changes to the program or supports for school personnel that will be provided for your child.
- **Participation with nondisabled children**. How much of the school day will your child be educated separately from nondisabled children or not participate in extracurricular or other nonacademic activities such as lunch or clubs? The IEP must include an explanation that answers this question.
- **Participation in state and district-wide assessments**. Your state and district probably give tests of student achievement to children in certain grades or age groups. In order to participate in these tests, your child may need individual modifications or changes in

how the tests are administered. The IEP team must decide what modifications your child needs and list them in the IEP. If your child will not be taking these tests, the IEP must include a statement as to why the tests are not appropriate for your child and how your child will be tested instead.

- **Dates and location**. The IEP must state (a) *when* services and modifications will begin; (b) *how often* they will be provided; (c) *where* they will be provided; and (d) *how long* they will last.
- **Transition service needs**. If your child is age 14 (or younger, if the IEP team determines it appropriate), the IEP must include a statement of his or her transition service needs. Transition planning will help your child move through school from grade to grade.
- **Transition services**. If your child is age 16 (or younger, if determined appropriate by the IEP team), the IEP must include a statement of needed transition services and, if appropriate, a statement of the interagency responsibilities or any needed linkages.
- **Measuring progress**. The IEP must state how school personnel will measure your child's progress toward the annual goals. It must also state how you, as parents, will be informed regularly of your child's progress and whether that progress is enough to enable your child to achieve his or her goals by the end of the year.

It is very important that children with disabilities participate in the general curriculum as much as possible. That is, they should learn the same curriculum as nondisabled children, for example, reading, math, science, social studies, and physical education, just as nondisabled children do. In some cases, this curriculum may need to be adapted for your child to learn, but it should not be omitted altogether. Participation in extracurricular activities and other nonacademic activities is also important. Your child's IEP needs to be written with this in mind.

For example, what special education services will help your child participate in the general curriculum—in other words, to study what other students are studying? What special education services or supports will help your child take part in extracurricular activities such as school clubs or sports? When your child's IEP is developed, an important part of the discussion will be how to help your child take part in regular classes and activities in the school.

## Who develops my child's IEP?

Many people come together to develop your child's IEP. This group is called the IEP team and includes most of the same types of individuals who were involved in your child's evaluation. Team members will include:

- **You**, the parents;
- **At least one regular education teacher**, if your child is (or may be) participating in the regular education environment;
- **At least one of your child's special education teachers** or special education providers;
- **A representative of the public agency** (school system) who (a) is qualified to provide or supervise the provision of special education, (b) knows about the general curriculum; and (c) knows about the resources the school system has available;
- **An individual who can interpret the evaluation results** and talk about what instruction may be necessary for your child;
- **Your child**, when appropriate;
- **Representatives from any other agencies that may be responsible** for paying for or providing transition services (if your child is 16 years or, if appropriate, younger); and
- **Other individuals (invited by you or the school) who have knowledge or special expertise** about your child. For example, you may wish to invite a relative who is close to the child or a child care provider.

Together, these people will work as a team to develop your child's IEP.

## So I can help develop my child's IEP?

Yes, absolutely. The law is very clear that parents have the right to participate in developing their child's IEP. In fact, your input is *invaluable*. You know your child so very well, and the school needs to know your insights and concerns.

The school staff will try to schedule the IEP meeting at a time that is convenient for all team members to attend. If the school suggests a time that is impossible for you, explain your schedule and needs. It's important that you attend this meeting and share your ideas about your child's needs and strengths. Often, another time or date can be arranged. However, if you cannot agree on a time or date, the school may hold the IEP meeting without you. In this event, the school must keep you informed, for example, by phone or mail.

**What should I do before the IEP meeting?**
The purpose of the IEP meeting is to develop your child's Individualized Education Program. You can prepare for this meeting by:

- **Making a list of your child's strengths and weaknesses,**
- **Talking to teachers and/or therapists** and getting their thoughts about your child,
- **Visiting your child's class** and perhaps other classes that may be helpful to him or her, and
- **Talking to your child about his or her feelings toward school.**

It is a good idea to write down what you think your child can accomplish during the school year. It also helps to make notes about what you would like to say during the meeting.

**What happens during an IEP meeting?**
During the IEP meeting, the different members of the IEP team share their thoughts and suggestions. If this is the first IEP meeting after your child's evaluation, the team may go over the evaluation results, so your child's strengths and needs will be clear. These results will help the team decide what special help your child needs in school.

Remember that you are a very important part of the IEP team. You know your child better than anyone. Don't be shy about speaking up, even though there may be a lot of other people at the meeting. Share what you know about your child and what you wish others to know.

After the various team members (including you, the parent) have shared their thoughts and concerns about your child, the group will have a better idea of your child's strengths and needs. This will allow the team to discuss and decide on: the educational and other goals that are appropriate for your child; and the type of special education services your child needs.

The IEP team will also talk about the *related services* your child may need to benefit from his or her special education. The IDEA lists many related services that schools must provide if eligible children need them. The related services listed in IDEA are presented . . . below. Examples of related services include:

- **Occupational therapy**, which can help a child develop or regain movement that he or she may have lost due to injury or illness; and
- **Speech therapy** (called speech-language pathology), which can help children who have trouble speaking.

**Some related services, as listed in IDEA:**

- Transportation
- Speech-language pathology
- Audiology services
- Psychological services
- Physical therapy
- Occupational therapy
- Recreation (including therapeutic recreation)
- Early identification and assessment of disabilities in children
- Counseling services (including rehabilitation counseling)
- Orientation & mobility services
- Medical services for diagnostic or evaluation purposes
- School health services
- Social work services in schools
- Parent counseling and training

Depending on the needs of your child, the IEP team may also discuss the special factors listed below:

- **If your child's behavior's interferes with his or her learning or the learning of others**: The IEP team will talk about strategies and supports to address your child's behavior.
- **If your child has limited proficiency in English**: The IEP team will talk about your child's language needs as these needs relate to his or her IEP.

- **If your child is blind or visually impaired**: The IEP team must provide for instruction in Braille or the use of Braille, unless it determines after an appropriate evaluation that your child does not need this instruction.
- **If your child has communication needs**: The IEP team must consider those needs.
- **If your child is deaf or hard of hearing**: The IEP team will consider your child's language and communication needs. This includes your child's opportunities to communicate directly with classmates and school staff in his or her usual method of communication (for example, sign language).

The IEP team will also talk about whether your child needs any *assistive technology devices or services*. Assistive technology devices can help many children do certain activities or tasks. Examples of these devices are:

- **Devices that make the words bigger on the computer screen or that "read" the typed words aloud**—which can help children who do not see well;
- **Electronic talking boards**—which can help students who have trouble speaking; and
- **Computers and special programs for the computer**—which can help students with all kinds of disabilities learn more easily.

Assistive technology services include evaluating your child to see if he or she could benefit from using an assistive device. These services also include providing the devices and training your child (or your family or the professionals who work with your child) to use the device.

As you can see, there are a lot of important matters to talk about in an IEP meeting. You may feel very emotional during the meeting, as everyone talks about your child's needs. Try to keep in mind that the other team members are all there to help your child. If you hear something about your child which surprises you, or which is different from the way you see your child, bring this to the attention of the other members of the team. In order to design a good program for your child, it is important to work closely with the other team members and share your feelings about your child's educational needs. Feel free to ask questions and offer opinions and suggestions.

Based on the above discussions, the IEP team will then write your child's IEP. This includes the services and supports the school will provide for your child. It will also include the *location* where particular services will be provided. Your child's placement (where the IEP will be carried out) will be determined every year, must be based on your child's IEP, and must be as close as possible to your child's home. The placement decision is made by a group of persons, *including you the parent,* and others knowledgeable about your child, the meaning of the evaluation data, and the placement options. In some states, the IEP team makes the placement decision. In other states, the placement decision is made by another group of people. *In all cases, you as parents have the right to be members of the group that makes decisions on the educational placement of your child.*

**Can my child's IEP be changed?**
Yes. At least once a year a meeting must be scheduled with you to review your child's progress and develop your child's next IEP. The meeting will be similar to the IEP meeting described above. The team will talk about:

- **Your child's progress toward the goals** in the current IEP,
- **What new goals should be added**, and
- **Whether any changes need to be made** to the special education and related services your child receives.

This annual IEP meeting allows you and the school to review your child's educational program and change it as necessary. But you don't have to wait for this annual review. You (or any other team member) may ask to have your child's IEP reviewed or revised at any time.

For example, you may feel that your child is not making good progress toward his or her annual goals. Or you may want to write new goals, because your son or daughter has made such great progress! Call the principal of the school, or the special education director or your child's teacher, and express your concerns. If necessary, they will call the IEP team together to talk about changing your child's IEP.

## Part IV. Re-Evaluation

### Will my child be re-evaluated?

Yes. Under the IDEA, your child must be re-evaluated at least every three years. The purpose of this re-evaluation is to find out:

- **If your child continues to be a "child with a disability,"** as defined within the law, and
- **Your child's educational needs.**

The re-evaluation is similar to the initial evaluation. It begins by looking at the information already available about your child. More information is collected only if it's needed. If the group decides that additional assessments are needed, you must give your informed written permission before the school system may collect that information. The school system may only go ahead without your informed written permission if they have tried to get your permission and you did not respond.

Although the law requires that children with disabilities be re-evaluated at least every three years, your child may be re-evaluated more often if you or your child's teacher(s) request it.

## Part V. Other Special Education Issues

Is the school responsible for ensuring that my child reaches the goals in his or her IEP?

No. The IEP sets out the individualized instruction to be provided to your child, but it is not a contract. The school is responsible for providing the instructional services listed in an IEP. School officials must make a good-faith effort to help your child meet his or her goals. However, the school is not responsible if your child does not reach the goals listed in the IEP. If you feel that your child is not making progress toward his or her goals, then you may wish to contact the school and express your concerns. The IEP team may need to meet and revise your child's IEP.

**What if I disagree with the school about what is right for my child?**

You have the right to disagree with the school's decisions concerning your child. This includes decisions about:

- **Your child's identification as a "child with a disability,"**
- **His or her evaluation,**
- **His or her educational placement,** and
- **The special education and related services that the school provides** to your child.

    In all cases where the family and school disagree, it is important for both sides to first discuss their concerns and try to compromise. The compromise can be temporary. For example, you might agree to try out a particular plan of instruction or classroom placement for a certain period of time. At the end of that period, the school can check your child's progress. You and other members of your child's IEP team can then meet again, talk about how your child is doing, and decide what to do next. The trial period may help you and the school reach a comfortable agreement on how to help your child.

    If you still cannot agree with the school, it's useful to know more about the IDEA's protections for parents and children. The law and regulations include ways for parents and schools to resolve disagreements. These include:

- **Mediation,** where you and school personnel sit down with an impartial third person (called a mediator), talk openly about the areas where you disagree, and try to reach agreement;
- **Due process,** where you and the school present evidence before an impartial third person (called a hearing officer), and he or she decides how to resolve the problem; and
- **Filing a complaint with the state education agency** (SEA), where you write directly to the SEA and describe what requirement of IDEA the school has violated. The SEA must either resolve your complaint itself, or it can have a system where complaints are filed with the school district and parents can have the district's decision reviewed by the SEA. In most cases, the SEA must resolve your complaint within 60 calendar days.

Your state will have specific ways for parents and schools to resolve their differences. You will need to find out what your state's policies are. Your local department of special education will probably have these guidelines. If not, contact the state department of education and ask for a copy of their special education policies. You may also wish to call the Parent Training and Information (PTI) center in your state.

### How can I get more services for my child?

Suppose your child gets speech therapy two times a week, and you think he or she needs therapy three times a week. What do you do?

First, you can talk with your child's teacher or speech-language pathologist (sometimes called a speech therapist). Ask to see the evaluation of his or her progress. If you are not satisfied with your child's progress, then request an IEP meeting to review your child's progress and increase speech therapy. Discuss your child's needs with the IEP team and talk about changing the IEP. The other team members will either agree with you and change the IEP, or they will disagree with you.

If the rest of the IEP team does not agree that your child needs more services, try to work out a compromise. If you cannot, then parents can take the problem beyond the IEP team. As was mentioned above, mediation, due process, and filing a complaint are ways to resolve disagreements. But always remember that you and the school will be making decisions together about your child's education for as long as your child goes to that school and continues to be eligible for special education services. A good working relationship with school staff is important now and in the future. Therefore, when disagreements arise, try to work them out within the IEP team before requesting mediation or due process or before filing a complaint.

### How can I support my child's learning?

Here are some suggestions that can help you support your child's learning and maintain a good working relationship with school professionals:

- **Let your child's teacher(s) know that you want to be involved in your child's educational program**. Make time to talk with the teacher(s) and, if possible, visit the classroom.
- **Explain any special equipment, medication, or medical problem your child has.**

- **Let the teacher(s) know about any activities or big events that may influence your child's performance in school.**
- **Ask that samples of your child's work be sent home.** If you have questions, make an appointment with the teacher(s) to talk about new ways to meet your child's goals.
- **Ask the teacher(s) how you can build upon your child's school activities at home.**
- **Give your child chores at home.** Encourage behavior that leads to success in school, such as accepting responsibility, behaving, being organized, and being on time.
- **Volunteer to help in the classroom or school.** This will let you see how things work in the school and how your child interacts with others. It will also help the school.
- **Remember that you and the school want success for your child.** Working together can make this happen.

## Rights and Responsibilities of Parents of Children with Disabilities

(*Source*: "Rights and Responsibilities of Parents of Children with Disabilities," ERIC Digests, published by The Council for Exceptional Children.)

### What are your rights, as a parent, in the special education process?

The Individuals with Disabilities Education Act (IDEA) enhances the rights of children with disabilities and their parents. It builds on the rights provided under Public Law 94-142, the Education for All Handicapped Children Act, of 1975. A fundamental provision of these laws is the right of parents to participate in the educational decision-making process. Currently this includes the right to:

- **A free appropriate public education** for your child. "Free" means at no cost to you as parents or to your child, except for incidental fees normally charged to parents of students without disabilities as part of the regular education programs. "Appropriate" means that your child's program must be individually designed to meet his or her unique educational needs.
- **Request an evaluation** if you think your child has an impairment that may require special education services. You also have

the right to get an independent evaluation if you disagree with the evaluation obtained by the school.

- **Be notified in writing** ("written prior notices") whenever the school proposes any of the following: an evaluation to determine whether your child has a disability; a reevaluation; or a change in your child's educational placement. You are also entitled to be notified in writing if the school refuses your request for an evaluation or change in educational placement for your child.

- **"Informed consent"** means you understand and agree in writing to the evaluation and educational program decisions for your child. Your consent is voluntary and may be withdrawn at any time.

- **Request a reevaluation** of your child at any time. The school must reevaluate your child if conditions warrant, or if you or your child's teacher requests a reevalution; but in any case, the school must reevaluate the child at least once every three years.

- **Have your child tested in the language he or she knows best**. For example, if your child's primary language is Spanish, this is the language in which he or she must be tested.

- **Have access to your child's education records**. A school must comply with a parent's request to inspect and review his or her child's education records within 5 days of the receipt of the request. Generally, schools must have written consent from the parent before releasing any information from the student's records. However, records can be released to certain education officials without the parent's consent. If you feel that some information contained in your child's records is inaccurate or misleading or violates your child's rights, you may request that the record be changed. If the school refuses, you then have the right to request a hearing, or you may file a complaint with your state education agency.

- **Be fully informed by the school of all rights** that are provided to you under the law and all safeguards that the school must follow to ensure that the rights of all are protected.

- **Participate in the development of your child's individualized education program** (IEP), or, if your child is under age 3, individualized family service plan (IFSP). You have the right to participate in all IEP or IFSP team decisions, or any other decision regarding your child. The school must make every possible effort to notify you of the IEP or IFSP meeting and then arrange it at a time and place that is convenient for both you and the school. The school is responsible for reviewing this plan at least once a year, but you have the right to request an IEP or IFSP meeting at any time during the school year.

- **Be kept informed about your child's progress**, by means such as periodic report cards, at least as often as parents of children who do not have disabilities.

- **Have your child educated in the least restrictive environment**. This means that, to the maximum extent possible, your child should be educated in regular classes with his or her nondisabled peers, and your child should receive supplementary aids and services in his or her neighborhood school. If education outside the regular classroom is determined to be most appropriate, your child should be educated in the most integrated setting possible.

- **Voluntary mediation** or a due process hearing to resolve differences with the school that cannot be resolved informally. Be sure you make your request in writing, date your request, and keep a copy.

**What are your responsibilities, as a parent, in the special education process?**

Parents have a key role in the special education process. The following suggestions may offer some guidance:

- **Develop a partnership** with the school or agency. Share relevant information. Your observations and suggestions can be a valuable resource.

- **Ask for clarification** of any aspect of the program that is unclear to you. Educational terms can be confusing so do not hesitate to ask.

- **Make sure the IEP or IFSP goals (f you have requested these) and objectives are specific and measurable**. This will ensure that everyone teaching your child is working toward the same goals. Take the IEP or IFSP home to think about it before you sign it. You have 10 school days in which to make a decision.

- **Make sure your child is included in the regular school activities program**. Do not forget nonacademic areas such as lunch and recess and other subjects such as art, music, and physical education.

- **Learn as much as you can about your rights** and the rights of your child. Ask the school to explain these rights as well as the policies and regulations in effect in your district and state before you agree to a special education program for your child.

- **Monitor your child's progress.** If your child is not progressing, discuss [your child's progress] with the teacher and determine whether or not the program should be modified. As a parent, you can initiate changes in your child's educational program.

- **Discuss with the school or agency any problems** that may occur with your child's assessment, placement or educational program. It is best to try to resolve these problems directly with the agency, school, or district. In some situations, you may be uncertain as to which direction you should take to resolve a problem. Most states have protection and advocacy agencies that can provide you with the guidance you need to pursue your case.

- **Keep records.** There may be many questions and comments about your child that you will want to discuss, as well as meetings and phone conversations you will want to remember. It is easy to forget information that is not written down.

- **Join a parent organization.** In addition to offering the opportunity to share knowledge, experiences, and support, a parent group can be an effective force on behalf of your child. Many times parents find that as a group they have the power to bring about needed changes to strengthen and broaden special services.

### As the parent of a child with a disability, what can you offer the IEP process?

Parents of children with disabilities can and should be involved in a number of ways, including the following:

- **Before attending an IEP meeting, make a list of things you want your child to learn.** Take notes about aspects of your child's behavior that could interfere with the learning process. Describe the methods you have found to be successful in dealing with these behaviors.

- **Bring any information the school may not already have** to the IEP or IFSP meeting. Examples include copies of medical records, past school records, or test or evaluation results. Remember, reports do not say all there is to say about a child. You can add real-life examples to demonstrate your child's ability in certain areas.

- **Find out what related services are being provided**, and ask each professional to describe the kind of services he or she will be providing and what improvement you might expect to see as a result of these services.
- **Ask what you can do at home to support the program.** Many skills your child learns at school can also be used at home. Ask to meet with the teacher when your child is learning new skills that could be practiced at home.
- **Discuss methods for handling discipline problems** that you know are effective with your child.
- **When you feel teachers and school personnel are doing a good job, tell them.**

**What resources are available to help you?**
Local and state education agencies have information to help guide you through the special education process. Since there is great variation in the specific criteria and procedures employed by school districts, it is important that you familiarize yourself with the information they provide. You will find your local director of special education and his or her staff helpful in accessing such information and guiding you through the process. (Please check the appendix for a state-by-state listing of Parent Training Centers funded by IDEA—these centers are for YOU and their purpose is to provide parents with information.)

## Change Begins with Parents and Teachers

Parents *must* find the time to learn as much as possible about AD/HD and then share this knowledge with educators, beginning with their child's teacher. Statistics show that for every classroom of children in the United States, one or two children will have AD/HD. If every parent of a child with AD/HD took the time to educate one teacher each year by providing him or her with information on teaching children with AD/HD, inviting him or her to attend a conference or workshop (or parent support group meetings), and donating a book on AD/HD to the school library, it would make an enormous difference, not just for our children but for future generations of children with AD/HD. Don't just talk about the changes that need to be made; reach out and educate.

# The Adolescent
# with AD/HD

DOLESCENCE IS defined as "the period of physical and psychological development between childhood and adulthood." For parents with teenagers, this is the time to let go—often a difficult concept for parents but particularly so for those with an adolescent who has AD/HD.

"How can I possibly let go?" asks one mom from Oklahoma. "I worry about my son from the time he wakes up until he goes to bed. He's still so unorganized. I have to remind him of everything, from taking his clothes to the cleaners to putting gas in the car to completing his homework. He can't even remember to take gym clothes to school. I worry about his driving, going out with the guys, having dates, etc."

"My daughter is always screaming at me, 'Get out of my face. Leave me alone,' " says Kathy from Salem, Oregon. "I know I need to give her some room, but who's going to help her if I'm not around. She wants to date, but she's so immature compared to other girls her age. I'm afraid some guy is going to come along and sweet talk her into having sex. What if she gets pregnant?"

"My son keeps saying he can't wait until he's twenty-one so he can drink," admits another mom from Arkansas. "I've read that children with

AD/HD, especially those who are hyperactive and impulsive, are at risk for abusing drugs and alcohol, so, of course, I'm worried."

"When my daughter drives without medication, she never sees a stop sign. With medication, she's a pretty decent driver," explains one mom. "The rule in our house is that if she wants to drive, she has to be current on her medication."

Yet like all parents, parents of teenagers with AD/HD know that their children are beginning to move on, and they, too, must begin the process of letting go. So how do committed parents let go?

Janet Robinson, RN, PhD, of Sylvania, Ohio, mother of an eighteen-year-old son with AD/HD, says, "At some point, we have to let them assume total responsibility, and the best way to do that is step by step, giving them as much as they can handle where it's appropriate. We don't own and we can't control the consequences of our kids' AD/HD. It's painful, but don't be afraid of your child's pain. Although we can walk through it with them, we can't take it away from them. Going through the pain does build character. The kids learn the lessons they need to learn."

## Letting Go Step by Step

How do you let go step by step? You begin by examining your child's history. Does he telephone you when he arrives at a friend's house as you have requested? Does he follow the house rule that says he must come right home from school? If you check on him, will you find him where he says he'll be? If yes, then he is ready for more responsibility; if no, then he must be taught to follow the rules before he can be granted more freedom.

Once a child is ready for more freedom, you begin letting go by negotiating the limits. If he wants to make a stop at a friend's house after school for a few hours twice a week and you are uncomfortable with two or three hours, reach a compromise. ("If you can show me that you will come home after spending one hour at your friend's house, then I will increase that time to two hours next month.") If your child wants to use the car on Saturday until midnight but you are uneasy about letting him stay out that late, give him permission to use the car but only until 10:00. Once he has proved that he is responsible and can get home by 10:00, then you can increase the time to 11:00 or later.

Once your child solicits more latitude, make sure the freedom you offer comes with clear-cut limits. For example, "Yes, you may use the car until 10:00, but you must tell me where you are going and call me when you arrive." Not only will you know where your child is, but you will find out if your child is responsible enough to follow the rules. When your child follows the rules, use praise to acknowledge his compliance. ("Thank you for calling me when you got to the mall. It shows me how responsible you are.") Remember to always praise the behavior you want to continue.

What do you do if your child abuses a new privilege? Don't overreact. Screaming or threatening will cause more harm than good. Stay calm, but take the privilege away from him. You might say, "I'm sorry you didn't call me when you got to the mall. Because you didn't call you may not use the car for one week. However, next week I will give you another opportunity to prove that you can follow the rules."

Monitor your child carefully and give one new freedom at a time. Don't tell your child he can use the car Saturday night to drive fifty miles to the school his friend attends and then spend the night.

## AD/HD Symptoms in Teens

Despite past predictions that children with AD/HD would outgrow this disorder when they reached adolescence, we now know that this is not always the case. Many children with AD/HD will have symptoms that persist into adulthood. As adults they will display, and have to cope with, many of the same symptoms that plagued them as children.

Some of the symptoms adolescents, as well as their families and teachers, will have to cope with are a short attention span, low frustration tolerance, impulsivity, a need for immediate gratification, distractibility, poor peer relationships, and low self-esteem. The symptoms of hyperactivity usually decrease as the child matures, but signs may still be evident and are often perceived as restlessness, such as tapping fingers. On the other hand, some teenagers may be underactive (sometimes referred to as "hypoactive"), often appearing lethargic or spacey.

### Short Attention Span

A short attention span creates problems for the teenager, especially in the school environment where students are expected to hear and remember instructions and complete more elaborate classroom and homework assignments. Often, teens with AD/HD do not remember or record assignments accurately and, consequently, the work is not completed. Other problems include being unable to distinguish between important details and not-so-relevant materials. Teachers generally describe these students as lazy, forgetful, or disorganized. This deficit may only affect specific subjects—the student may do well in other classes—which is confusing to those closest to the student, like parents and teachers.

Says Stephanie, the mother of a sixteen-year-old, from Lincoln, Nebraska, "My son never had any real difficulties in school until he reached ninth grade, then suddenly he was having all sorts of problems. He became so frustrated, despite the fact that he was trying. Eventually he fell behind in his schoolwork and his self-esteem was very low. One day I had a call from the school. They wanted to know why he wasn't in school. As it turned out he had skipped several days of school. When we confronted him, he said there was no point in going to school as he couldn't do the work even when he really tried. We found a tutor for him and that has made a difference. This year his more difficult classes are now in the morning and that seems to have made a difference also."

Poor grades can result in depression or in unacceptable behaviors, such as truancy. A tutor may be the answer in many cases, or the child may need to be placed in special education classes. Summer school is an option for other students. This allows the student to concentrate his efforts on one subject for a shorter time.

## Low Frustration Tolerance

Students with AD/HD may become especially frustrated when attempting to complete a major assignment, especially one that is boring or complicated, because they are so impatient and their frustration threshold is very low. They also may have difficulty waiting in traffic, obeying stop signs, and adhering to speed limits because they are in hurry to get where they are going. A high percentage of adolescents with AD/HD have an accident in their first year of driving. In fact, many teens with AD/HD are involved in car accidents each year—a result of their short attention span, their impulsivity, and their low frustration tolerance. My son opted to wait to get his license until age eighteen because he felt he wasn't ready to drive. However, even postponing didn't help. He officially joined the ranks when he had his first car accident within eight months of getting his license.

## Impulsivity

Teens may have little self-control and often act without thinking first. Poor impulse control may make it extremely difficult for a teenager to say no to peers who encourage him to try drugs or have a beer or two before driving to a party. "I've taught my daughter to stop and think before deciding to do something," explains Leah from Eau Claire, Wisconsin. "If she makes the wrong decision, I help her examine the consequences. I encourage her to look at the behavior and think of other ways, other options, she might have chosen instead. You can't just tell your child *once* to stop and think, you must do it repeatedly so it becomes second nature. The earlier you begin working with your child on poor impulse control, the easier it will be for her during adolescence."

## Immediate Gratification (Insatiability)

Like the younger child with AD/HD, a teenager may also beg and plead for something he wants now. "I spent an entire day with my daughter looking for the perfect dress, but once we got home she decided the outfit wasn't really quite right for the dance and she begged me to take her shopping again to find something else," explains Barbara, the mother of a seventeen-year-old. "This is really typical for my daughter. Once she gets what she *must* have, she often is not satisfied."

Sometimes, in teens with AD/HD, the need for immediate gratification leads to far more serious behavior. One AD/HD adult I know was extremely handsome as a teenager, had a sense of humor, and was considered quite a catch. He admits that when he wanted to sleep with a girl he usually got his way. How? He begged and pleaded and wouldn't give up until the girl consented. However, once he had sex with her he was no longer interested because there were many other girls who were just as appealing. Consequently, at ages fifteen and seventeen, he fathered babies (which were placed for adoption at birth).

## Distractibility

Children with AD/HD are easily distracted. In class, their attention may be diverted from the teacher by noises in the hall or by another student in the room. One teenager, Tracy, said that she would enter math class and tell herself to pay attention. "The next thing I knew the class was over and I hadn't heard a word the teacher said. Yet I did hear the two girls behind me whispering and I heard the pencil drop in the back of the room and I remember seeing the janitor walk past the door," she says. One mother of a sixteen-year-old said it was not uncommon to send her daughter to the grocery store to pick up three items and have her return with only two, which often were not the items she had specified. "Unless I write the items down, she can't remember them," the mother says. "Once I sent her to the grocery store and she went to the post office instead." To avoid this, make directions clear, simple, and brief. Have your adolescent repeat the directions back to you or, better yet, write them down. My youngest is always willing to run into the store for me to pick up a few items, while I wait in the car. He's usually in the store about five minutes when my cell phone rings. "What did you say you needed, Mom?" He really means well, so we now keep a small pad of paper in the car for times like this.

## Poor Peer Relationships

Like children with AD/HD, some teenagers with the disorder are immature for their age, often displaying inappropriate age behavior, and have younger friends. If these same teenagers are also demanding and bossy, it is easy to understand how they can alienate their peers. Adolescents who are not liked by their peers appear to be at risk for engaging in antisocial behaviors that result from poor self-esteem. Some may also be at risk for developing psychological problems. Studies have shown that young children with poor social skills usually have poor social skills as teenagers and adults.

Children who were extremely aggressive with peers as youngsters sometimes do not outgrow their antisocial tendencies. They are often at increased risk for substance abuse and criminal behaviors as teenagers. (The use of medication in the treatment of AD/HD does not lead to substance abuse. On the contrary, failing to medically treat AD/HD may lead to substance abuse or criminal behaviors in some individuals.)

"Parents should model appropriate social skills and make their child's friends feel welcome in their home," suggests Sally, the mother of a sixteen-year-old daughter. "Demonstrating appropriate social skills to their friends will help your child learn how to be nice to his friends and teach him how to welcome friends into his home. Obviously we can't make a child become a friend to our daughter, but we can help set the stage for a comfortable and pleasant interaction. As parents, we can also teach our children how to start a conversation and, especially, how to end one. My daughter, who easily gets distracted, would just walk away in the middle of a conversation or, if on the phone, would abruptly say 'good-bye' and hang up. It's not easy to teach these skills, particularly if one spouse has AD/HD and has difficulty with social skills. My husband, who has AD/HD, often gets up in the middle of a conversation with my daughter or me and makes a phone call. My daughter has witnessed this repeatedly. Teaching her the proper way to talk with people was not easy because of the way her father handles situations. But with work, patience, and time, I did get through to her."

## Low Self-Esteem

Frustrations that arise from troubles with schoolwork, underachievement, the inability to make or keep friends, continuous negative feedback, and the realization that they are different than others, will adversely affect the adolescent's self-esteem. Over the years, it becomes easy for him to see himself as a failure, even in areas where he may excel. It's imperative that parents focus on their child's strengths and abilities and encourage him to develop them more fully. Express pride in their accomplishments and note areas of improvement.

"When my daughter expresses frustrations about not being like the other girls, I run through my mental list," offers Sandy from Spokane, Washington. "For instance, if she tells me how well her friend does in math, I remind her how well she does in drama. Parents can always find something about their child that is particularly positive to compliment."

Parents of teenagers with AD/HD should be aware that poor self-esteem and feelings of failure, anger, and isolation can result in depression. Depressed teenagers may turn to drugs or alcohol, exhibit out-of-control behavior, or even harbor thoughts of suicide. Parents who are troubled by their teen's behavior should not hesitate to seek professional intervention. Parents who are having considerable difficulty reaching their teenager, losing self-control when faced with noncompliant behavior, or retreating to inappropriate techniques that perpetuate unacceptable behavior should also seek professional help. Through therapy, parents can improve their self-control, for instance, and learn how to teach their teenager self-restraint. Through therapy a teenager's self-esteem can be bolstered. The adolescent can also learn strategies for dealing with the stress that results from heightened demands.

## Some Suggestions for Parent-Teacher Activities

(*Source*: NICHCY's Transition Summary, no. 7, Sept. 1991.)

To feel good about what one has to offer as an individual, one has to feel good about oneself. Therefore, parents and teachers can start teaching self-determination by focusing on the individual's disability. Parents and teachers should keep in mind the following when helping children and youth feel good about being a person with a disability:

- **Be open about the disability**. Your view of the disability will be reflected in your child's body image and self-concept. If you cannot accept the disability or overreact to it, your child will react the same way.
- **Avoid demeaning and negative terms like "hardship" and "burden."** If you perceive the disability as something negative, so will your adolescent.
- **Don't hide the disability**. Both of you know the disability is there. You are the best source of accurate information regarding his disability and can help him understand it. If the teenager cannot get the information from you, he will try to figure it out alone or ask others who may give erroneous answers.
- **Avoid comparisons with others**. Phrases such as "Why can't you be like . . ." and "If John can do it, why can't you?" not only focus on an ability the child does not have but implies that this ability is something that the parents value and see missing in their teenager.
- **Stress positive, coping strategies**. Get to know good role models. Your teenager can learn many positive things from adults with disabilities who live and work in your community.

The second step is for parents to provide their teenagers with opportunities for structured choice. [For example, you might tell your teen,] "You get to plan dinner for Tuesday. This is the menu for the rest of the week, and this is our budget for food." (This reflects a higher level of decision making, because the teenager needs to know something about nutrition and the price of the food. This task also reflects the importance of the teenager's input for the good of the family unit.)

Parents can assist in planning activities that the teenager can perform independently by (1) providing a checklist of the steps the child needs to follow or (2) using an approach where a parent, mutual friend, or more responsible peer "shadows" the teen as he proceeds through the activity. The "shadow" intervenes only if necessary. Both of these procedures should provide the teen with enough flexibility to begin taking some independent action, but there should be sufficient structure, if necessary, to guide the teenager.

As early as possible, parents should involve the child in meetings and conferences that are directly related to the child's well-being (IEP, [or individualized education program, parent-teacher conferences,] etc.). Parents may need to help professionals relate to their child by requesting that they phrase their comments so that he can understand what is being said and its implications. The child may not want to or know how to contribute meaningful information during the meeting, but by observing the interactions of others, there is an opportunity to learn by example. Parents who communicate effectively can also pattern assertive behavior without being overly aggressive.

Skills necessary for self-determination *must* be taught to all children and youth; it is especially important for children and youth with disabilities. Expecting youth who have been overprotected and restricted in terms of self-determination to be functioning, independent adults is akin to expecting a nation that has lived under an oppressive, totalitarian system for centuries to govern by democratic principles immediately after a revolution. Self-determination just doesn't happen; it requires a great deal of preparation and practice.

## Discipline Strategies That Work with Teenagers Who Have AD/HD

You don't have to be a genius to understand that many of the discipline techniques (token and chart systems, for example) you use with the younger child who has AD/HD lose effectiveness as the child matures. Other strategies that you might have been using may continue to be effective into the teenage years (see chapter 7 for techniques that work with younger children). The following list includes some of those strategies but also others that are appropriate for use with teenagers:

## Time-Out

While it's true that time-out is most appropriate for younger children (ages two through ten years), you may find it works with your teenager (especially if you have used it consistently for years). If your older child still complies when sent to time-out, then by all means use it. "My daughter is seventeen, almost eighteen, and we still use time-out," comments Barbara from Omaha, Nebraska. "We send her to her room when she needs to calm down, to collect herself. And she goes without an argument. We don't use the term 'time-out' anymore. At this age, we just tell her to go to her room."

## Grounding

Grounding is a popular punishment for all teenagers, and it does work with adolescents who have AD/HD when it is used properly. The problem with grounding is that many parents do not use it appropriately, probably because they don't understand how it is meant to be used. A parent who grounds for one month his or her teenager for coming home ten minutes late on Saturday night has misused the grounding technique. Not only must the teenager stay home for four weeks, but he also misses contact with friends for one month. So what? you say. Consider the facts.

Withdrawing your adolescent from friends and activities for long periods can seriously impair his social network. Remember, teens with AD/HD sometimes have difficulty with social skills. If he has one or two close friends, he's probably worked hard to make and keep those relationships. Cutting him off from his friends for weeks may cause his social network to collapse. He may also rebel or fall into a state of depression. Besides, grounding your teenager for extended periods is hard work for parents to enforce.

So how should grounding be used? Grounding works best when the rules have been established first and the teenager is forewarned that if he is late he will then be grounded next Friday and Saturday night, or he'll be grounded for the rest of the week. Grounding is most effective when used for only short periods.

## Withdraw the Use of the Car

Driving is a privilege. Driving and using the family car is an even bigger privilege. When a teenager abuses that privilege, then it may become necessary to withdraw it entirely. If your teenager gets a ticket for speeding, has been drinking and driving, is responsible for causing an accident, or uses the car to go someplace other than where he said he was going, it is appropriate to suspend the use of the car. Be sure your child knows the rules regarding the use of the car and the consequences of abusing those rules.

## Ban the Use of the Telephone

Suspending the use of the telephone is another common discipline technique. A teenager who abuses the privilege of using the family telephone after being warned not to tie it up for more than the allotted time, or fails to do homework because he is on the phone all evening, should lose the use of the telephone for a few days. This is a logical and fair removal of a privilege. Losing the use of the car for one month would not be a reasonable or just price to pay for violating phone privileges. Losing the telephone for a month also would not be fair. Always be sure the crime fits the penalty.

## Write a Contract

Contracts can be made with teenagers. A negotiated agreement is made between the parent and the middle or high school student and can work for such things as violating curfews, skipping school, and other similar major infractions. Let's say your daughter has been bugging you to let her get her hair colored and so far you've resisted because she's been skipping classes. The contract might read

I, Heather, agree to go to my classes every day.
When I go to all my classes for one month, I can go to the beauty salon and have my hair highlighted.

Signed,    *Heather*

## Negotiate

You can negotiate with your teenager as long as both parties are willing to work to find a solution to the problem. Both parties must be willing to compromise. To negotiate, you first must define the problem. Then in a respectful manner, together, you find some solutions to the problem and discuss the pros and cons of each until you reach an acceptable conclusion you both can live with. Once you've reached an agreement, set a defined time for a trial period, then renegotiate the terms if necessary.

## Use "I" Statements

Remember, "I" statements focus on you not on your teenager. "When you miss your curfew and don't call to tell me where you are, I feel frightened because I'm afraid you've had an accident." (See chapter 6 for more information on "I" statements.)

## Cost-Response

Cost-response appears to work well with teens who have AD/HD. Instead of earning rewards, rewards are given first and the child must work to keep them.

You can give teens a number of hours per week that they can use the telephone or car. The teenager then works to keep those hours but is penalized for not doing chores, abusing privileges, etc., by losing precious time from this weekly allotment. (A weekly allowance can also be handled the same way.)

## Family Meetings

Plan a meeting once a week for all family members. A secretary should be chosen at each meeting to take minutes, so that there is always a record of important decisions and rules. Use the meeting to go over the family rules, and solicit your teenager's input. Show respect for his opinion. If a rule needs to be changed, make the necessary changes. If you don't feel comfortable with a change at this point, explain why, but write it down. Consider all ideas. This will show your teenager that his opinion is valuable.

Meetings also can be used to allow all members of the family to discuss whatever is on their minds (routines that need to be readjusted, mom needs more help with housekeeping chores, where to go on vacation, who will help a sibling with a scouting project, etc.). The family meeting focuses on all family members, not just the child with AD/HD. Set rules for meetings, such as no prolonged arguments will be permitted and respect must be shown for others' opinions. Remember though, a family cannot be a true democracy; parents must keep some executive veto power. If you find you must veto, make sure you explain your reasons for refusing to consent. For detailed information on the family meeting, refer to *The Parent's Handbook* by Don Dinkmeyer and Gary D. McKay (Circle Pines, MN: American Guidance Service, 1989).

## Offer a Choice

Offering a choice of activities is a great technique for oppositional teenagers ("Would you like to prepare lunch or dinner today?" "Would you like to run the vacuum or fold the laundry?" "Would you like to plant the flowers or trim the bushes?"). Although your teen has a choice, be sure he realizes that if he doesn't choose one of the tasks, you will assign one. As mentioned in chapter 6, offering mini choices also directs debate away from important nonnegotiable rules.

## What Not to Do

If your child has a special talent or interest, such as playing the piano, *do not take this away* from him. This one precious gift is just too relevant and necessary for your child's self-esteem to be used as a punishment for undesirable behavior. (Too often parents react hastily and take away the first thing that comes to mind—usually, whatever is most important to the child. Often the undesired behavior can be changed with the loss of another privilege.) Restricting or pulling your teenager out of something so important to him will yield only negative results. When your teenager has something in his life that he feels good about, he is more apt to have positive feelings about himself, his schoolwork, and his family. If you take away that one activity, your child may have nothing worthwhile left.

If your teen has a part-time job he particularly enjoys, do not force him to quit. You may ask him to reduce his hours if he's working too late or is falling behind in his homework. Parents should consider the job's role in fostering their teen's sense of independence. A job not only teaches responsibility it enables a teen to acquire valuable skills and knowledge and earn and manage money.

Do not preach, nag, lecture, or argue because your adolescent will only tune you out. (Remember the many times you didn't listen to your parents? And when you did listen, you probably disagreed, verbally or mentally, with everything they said to you.) Arguing with your teenager is a no-win situation.

If you have the urge to argue, nag, lecture, or preach, leave the room immediately! If the problem is something that must be addressed, do it later. When everyone has settled down, arrange a meeting with your teenager. A restaurant is an excellent spot for this type of conversation because participants are more apt to keep themselves under control in a public place. Or write your teen a note explaining your feelings and arrange to talk (possibly before bed or after dinner).

If you find yourself arguing, nagging, preaching, or lecturing more often than not, you *must* alter your behavior. These tactics only perpetuate the unacceptable behavior you are trying to modify. Concentrate on changing your normal response patterns. I know how difficult it is to change your behavior when you have a child who is difficult and strong-willed. But I'm also familiar with the guilt one feels after such episodes. It takes time, effort, desire, and awareness to change negative responses into positive ones, but it can be done.

## Living with the Teen Who Has AD/HD

Several parents have offered excellent suggestions and advice for living with teens who have AD/HD. Here are some of the most helpful:

- **Follow through.** "Don't threaten your son or daughter unless you plan to enforce the threat," suggests Bill from Knoxville, Tennessee. "Threats that are made [often in anger] but never implemented teach your child that you do not mean what you say. If the infraction is serious, tell your teenager that you need to think about the situation and discuss it with the other parent before delivering the consequence." It is imperative that parents follow through because teens with AD/HD need the stability of knowing what to expect.
- **Set realistic expectations.** Think AD/HD and you are less apt to expect perfection. Always focus on your child's assets and abilities, rather than on his shortcomings. Believe in your child, even when he doesn't believe in himself.
- **Be flexible.** "Remember, there is more than one way to do something," cautions Faith from Marietta, Georgia. "Our way is not always the best, even though we'd like to believe it is." Parents of children with AD/HD become accustomed to telling their children how to do things. As children mature, we must accept the fact that they may have found their own way of handling life's challenges.
- **Listen to your child.** Children who talk but are not heard by their parents often drift away from their families over the years. Be open to what he has to say. Don't be judgmental. Teens with AD/HD need to be *heard*—possibly even more than other teens—because *they* are always listening to others' instructions.
- **Look ahead.** "When your teenager enters high school, look ahead with him at career choices, colleges, junior colleges, or no college," suggests Helena from Hartford, Connecticut. "Too many parents leave this job to school guidance counselors. Nobody knows your teenager better than you. Many AD/HD symptoms are qualities that are greatly admired in adults and there are occupations that people with AD/HD experience relatively few problems with." There are AD/HD adults who head corporations, are police officers, attorneys, and great salespeople. Some are computer programmers, hairstylists, entertainers, construction workers, truck drivers, psychologists, and teachers. Some of these people have AD/HD and are also learning disabled. So don't lose hope.
- **Prepare your teen.** Talk with your younger teen about potential problems he may encounter. Children learn about drugs and

alcohol, drinking and driving, AIDS, and teenage pregnancy in school, but parents need to reinforce these issues. Let them know about the temptations they will face when they begin dating, how their impulsivity may come into play, and the choices they'll have to make. Give them time to consider these choices before they're confronted with them. They're more apt to listen to you before a problem develops, rather than after when they often become defensive.

- **"Set ground rules for dating,"** advises Allison from Council Bluffs, Iowa. "Ask your teenager to tell you about the person he or she wants to date. Tell your daughter that you want to meet the fellow she's planning to go out with (he's to come up to the door when he picks her up, for instance). Likewise, tell your son you want to meet the girl he's dating. Make sure you know the date's name and where he or she lives. [Try to meet the other parents also or, at the very least, talk with them on the telephone.] After the date, encourage your teenager to tell you how the date went. Know where your teenager is going (be sure he knows what types of places are off limits) and what time he plans to be home, or give him a time to be home. [Make sure he has money to call home if needed, or let him take a cell phone.] Decide how often he or she can date (once a week, for instance, during the school year, and twice a week during summer vacation). If you haven't done so already, talk with your son or daughter about sex." Although establishing and periodically reiterating rules usually works with most teens, those with AD/HD need to hear rules much more frequently (possibly before every date). Because teens with AD/HD may have poor self-control, be impulsive and insatiable, and have difficulty delaying gratification, repeating rules and expectations will help them avoid situations that may lead to an unwanted pregnancy, drug abuse, or other problems that can result from socializing and peer pressure.

- **Help structure and organize.** "Remember your teen needs structure and that he has trouble with organization," continues Helena. "Establish rules, give clear, simple directions for tasks, and teach him ways to organize himself [if he can't do this entirely on his own yet] and manage his environment. Encourage him to make use of bulletin boards, calendars, and daily planners and to make notes for daily tasks, activities, and schoolwork. He may need to use lists [of things to do] and daily planners for his entire lifetime." If you are having problems teaching your child to organize himself, look for classes in the community that teach organization skills. Memory skill classes are also available.

- **Teach them to advocate for themselves.** "For years, when our children are younger, we are their advocates," says Judy, a former high school teacher in Toledo, Ohio, and parent of a child with AD/HD. "It's imperative that parents teach their teenagers to advocate for themselves in school [and later, on the job or in a marriage]. When an older student comes to a teacher and says, 'I have attention deficit problems and I can't organize my schoolwork very well,' or 'I have problems with spelling and writing. I try my hardest, but I may need more time than the average kid to complete essay questions,' or whatever the problem is, teachers are very impressed and are willing to help in any way they can. Somehow it's different when the student makes the appeal in high school than when the parent does. Maybe it shouldn't be, but that's the way it is for a lot of teachers."

- **Analyze your fears.** "Look at your fears," advises Jolene from Madison, Wisconsin, "and analyze how realistic they are. Ask yourself, 'What is the very worst that can happen and how likely is it that it will happen?' Talk about your fears with others in a parent support group or with a therapist. It will help you deal with your fears and to take control of your feelings."

- **Give your teen attention.** "Always be available for your teenager to help keep him on task with homework, chores, daily tasks, etc.," says Leslie from Huntington, West Virginia. "Set aside fifteen minutes a day and give your teenager your undivided attention. Like youngsters, older children appreciate special time with mom or dad."

- **Make explicit the teen's family role.** Elicit their compliance on the basis that everyone is responsible for the family's success. For example, "If you limit your time on the telephone and help me around the house, I'll have enough time to make arrangements to have your friends over this weekend."

## The Adopted Teenager with AD/HD

Teenagers who were adopted will be dealing with a number of issues during adolescence that parents should be aware of. (Of course, younger children may also wrestle with adoption-related issues, which will likely differ.) These include, but are not limited to the following:

- **Sense of identity.** A struggle to develop a sense of identity because they have been separated from their biological families ("Who do I look like, what do my birth parents look like, and how alike or different am I from my adoptive parents?").
- **Different from adoptive family.** The realization that things may have been different had they stayed with their birth families, especially if they are the only person in the adoptive family who has AD/HD, learning disabilities, or both. For example, would their biological parents be more like them? Would they have been better equipped to understand their AD/HD symptoms (and problems) than their adoptive parents? Some teenagers may be angry at their birth parents for the role they may have played in passing along their impulsivity to them. Be sure you let them know that no one is to blame for the AD/HD.
- **Different from peers.** The teen feels different than other teenagers and does not fully understand the effects a learning disability or AD/HD may have on him and often labels himself as stupid or dumb, which he may then view as the reason he was placed for adoption in the first place. Not only will he feel different because of the AD/HD or learning disability, but he will also feel different because he was adopted. His self-esteem is then hit doubly hard.
- **Acceptance.** Teenagers may wonder if they really fit in with their families, especially if they exhibit major differences in their abilities, interests, and personalities than their adoptive families.

The child with AD/HD who has an average IQ, for instance, may wonder if his adoptive parents are disappointed in him, especially if they are professional people with advanced degrees. The day will come when the adoptive child will realize that his parents could have adopted a different child—one with a higher IQ or one who did not have AD/HD. The child may ask himself, "Would they have been happier with another child? Am I good enough for them?" Adoptive parents must let their teen know that they love and accept him for the very special and unique person he is.

Whether your child was born to you or adopted, you must remember that he did not choose to have AD/HD. But with the proper intervention and lots of love, patience, and understanding from the people who love him the most, your child has a good chance at having a great life.

## What's Next?

(*Source*: NICHCY's Transition Summary, no. 7, Sept. 1991.)

This section presents suggestions for how students with disabilities can work with their families and school professionals to put together an action plan for transition after high school. The key words here are *plan* and *action*. There's a saying that goes "Plan your work, and then work your plan." Planning requires action—information gathering, self-assessment, weighing of alternatives, decision making. "Working the plan" also requires action—following through on decisions that have been made, evaluating progress, gathering more information and making new decisions, as necessary.

Leaving secondary school is an eventuality that all students must face. Under IDEA [Individuals with Disabilities Education Act], preparing for this transition has become more than a personal choice. Each student's IEP must now include a statement of the transition services needed by the student, beginning no later than age sixteen. The transition plan must also include, where appropriate, a statement of interagency responsibilities or linkages (or both) before the student leaves the school setting. [Much of the following is excellent advice for all students, not just those with IEPs.]

### In Junior High School: Start Transition Planning

- **Become involved in career exploration.**
- **Visit with a school counselor** to talk about interests and capabilities.
- **Participate in vocational assessment activities.**

- Use information about interests and capabilities to make pre-liminary decisions about possible careers: academic versus vocational, or a combination.
- Make use of books, career fairs, and people in the community to find out more about careers of interest.

## In High School: Define Career/Vocational Goals

- Work with school staff, family, and people and agencies in the community to define and refine your transition plan. Make sure that the IEP includes transition plans.
- Identify and take high school courses that are required for entry into college, trade schools, or careers of interest.
- Identify and take vocational programs offered in high school, if a vocational career is of interest.
- Become involved in early work experiences, such as job tryouts or internships, summer jobs, volunteering, or part-time work.
- Re-assess interests and capabilities, based on real world or school experience. Is the career field still of interest? If not, redefine goals.
- Participate in on-going vocational assessment and identify gaps of knowledge or skills that need to be addressed. Address these gaps.

If you have decided to pursue postsecondary education and training prior to employment, consider these suggestions:

- Identify postsecondary institutions (colleges, vocational programs in the community, trade schools, etc.) that offer training in any career of interest. Write or call for catalogues, financial aid information, and applications. Visit the institution.
- Identify what accommodations would be helpful to address your special needs. Find out if the educational institution makes, or can make, these accommodations. Many colleges maintain advisors and tutors for individuals with learning disabilities.
- Identify and take any special tests (e.g., PSAT, SAT, NMSQT [Preliminary SAT, Scholastic Assessment Test, and National

Merit Scholarship Qualifying Test]) necessary for entry into postsecondary institutions of interest. SATs can now be taken untimed by youth with AD/HD.

For a complete source of information on teens with AD/HD, please refer to my book *AD/HD and Teens: A Parent's Guide to Making It Through the Tough Years,* published by Taylor Trade. In the book you will find many proven techniques for dealing with emotional, academic, and behavioral problems. You will also find an excellent chapter on medications, written by Paul T. Elliott, MD. I highly suggest that you *not* put off future reading just because your child is only five or six or eight years old. You should definitely read this book before your child becomes a preteen.

# Medications for the Treatment of AD/HD: Challenges, Opportunities, and Strategies

## LOUIS B. CADY

RAVELING ON an airplane and letting people know you are a psychiatrist—particularly a child psychiatrist—has its blessings and challenges. Nowhere did this snap more clearly into focus for me than on a delightful trip out of Idaho where my traveling companion, upon learning what I did for a "day job," confessed that he had a beautiful nine-year-old daughter for whom a well-known AD/HD[1] medication was not working. What alarmed me, however, was that his daughter was having some brief staring spells and that from time to time her eyelids would twitch.

Before sallying forth on a chapter regarding the medication treatment of AD/HD, some words of caution are in order. First of all, the diagnosis of AD/HD must be precisely and carefully made. As Ms. Alexander-Roberts has previously touched on, this requires the presence of six symptoms in the nine-symptom complex of either hyperactivity or inattentiveness for at least six months in two settings (school and home, for example) and *not accounted for by any other medical or psychiatric condition*.[2] Medication strategies, if embarked upon, should be done cautiously, carefully, and precisely and with an open mind toward changing the presumptive diagnosis of AD/HD. In this chapter, we will cover how to do exactly that.

An obvious point of confusion is that frequently diagnostic possibilities, and even diagnoses themselves, overlap. That is why folks who like things neat and tidy in their diagnosis, where they can isolate the presumptive germ in a culture dish, tend to avoid psychiatry. It is a discipline where an open mind must be kept and intellectual humility—with the ability to admit at any time that you are wrong—must be practiced and maintained.

Contemporary diagnostic problems for AD/HD include the presence or possibility of bipolar disorder, a simultaneous learning disability, auditory processing difficulties, depression, post–traumatic stress disorder, anxiety disorder, mental retardation, sleep apnea, thyroid disorders, or other neurologically based disorders with clear signs and symptoms of their own—to name but a few. Pathologically low levels of essential fatty acids, as well as IgG (delayed reaction) food allergies,[3] are now clearly in the scientific literature as exacerbating influences on AD/HD. Petit mal epilepsy with absence seizures—what my friend's daughter might have been experiencing—must also be considered with a relevant clinical history.

In short, one must pause before making a diagnosis of AD/HD and consider what else may be going on. Hence, the touchstone of any medication strategy is a bulletproof diagnosis of pure AD/HD, or at least the relatively major contribution of this diagnosis to the psychiatric mélange of confusing possibilities. This can only be properly done by either (a) a physician who can exclude biological causes for the symptoms by making a physical exam and taking a medical history (or reviewing one), and not just totting up symptoms on a checklist, or (b) an expert psychologist or therapist specializing in the diagnosis of AD/HD after a child has been *thoroughly* evaluated by a physician who is comfortable excluding all other physical, psychiatric, and medical problems. To be ridiculously obvious, pinworms can make a child wiggle and possibly push the child over the top in terms of the number of diagnostic symptoms of AD/HD.

One must be careful that it is true AD/HD, not pinworms on a kid's bottom, that is causing him or her to squirm and have trouble sitting still.

If there are sources of confusion in terms of the exact cause of a symptom complex that looks like AD/HD but that may represent other, more fundamental nutritional or dietary causes, a number of strategies exist that might prove very useful and do not involve the use of medications.

## Nutritional and Functional Medicine Evaluation and Treatment Considerations

There are notable themes in the peer-reviewed psychiatric literature that amino acid manipulation[4]—either their addition or subtraction in experimental protocols—can have *radical and profound* impacts on the brain. These effects include changes in concentration, mood, and mental efficiency. The use of L-tyrosine and DLPA (DL-phenylalanine) to boost both norepinephrine and dopamine in the brain, as well as 5-HTP (5-hydroxytryptophan) to boost serotonin in the brain, are well established in the medical literature. The level of practicality of doing this for the average AD/HD patient, however, as well as the limited duration of action of the actual beneficial effects of the dosing, makes it a less than practical first-line therapy. The role of GABA (or lambda-aminobutyric acid, which is actually the only neurotransmitter you can buy in a bottle over the counter) is increasingly being explored in the literature for use in numerous other psychiatric conditions, as well, and may have relevance in a "calmer-downer" approach to hyperactive and impulsive kids.

Similarly, the roll of fish oil supplementation is now well established. Levels of two critical fatty acids, EPA (eicosapentaenoic acid) and DHA (docosahexaenoic acid), can be obtained from multiple labs. My favorite test is the Comprehensive Essential Metabolic Fatty Acid Analysis from Great Smokies Diagnostic Laboratories. I have two favorite laboratories that I frequently use to run tests for my patients: Immuno Laboratories in Florida, to conduct a definitive food allergy panel to evaluate IgG food allergies, and Spectracell Laboratories in Houston, Texas, which carries out a nutrient analysis on a functional, intracellular basis. Details of these tests are available on the laboratories' websites.

After eliminating or treating these potentially confusing and simultaneous problems, conventional psychiatric medications for the treatment of AD/HD break down rather simply and straightforwardly.

## Medication Concepts: Why Use Them?

How enthusiastic am I about prescribing medications for AD/HD? Answer: very! A review of the published scientific literature, including a recent groundbreaking study called the Multimodal Treatment Assessment, is very clear that *absolutely nothing works better to bring AD/HD under control than medication*. Not parent training. Not coaching. Not behavioral therapy. Zip. Nada. Nothing. I once heard the noted PhD psychologist Russell Barkley, in a lecture at Mayo Clinic, say that, as a psychologist, it broke his heart to concede that no form of therapy worked better than medication, but that was what the literature stated at the time (and still states).

All that being said, it is very important to tease apart AD/HD look-alikes—which can certainly include bad parenting, bad (and boring) teaching and teachers, processing difficulties, nutritional and fatty acid problems and food allergies—versus the real thing. While medications may help AD/HD look-alikes, it's sloppy practice to go after these with a pill on one hand and a lousy history and clinical exam on the other. Such sloppy practices may also delay recognizing and treating other conditions, such as thyroid problems, anxiety, depression, and subtle physical and medical problems. In these cases, medication intervention at the outset is a lousy idea, and every other strategy and diagnostic consideration noted by Ms. Alexander-Roberts in this book should be considered *first*.

Finally, even if AD/HD is the real thing, many times pills are not sufficient unto themselves. There can be profound disturbances in relationships between the child and parents, child and teachers, and child and society in general. The frequent explosions or inexplicable bottom-scraping grades in school have worn down parents. Teachers and school administrators can be burned out, hopeless, or at times actively hostile. In almost all of these cases, therefore, even though I would happily and enthusiastically prescribe medication, all the strategies and concepts Ms. Alexander-Roberts reviewed in this book will be critical for a complete, balanced, and holistic approach to serve the child's needs ultimately, efficiently, and completely.

## The Different Types of Medications

Two basic classes of AD/HD medications exist: stimulants and non-stimulants. The classic agent loathed and despised by generations of AD/HD kids who got too much of it—or for whom it wasn't the correct medication—is Ritalin (methylphenidate). This agent predominantly boosts dopamine in the brain, which our current models of AD/HD show to be critically lacking in adequate quantities.

The other class of stimulant is the amphetamine class whose members—Dexedrine (dextroamphetamine), Desoxyn (methamphetamine),[5] and Adderall (mixed salts of amphetamine)—are all available. The amphetamine class of medication boosts dopamine and norepinephrine, and it is more potent. As a result, it takes approximately half as much, in milligrams, of an amphetamine compound to get the same effect as a Ritalin compound.[6] Cylert (sodium pemoline) is a weak stimulant that was used for a while but has largely fallen out of favor because of problems with liver toxicity and the resultant repetitive blood tests required to monitor its safety.

Methamphetamine is actually an FDA-approved, totally legit medicine to treat AD/HD. It's the amateur crank labs and the mass production of street-level methamphetamine that is horrific, addictive, and quite possibly destructive to nerve cells in the brain. The appropriate use of this drug and precise dosing under careful psychiatric monitoring can be literally lifesaving in some severe cases of AD/HD. It is also not addicting—just like any other stimulant when prescribed appropriately is not addicting—if given in low doses, under medical supervision, for the treatment of AD/HD. It is only when stimulants are used in quantities to amp up the user or to give superhuman amounts of energy or the unnatural ability to stay awake for longer than humans were designed to do that these drugs are addicting.

Another stimulant, which is so novel it deserves its own mention, is Focalin (dexmethylphenidate), which is the active part of the molecular mix of what is known as Ritalin, or methylphenidate. The two different forms of this molecule, for purposes of our discussion, are like a guy waving at himself in the mirror. The right hand of our waving friend actually appears as the left hand of the figure waving back in the mirror. In the same way, there are right-handed and left-handed forms of particular molecules. In the case of Focalin, the right-handed form is the active form and the left-handed form is inactive. Purifying it to *only* the right-handed form makes it twice as potent, with arguably fewer side effects.

The major news on the market in the last several years has been the emergence of Strattera (atomoxetine). The rate of success with this drug is highly variable. For this reason, I consider Strattera a miracle drug:

it's a miracle *if* it works (at least, as well as the other agents), and to be absolutely fair, it can be a miracle *when* it works—and it does work spectacularly well in some children and adults. Eli Lilly is to be commended for its research in bringing this drug to the marketplace.

It also appears that within the next year there will be a new class of medication available for AD/HD—a rebranded version of the current drug Provigil (modafinil). This drug, while not a stimulant per se, is a wake-promoting agent, which is appropriate for people who contract a devastating condition called narcolepsy, in which they literally can't stay awake even if they want to. You can think of Provigil as the exact opposite of Benadryl: instead of blocking your histamine receptors, it increases the level of histamine in your brain.[7] For AD/HD, it serves as a "waker-upper" for all of the brain, including the frontal lobes—an approximately two-cup-sized area of your brain right behind your forehead, responsible for planning and organization. (If it were a truck-camper combination, you could consider this portion of the brain analogous to the part of the camper that hangs out over the truck cab.)

"Waking up" the frontal lobes is about the same thing as giving tired executives a coffee break so that they can whip out their planners and start organizing their day's activities. If you are a kid, this includes such important things as sitting still, paying attention, not sassing the teacher, and not thumping your brothers and sisters. Without this pharmacological wake-up call, this important area of the brain—the executive control system—is asleep at the switch.

It's simultaneously significant and important to note that not all drugs that have waker-upper effects on the executive control center of the brain are stimulants and not all stimulant-type drugs (caffeine, for example) have solid waker-upper effects on the brain areas in question. (If caffeine worked uniformly for the treatment of AD/HD, the pharmaceutical companies would be out of business and everyone would simply go to Starbucks several times a day to treat their AD/HD. It doesn't happen.) Thus, the whole idea that we are treating innocent children with speed and amping them up to treat their AD/HD is simply hogwash.

Sometimes I have to do some fast talking and "power shrinking" with parents when I propose to put their munchkins on typical meds. They are frequently concerned that I will turn their children into zombies—and with good justification, based on other people's experiences and the frequently overly high doses prescribed and poor selection of many of these medications. I point out to them, if appropriate and after a careful review of the case, that it appears the child, for whatever reason (and it is generally genetic transmission of AD/HD—a transmission that is extremely potent), has what we understand to be a deficit of some specific neurotransmitters in his or her brain that I can fix by giving the child a medication to boost these brain chemicals. In this sense, the use of medications to treat AD/HD amounts to a straightforward medical intervention to a medical problem. Other examples of such intervention are glasses for nearsightedness and insulin for diabetes. It would be unreasonable to demand of a child, "Just make yourself see better" or "Just make your blood sugar go down by pumping out more insulin," while ignoring, of course, that the child may be blind as a bat without glasses or have a pancreas that isn't pumping out insulin. It's therefore important to realize that the medication treatment of AD/HD is not some sort of malevolent, drug-pushing, puppet-master control of a child, but a restoring of normal levels of inarguably required neurotransmitters to get objective, demonstrably better results. It's the same as getting your kid glasses or insulin if needed.

Accurately prescribing these medications is not difficult and can be done relatively easily *if the physician knows what he or she is doing and why.* It goes without saying that there are numerous intellectually vigorous and compassionate physicians who are excellent at what they do, many of whom are simply intuitively good at it. However, if your child is being treated by one who is not or if you are reading this to figure out what is the best road on which to proceed, read on.

## Two Fairy Tales and Your Child's Medications: Things You Need to Know

Everything that needs to be learned about drug therapy for kids with AD/HD (and adults) is contained in two fairy tales: "Goldilocks and the Three Bears" and "Cinderella." Don't laugh. The message is profound as well as sophisticated.

Goldilocks, if you recall, discovered three bowls of porridge: one was too cold, one was just right, and one was too hot. That's the way medication should be prescribed. It should always be started at a low dose. Only God Almighty—or the deity of your choice—knows what dose and drug your kid should be on. The kid doesn't. The parent doesn't.

And the doctor *certainly* doesn't. This is where the art and science of medicine meet.

The science is simple: form a hypothesis, do an experiment, get a conclusion. This experiment will be done on your child. There is no other way. The art is the intuitive feel, based on the history, past clinical experience with different drugs, and a gut level hunch, as to which class of medications, or stimulants versus nonstimulants, would be the appropriate medication to select.

The smart (and humble) physician always starts at incredibly low levels, no matter what the dosing charts say. For small kids, I've been known to start them as low as one-fourth of a five-milligram Ritalin tablet, or one-fourth of a five-milligram brand tab of Adderall or Dexedrine. We go up from there. In this manner, we visit the first bowl of porridge, which is almost always too cold: the medication doesn't work but neither does it give side effects. It is imperative to find a medication that can be *tolerated* before obsessing about whether it will adequately control the symptoms. What difference does it make if the kid can concentrate wonderfully but he feels miserable and sick at his stomach or like his head is in a vise for the better part of the day?

The second bowl of porridge is the golden realm of good, solid drug therapy. This is the dosing level where the medication works *perfectly*, at least for a time. It is neither too hot nor too cold. All symptoms that could reasonably be expected to be treated with a medication are under superb and perfect control, and the child, or adult, has *no side effects*.

If there are side effects, we are now in the too-hot bowl of porridge, pharmacologically speaking. This means that no matter how well the drug works, there are side effects. I do not tolerate side effects in my practice. Children do not tolerate them well either—at least, not happily. This is where the oft-heard lament "Please don't turn my kid into a zombie" is heard. The "zombification" of kids occurs because of sloppy and unimaginative prescribing by unenlightened, cognitively dull practitioners who don't seem to care whether their pint-sized, or even adult-sized, patients feel like death warmed over on their potions or not. Do not tolerate this type of medication side effect in your child or in yourself. It is unnecessary and the mark of a sloppy practitioner.

The tale of Cinderella is somewhat more straightforward. In the Doc Cady version of this tale, Cinderella has the wicked stepmother and stepsisters. The fairy godmother comes by, waves her wand, fits her with the fancy duds, and sends her to the party. But at the stroke of midnight, as one of my munchkin patients told me, "She turns back into Cinderella."

That actually is not the point of the story. The point is, the spell is *over*! There are three take-home points:

1. How fast does the spell take effect?
2. How long does it last?
3. How fast does it fade?

In Cinderella's case, the answers are, respectively, the following:

1. Instantly
2. Until the stroke of midnight.
3. "When the clock strikes twelve." All at once. Catastrophically.

Between these two fairy tales, there is almost nothing left to discuss in terms of picking medications. The first strategy is that *whatever* is picked needs to be tolerated, needs to get the job done, and needs to give *no* (or easily manageable[8]) side effects.

It's when you look at Goldilocks and Cinderella together that a cohesive understanding of the issues involving sophisticated and tactful prescribing emerges. Here are some quick points:

- **Ritalin lasts four hours** by itself. Dexedrine, about the same. Focalin, the right-handed, purified form of Ritalin, also lasts about four to five hours.
- **Adderall tablets last from six to twelve hours**, depending on how high you push the dose (and how well it is tolerated). Adderall XR lasts either eight hours or twelve hours, and all points between, depending on the patient's brain chemistry.[9]
- **Desoxyn lasts between four and six hours.**
- Focalin, even though it may be much better tolerated than conventional Ritalin, lasts in its current formulation for only about four to five hours.
- **Provigil will probably last anywhere from eight to twelve hours** when it emerges on the market in 2006 or 2007 in its rebranded form as Attenace (specifically for the treatment of AD/HD). It is unclear if multiple doses throughout the day will be required.

## Picking and Choosing a Medication

The fun in picking out what to prescribe is, first of all, to select a *class* of medications. Currently this boils down to, among only FDA-approved agents, the methylphenidate (Ritalin) class, the amphetamine class, or Strattera. I almost always put Strattera last because I am underwhelmed about the low probability of success. No currently published studies in the literature support the notion that Strattera is *ever* superior to a branded stimulant. Two head-to-head trials have been done with it against Concerta (twelve-hour sustained-release methylphenidate) as well as branded Adderall XR. Neither was pretty.

In making this first medication selection, I'm guided by the patient's history. Are there any blood relatives who have been on an AD/HD medication, and, if so, how did they do? Has the child, or adult, ever been on a previous trial of medication? If the patient is a teenager or older, I particularly pay attention to any history of illicit drug use, because I don't want to compound the problem by adding something that has the *potential* to be abused by someone who has a documented history of deliberately wanting to induce an altered state for purposes of warped enjoyment.

Following the selection of the class of medication, the real fun begins. Decisions that have to be made include the following:

- **How fast** does it need to kick in in the morning?
- **How long** does it need to last?
- **Does the child need fast or slow onset?** That is, does he seem to do better with a type of medication where there is fast onset and a blood level that peaks early or with a slower onset with a gradual upward trend during the day? (I refer to this as "curve matching": finding the right dosing "curve" of a medication to correspond to a patient's clinical needs.)

Here are some examples.

Concerta is probably the most elegant dosing form currently available. The delivery vehicle was so creative that it was patented and essentially created a company, Alza Pharmaceutical. Concerta looks like a little bitty cylindrical tablet, with an immediate-release coat of methylphenidate on the outside, a laser-drilled hole underneath, and a spongy compartment inside the pill that sucks in gut juice as the pill traverses the gastrointestinal tract. The first thing that happens is that the outside coating delivers a small burst of methylphenidate to the patient's system, much like the space shuttle's solid-fuel rocket boosters, helping it to get going. After that, the secondary delivery vehicle takes over. As the sponge inside the tablet sucks in gut juice, it expands, pushing the methylphenidate inside the tablet out the laser-drilled hole on the end, like an itty-bitty caulk gun (or cake-icing dispensing tube). For this reason, Concerta (referred to generically as OROS-methylphenidate) is consistently the most reliable medication for twelve hours of effect.

Nothing is perfect in pharmacology land, however. For some kids, the lower amount of methylphenidate in the morning, with a higher level in the afternoon, presents one of two pictures: either lack of effectiveness in the morning and then effectiveness in the afternoon or perfect effectiveness in the morning and then side effects in the afternoon when the medication peaks. There are strategies that are available to the sophisticated prescriber to easily deal with this, however.

Other types of Ritalin delivery vehicles have their own quirks. Ritalin LA, by Novartis, is a fifty-fifty release of Ritalin—half the total dose of the capsule delivered every four hours. It's exactly the same as taking the gold standard dosing of equal doses of Ritalin four hours apart. That's the good news. The bad news is that (a) sometimes kids don't need that much in the morning and it hammers them and (b) it lasts only eight hours. Concerta lasts twelve. And some studies actually suggest that Concerta has benefits on teenage driving extending out to an incredible sixteen hours or more! On the other hand, some kids need the higher level of medication in the morning, and Concerta will not be effective for them. You can't have it all!

Metadate CD, from Celltech Pharmaceuticals, is the only other game in town. It initially releases 30 percent of the methylphenidate and then the remaining 70 percent over the lifetime of the tablet. Think of it as an eight-hour version of Concerta.

Focalin, although not available as a sustained-release (SR) preparation in early 2005, is being researched and prepared by Novartis for a launch later in 2005 in SR form. The estimated duration of this drug, as of early 2005 estimates, is eight to twelve hours.

In the amphetamine class, Adderall (available as either a branded formulation of mixed salts of amphetamine in an instant-release form or as Adderall XR, which delivers half the dose every four hours), fairly well owns the market. I have seen this medication work when basically nothing else, short of methamphetamine, would. In most cases it is remarkably well tolerated and "smooth." Indeed, the introduction of the instant-release tablet form of this drug to the market was heralded on the CompuServe AD/HD forum—on which I met the author of this book in 1993—as a medication that was nothing short of a miracle, working when conventional Ritalin and Dexedrine did not. Shire, the maker of Adderall and Adderall XR, has probably done more than any other company to develop educational products for patients, families, and doctors regarding AD/HD and its treatments. This company is also at work on patch forms, which can be absorbed through the skin, of Ritalin (methylphenidate) and mixed salts of amphetamine (Adderall).

But we are forgetting Cinderella at the ball. If you recall, she had to get out of there because when the clock struck midnight it was *over*. This relates to "how fast does the medication run out at the end of the day?"

In general, the medications lasting four to five hours have their spells wear off rapidly, and the eight-hour meds tend to run out faster than the twelve-hour ones. Both Concerta and Adderall fade much better at the end of the day, resulting in less—or no—stimulant rebound. "Stimulant rebound" is that dreaded event where all the AD/HD hyperness, or ADD inattentiveness and flakiness, come out in force at the end of the day after having been stuffed into their container all day like a misbehaving genie in his magic lamp. If the transition back into uncontrolled AD/HD or ADD is sudden and abrupt, a child (or adult) can go from the sweet light of reason to a snarling little terror with a hair-trigger temper in five minutes. If the effects fade more gently, the transition is generally much more palatable for all concerned.

## Other Off-Label Possibilities

Several other medications are useful to think about. All of the following discussion of these agents is "off label." That means that the FDA does not specifically approve them for these purposes but it is conventional practice to use them because the peer-reviewed medical literature supports their use and reasonable studies have been done that show that *these agents are safe and effective for these uses.* These medications may work for the following:

- **Adjunctive or even exclusive control of AD/HD,** in mild cases
- **Treatment of sleep problems** either as a result of the primary medication or, in most cases, the fading of AD/HD medications *before* bedtime
- **Appetite boosting**
- **Temper and explosiveness control** (including bipolar disorder existing alongside AD/HD)

Clonidine (brand name Catapres) and guanfacine (brand name Tenex) are both agents that masquerade as little norepinephrine molecules in the brain and bind to specific receptors, called the alpha 2 receptors. This actually has a number of interesting effects, including, theoretically, the release of increased amounts of norepinephrine as well as serotonin from neurons in the brain. In this sense, both of these drugs can be thought of as releasing the brakes on these two types of neurons to allow more of their good neurochemicals to be released. This can result in better concentration, less hyperness, less irritability, and a generally improved disposition.

Clonidine lasts around four hours; guanfacine lasts at least eight to twelve hours or even longer. Both of these agents can drop blood pressure if overenthusiastically prescribed. Therefore, slow upward adjustment and not unimaginative prescribing is advisable. Both of these agents can be used for additive control of stubbornly resistant AD/HD symptoms during the daytime and for sleep problems at night when daytime medications are wearing out.

Appetite boosting is another area for medication intervention, if required. It can be accomplished, most conservatively, by the safe and benign cypropheptadine (brand name Periactin), an antihistamine. This agent essentially fools the brain into thinking there is not enough serotonin in the body, causing the brain to send out signals to eat more carbohydrates. Carbs represent the building blocks of serotonin. Hence, the patient wants more carbs and begins to gain weight.

A more radical approach is to take the good news–bad news duality and to work it to advantage. The atypical antipsychotics, as a class, have been noted by the FDA to sometimes cause unacceptable munchiness and severe weight gain, leading to morbid obesity and the explosive onset of full-blown adult diabetes. As a rule, the most offending members—as well as two of the best in terms of antipsychotic effectiveness, to be fair— are Zyprexa (olanzapine) and Risperdal (risperidone).

I will typically use *microdosing* of these agents for creating more munchiness in my patients. My favorite for this tends to be Risperdal, largely because it is available in the tiniest prescription strength. To put this in context, a typical adult schizophrenic or bipolar patient who needs complete symptom control with full-bore dosing will require from two to six milligrams of the drug and sometimes more. I start my small patients who need it with a quarter of a one-quarter-milligram tablet, or one-sixteenth of a milligram. That is one thirty-second of the smallest dose in the lower range for adults, and one ninety-sixth the top dose in an adult. (This is the equivalent of giving a "one cent" dose instead of a "dollar" dose, to a rough order of approximation.) Incredibly, that very small dose can have potent benefits—both in inducing appetite as well as controlling irritability. It may also be useful for sleep. Dosing can be adjusted in a Goldilocks strategy. This is the soft touch in psychiatry: the child is not hammered with the drug, but the dosing is just high enough to do the job without the child feeling drugged.

One final agent, specifically for sleep, is trazodone (brand name Desyrel). This was a fairly unsuccessful antidepressant, which, although it worked reasonably well—if patients could tolerate it—had the nasty habit of conking out many people out during the daytime. In the competitive antidepressant marketplace, it had limited usefulness. However, by using smaller doses of this medication one to two hours before bedtime, its ill effects could be used to an advantage: it could actually help your child or teen fall asleep faster or stay asleep during the night. My dosing ranges are from one-quarter of a fifty-milligram tablet in small munchkins up to as much as one hundred to two hundred milligrams in older teens who are having severe sleeping problems.

Again, Goldilocks must apply. If the child feels hammered the next morning, the dose is too strong. One caution applies: priapism[10] can occur in males. I have never seen a case of it in children nor do I know any of my colleagues who have, but it's listed as a potential side effect in the package insert and you need to know about it.

In terms of stabilizing symptoms of bipolar disorder—which can occasionally co-exist with severe AD/HD—the two classes of medication that are frequently useful are the mood stabilizing drugs (lithium and the anticonvulsants) as well as the atypical antipsychotics. These are beyond the scope of this book and this chapter.

Many times, parents come across physicians who want to prescribe SSRIs (selective serotonin reuptake inhibitors) or other antianxiety agents for kids with AD/HD. Remember that these are not AD/HD meds. They are for other conditions. If your child is depressed or anxious, these medications may well be appropriate. Generally speaking, I find that Lexapro (escitalopram) is the cleanest and best tolerated. It is also available in liquid form, meaning that I can give it in as small a dose as I like. With kids, I will frequently start at one milligram, which is one-tenth the standard adult starting dose.[11] A review of the pros and cons of all of the antidepressants and antianxiety drugs is also outside the scope of this book.

## The Risk of Medications

Finally, a chapter on medication would not be complete without some mention of risk. In general, nothing is safe in life. The very fact that you are above ground and breathing means that something bad may happen to you. Airplane parts have come crashing out of the sky and gone through people's roofs, so even staying in bed with the covers pulled up over your (or your child's head) is not 100 percent safe.

Essentially, when I start medications, my standard line is that "anyone can have any side effect on any medication, including seizures, coma, and death." Generally speaking, the side effects I encounter are not nearly that catastrophic, although I have had patients have seizures on medications for which that was not even listed as a risk factor in the drug information sheet (the package insert) that comes with it.

In terms of the stimulants, two recent reports are of note:

Recently, two verified case reports have emerged of patients having liver problems with Strattera. These problems went away when Strattera was removed, came back when Strattera was reintroduced, and went away again when the drug was removed. It should be noted that out of all of the millions of scripts issued these are the only two case reports recorded. These two reports were identified as idiosyncratic reactions—which means that, by pure dumb bad luck, these two people's systems could not handle this particular medication for some reason. These types of reactions do occur. They are impossible to predict. They are also *rare*. Statistically, these amount to one of those "it's just one of those things"—but it's big news if it happens to be your or your child's liver on the line.

Also recently, for no definable scientific reason, Health Canada removed Adderall XR from the market in Canada. I have seen the data used to justify this decision. In my opinion, Health Canada's decision was bogus and without scientific merit. In fact, the net statistical information currently available is that, incredibly, you have *less* of a risk of dropping dead from sudden cardiac death if you are on Adderall XR than if you are unmedicated. Clearly, that can't be right. But it certainly doesn't appear that this is a killer drug. For all medications, of course, it is absolutely critical to take a solid medical history, screen for family histories of heart disease or other abnormalities, and then proceed calmly, deliberately, and cautiously.

In closing this chapter on medications, it is useful to reflect on two other areas: future research and continuity with the past.

In terms of state-of-the art research, marvelous progress is being made by people like Daniel Amen, MD,[12] Robert Hunt, MD,[13] and others in terms of SPECT imaging of the brain. SPECT stands for single photon emission computed tomography, and it has significant advantages over some of the more well-known types of brain images. Among other things, the precise location and amount of activity in the brain when the patient is *doing something*—such as concentrating on a tough computer test, which shows ability to pay attention, or even playing a piano or writing poetry with a pen in hand—can be frozen in time shortly after the mildly radioactive (and apparently very safe) testing chemical is injected intravenously. This is something that is impossible to do with any other available scanner, because with the rest of them the patient must be doing the activity *inside the scanner*. That significantly limits the scope of what can be done. There are also technical aspects of these studies that make them easier and less costly than the other types of brain scans.

To be sure, other forms of examining the living brain are useful; these include PET (positron-emission tomography) scans and functional MRI (magnetic resonance imaging). Essentially, however, SPECT offers what no other brain-scanning technique for looking at the living brain can offer: a view into the brain's function, frozen like a fly in amber, at a precise moment *when its owner was doing something*. All of the brain-scan techniques that show what a living, functioning brain is doing are useful, and they can reveal certain areas of the brain that appear to be functioning too poorly or too excessively.

With regard to SPECT, Daniel Amen was the first to develop this technique and publish on it. As a result of the greater sensitivity of picking up brain dysfunction by looking into the living, functioning human brain, and also of scrupulously correlating symptoms reported by patients with what he saw on SPECT scans of the same patient, he described not two but *six* types of AD/HD: inattentive, hyperactive, over-focused, temporal lobe, and limbic types and the ring-of-fire subtype. Read his book *Healing ADD* for more information.[14]

Finally, we cannot forget the past. Many years ago, Stanley Greben wrote a masterpiece in the psychotherapeutic literature: a nifty little paper called "On Being Therapeutic."[15] He found that no matter what their theoretical orientation, all of the most potently effective psychotherapists had the same character: the qualities of empathy and concern, warmth, interaction, the ability to arouse hope, the positive expectation of improvement, not giving up, reliability, and friendliness. After all, what else is there?

Ultimately, no matter how good the pills are, the final outcome will be in the hands, minds, and skills of the practitioners who deploy them. Nowhere is this summarized more eloquently than in the words of William J. Mayo, MD, in 1935.

> Perhaps the ability not only to acquire the confidence of the patient, but to deserve it, to see what the patient desires and needs, comes through the sixth sense we call intuition, which in turn comes from wide experience and deep sympathy for and devotion to the patient, giving to the possessor remarkable ability to achieve results.

In evaluating medication strategies for your child, remember, it's not the pills, it's the skills. Accept nothing less than total optimization with minimal to nil side effects. It's theoretically practical and eminently doable. Your child deserves nothing less.

## About the Chapter Author

*Dr. Louis Cady obtained his medical degree in 1989 from the University of Texas Medical Branch in Galveston, Texas. He then trained in psychiatry at the world famous Mayo Clinic, beginning his practice of child, adolescent, adult, and forensic psychiatry in Evansville, Indiana, in 1993. In addi-*

*tion to his conventional medical training in medicine and psychiatry, Dr. Cady has subsequently received additional training in age-management medicine from the Cenegenics Medical Institute in Las Vegas, Nevada. In 2005, Dr. Cady founded the Cady Wellness Institute.*

Dr. Cady is a highly sought after speaker for the pharmaceutical industry, particularly in his expertise in the treatment of AD/HD as well as severe and resistant depression, and an author. You are invited to visit his websites at www.drcady.com and www.cadywellness.com.

## Notes

1. In this chapter, the relatively standard abbreviation of *AD/HD* will refer to all types of attention deficit disorder, including those with and without hyperactivity, or as one of my moms put it, "The AD/HD without the *H*."

2. *DSM-IV-TR*. American Psychiatric Association, 2000.

3. L. Cady, "Food Allergy Testing for AD/HD and Autism," *The Autism File*, no. 13, *www.autismfile.com*.

4. Amino acids are the fundamental building blocks of protein—there are about twenty of them in the human diet. You get them when you eat protein, soy, hot dogs, turkey, fish, beans, etc.

5. Yes, you read that right.

6. J. Biederman, "Practical Considerations in the Stimulant Drug Selection for the Attention-Deficit/Hyperactivity Disorder Patient—Efficacy, Potency and Titration," *Today's Therapeutic Trends* 20, no. 2 (2002): 311–28.

7. Recall that Benadryl is an antihistamine—which means it blocks histamine receptors and dopes you up. Provigil is kind of an anti-antihistamine. That means it actually *increases* histamine levels in the brain. This is associated with waking you up. That's why it works great for narcoleptics. It's also why "waking up the brain" in those with AD/HD seems a reasonable purpose for this drug.

8. "Easily manageable," in my practice model, means that the patient does not end up ultimately experiencing unsettling side effects that are intolerable and compromise his or her quality of life. I'm willing to tolerate a *little* loss of appetite, as long as the child will make up for it later in the day. I'm unwilling to tolerate headaches, stomachaches, head-in-a-vise feelings, etc. Nor should you!

9. A frequently overlooked nicety with Adderall is that if the patient is particularly and exclusively sensitive to the dextroamphetamine sulfate component of the medication, the effect is four hours of good control with an uncertain amount of potential misery or side effects after it. This is why some people do not benefit from Adderall XR past eight hours—it is, in essence, two releases of mixed amphetamine salts four hours apart. With many people, this

works spectacularly well, but a *few* respond only to the dextroamphetamine sulfate component and not to the rest of the salts.

10. Priapism is a case where a certain portion of the male anatomy goes up but doesn't go down. While this might appeal to the Hugh Hefner types, it is considered a medical emergency because *gangrene can occur*. This could ruin your whole day. Generally, a trip to the emergency room is required with an injection in a most alarming location.

11. Again, note that this is an off-label use of this medication, which is not FDA approved for use in children. The peer-reviewed medical literature almost uniformly supports its safety, efficacy, tolerability, and the logic of using it for both depression and anxiety in kids. It may also be a less potent drug than the heavy hitters, such as Depakote or Risperdal, for quelling severe temper, irritability, and explosiveness. It is one of the "ultimates" for treatment of premenstrual dysphoric disorder in adolescent females, which can certainly exacerbate AD/HD symptoms. Zoloft (sertraline) is the next best alternative. Both drugs are relatively clean in terms of interactions with other medications.

12. www.amenclinic.com; www.brainplace.com. Also, Daniel G. Amen, *Healing ADD: The Breakthrough Program that Allows You to See and Heal the Six Types of Attention Deficit Disorder*. New York: Putnam, 2001..

13. The Center for Attention, Nashville, Tennessee (www.centerforattention.com).

14. Daniel G. Amen, *Healing ADD*

15. S. Greben, "On Being Therapeutic," *Canadian Psychiatric Journal* 22 (1977): 371–80.

# 10

# The Impact Children with AD/HD Have on Their Families

## Managing Life

**T**HE FAMILY raising a child with AD/HD encounters an immense task—keeping the family unit as normal as possible with a child who does not conform or meet expectations (yours and society's). Families need balance to progress, yet children with AD/HD manage to keep families unbalanced in varying degrees. These degrees change, often daily, and confusion develops. One thing is always certain, that nothing is ever certain. We often can't predict how our child will act from one situation to the next, or one day to the next, which leaves parents feeling like they are on an emotional roller coaster. Visiting friends, going to the grocery store, attending your place of worship, or going out for dinner, is not a matter of just picking up and going. This is a privilege that belongs to other families. Instead, decisions to leave the house with the child who has AD/HD are usually made, and well thought out, in advance. To not think ahead may result in a disastrous experience for all.

Because of the uncertainty and confusion, as well as the ramifications of inappropriate behavior and a parent's reaction to the stress, numerous problems often confront the family. Some families are drawn and stretched in every direction. The child usually becomes the center of the attention, with other family members (usually mom) trying to pull it all together and maintain a sense of balance.

Balancing a family in which one or more members have AD/HD is like trying to put together a solid green jigsaw puzzle made up of fifteen hundred pieces. The difference, of course, is that you can dump the puzzle back into the box and forget about it. When it's your family, you have to keep working at it day after day. Every member of the family is affected. The mother's role usually needs to be redefined (with other family members taking on some of the responsibilities of caring for the child) or the child with AD/HD becomes her all-consuming focus. Role overload is the result, a situation that can become highly problematic for some mothers and even result in depression or drug abuse. Mothers of children with AD/HD are often critical of their parenting skills and are apt to blame themselves for the difficulties their children experience.

Unless you or your spouse grew up with a family member who had a disability, you are not equipped for parenting a child with special needs. You are not prepared to lose your parental autonomy to well-meaning professionals, and feelings of resentment and loss of self-esteem often develop. Your child with AD/HD may require special education classes, which means you will be more involved in his education than most other parents and this adds additional stress. You may recognize the need to reach out to other families with children who have AD/HD for support yet hesitate because you are uncomfortable sharing family matters with others. Marriages often are at risk because of the constant turmoil, stress, and the unpredictability of daily living. As noted in other chapters, siblings of children with AD/HD suffer also.

The intent of this chapter is not to paint a bleak picture for families struggling to raise their children, but to provide insight into the various feelings experienced by family members and the types of situations that can develop within the family. You may want to look at this chapter as preventive medicine.

## Privacy between Spouses

With the addition of children to the family, husbands and wives find that their sexual intimacy is affected. Spontaneity is abandoned. Workload also becomes a consideration, as mom becomes, in many cases, the primary caretaker. If mom has a full-time job outside of the home, plus the responsibility for the majority of housework and meeting the needs of all her children, she then has two jobs and is often too exhausted to engage in sexual intimacy with her spouse. Now add a child with AD/HD, the focused time that must be spent with the child, financial concerns, and job-related pressures, and you have a horrendous strain on the marital relationship.

In the 2000s, almost all couples have less time to spend together, due to job and child care demands. However, parents of children with AD/HD need to examine issues that may be less obvious to them such as anger, frustration, and disappointment—intense feelings that may unconsciously affect your marital relationship. Resentment or frustration can build if one spouse feels the other is not a contributing partner in managing household chores, shopping, homework, and caring for the overall needs of the children. When negative feelings become overwhelming and a spouse finds fault with the other, avoidance may be the outcome! (See the introduction, by Mary D. Squire, PhD, for additional information on the strain on marital relationships and the family.)

"Our sexual relationship was greatly affected by the birth of our son," says a woman from Kansas. "We expected some changes initially, but felt that once our baby began to sleep through the night, we would have more time for each other. He was almost thirty-six months old before he began sleeping through the night. During those months we were both totally exhausted from a lack of adequate sleep. Sex was the last thing on our minds. Unfortunately, our sexual life never returned to where it once was. Now, at age five, our son who is very impulsive and hyperactive, leaves me exhausted by the end of the day. I usually go to bed early, an hour or so after he falls asleep, because I am so tired and he awakes so early each morning. One of us has to get up with him, and since my husband won't, he's my responsibility. For all practical purposes our sex life is over."

In retrospect, this mother advises that parents make an extra effort to keep their sex life alive. "Take advantage of grandparents who offer to babysit your child," she adds. "Ask if your child can spend one night every other weekend. Drop him off a few hours before his bedtime and pick him up first thing Saturday morning, for instance. In reality they are watching your child a total of only a few hours, but you have all night with your spouse. Or find a babysitter who will spend the night while you check into a nearby motel."

One very frustrated parent told a good friend of their dilemma. One day when the friend was watching the nine-year-old, she asked the child what she did when she awoke during the night. The child replied that she always went to her parents' room. When the friend asked why, the child shook her head and said, "I don't know. I just always do." The friend suggested that the next time she awoke she just use the bathroom and go back to bed. She explained that unless it was an emergency she shouldn't go into her parents' bedroom because they needed their sleep to care for her the next day. The child said, "Okay." From that day on the child no longer wandered into her parents' bedroom during the night. Sometimes it takes a supportive and caring friend, a therapist, or the child's doctor to reach your child. Please don't be afraid to reach out to others who are in a position to help.

## Uncooperative Grandparents

"I've given up on my mother and father," says another mother. "They don't believe that my daughter has a medical problem and see my husband and me as the reason she acts the way she does. Consequently, we don't do much with them because every time we are all together the strain is unbearable. They become upset with my daughter and raise their voices. She cries and it hurts to see her get so upset. We visit them but only for a short period of time—a half hour here and there. Hopefully, as she matures, we'll be able to spend more time with my family. I really could use the emotional support that my parents could offer us if things were different."

Some parents were raised during the time when children were to be seen but not heard. If this is true in your case, you have probably received more than your share of questions and suggestions about your child-rearing practices. ("Why can't you control that child? What that child needs is a good spanking. Then he'll learn who's the boss in your house. When you were younger, we never let you . . .") If this has gone on for some time, you may already resent your parents' interference in your family's life.

As discussed earlier, grandparents need to know the truth so they can understand that not all children can be parented the same. You and your spouse are probably the only people who are going to teach your parents about AD/HD. Provide them with reading material or videos on AD/HD, invite them to attend a support group meeting with you or ask them to attend an AD/HD conference, or introduce them to other parents with AD/HD children. It may take a long time before you reach them, but once you get through life will be much better.

I knew I had finally reached my father when one day my son came flying through the house and a relative raised her voice to him. My dad responded, "Raising your voice won't help, because his medication wore off twenty-five minutes ago. He can't help it. He's not running to make you angry." It took me seven years—and my patience was tried many times during those years—but I was eventually heard. Persistence can and does pay off.

"My mother-in-law is a former teacher. I expected her to understand AD/HD, but she didn't," says one father. "Every time she started questioning why we did this or that or offering suggestions, I calmly explained why it wouldn't work with our daughter. I finally got through to her, and as it has turned out she's an excellent grandmother to our daughter. She's very patient and will explain or repeat directions calmly. Even the temper tantrums don't get to her. She remains calm and can settle our daughter down quickly when necessary. Parents need to realize that instead of getting upset with grandparents' reactions to their child, they must patiently teach their parents about AD/HD, even if it takes years. Children need grandparents in their lives."

"We have had critical grandparents to deal with," says Julie from Newark, Ohio. "I inundated my mother-in-law, who lives far away, with literature about AD/HD. After she read it all (and I hope understood AD/HD more), she rarely criticized our parenting methods or our choice to use medication for our son."

But what about grandparents who believe you are literally abusing your child by medicating him? Like Julie, from Newark, Ohio, you can flood them with information and hope they'll take the time to read it. Or you can take the tough-guy approach and tell grandparents in no uncertain terms that your child is your responsibility and that you will no longer listen to their criticisms or accusations. You might phrase it like this: "Mom and Dad, you know nothing about attention-deficit hyperactivity disorder. John and I have conferred with Jessica's pediatrician, a child psychologist, and a pediatric neurologist and they have recommended that Jessica take medication so she can succeed in school. Despite what you may think, we did not make this decision haphazardly. We can no longer tolerate your interference in this matter. John and I will send you information on AD/HD. We hope you will take the time to become informed. Until that time, we do not want to discuss this with you nor do we intend to listen to your criticisms. I'm sorry it had to come this, but we find your remarks very upsetting. We need your love and support, not your accusations." Sometimes it becomes necessary for parents to cut ties with family for an indefinite period of time to maintain their own sanity and concentrate their energies on their child and their family unit.

## Unique Demands from Non-AD/HD Siblings

When a child becomes the focus of mom's and dad's attention, stress-related problems will develop with other siblings. Factors that will influence the amount of stress a sibling feels depend on many variables, including the following:

- **The severity of the AD/HD** (mild, moderate, severe) and how it affects the lifestyle of the family. Is the family often governed by the behavior of the child with AD/HD? Is the family limited by the number of things they can do together as a unit because of the child?
- **The age of the child with AD/HD.** Is the child the oldest or the youngest, for instance?
- **How the parents react to the child with AD/HD.** Are parents patient and understanding? Or do they frequently display anger and frustration with the child?
- **The temperament and personality of the child with AD/HD.** Is he demanding and nasty? Does he constantly pick on or grab at the sibling, disregard rules of privacy, etc.? Or is he basically a pleasant child, but inattentive?

Siblings should be encouraged to express their feelings about their brother or sister with AD/HD, even if those feelings are negative. Parents should listen carefully and express empathy. You might say it this way: "I know it's difficult to see and hear your brother running around the house causing trouble and upsetting everyone. We all need to be patient until he learns that those behaviors are not appropriate. Thank you for sharing your feelings with me." Encourage your child to treat his sibling with kindness and compassion—the same way he would treat a friend who had a medical problem.

In general, most older non-AD/HD children will feel empathy for their sibling with AD/HD, especially when parents have made a point of explaining the disorder to them. Yet depending on how parents manage home life, some siblings may feel unimportant, ignored, and even angry at times because of the amount of focused time that is bestowed on the child with AD/HD. Parents must make an effort to spend quality time alone with each of their children, not just with the child who has AD/HD.

Many parents say that the biggest problems they experience with their non-AD/HD children is related to behavior. Not surprisingly, when the non-AD/HD sibling was younger, parents report that the sibling copied or mimicked the behavior of the child with AD/HD in what they felt was an attempt to get the same attention, even if the attention resulted in punishment. Remember, charts work just as well with children who do not have attention deficit or hyperactivity as they do for the child with AD/HD. Other parents expressed concern about the younger sibling. Was the younger sibling really mimicking the inappropriate behavior or actually displaying his own symptoms of AD/HD?

One mother reported her daughter suddenly couldn't do her homework once she realized that her older brother had a tutor. "She wanted a tutor also, so for a time I acted as her tutor while continuing to emphasize the good work she did on her own. Eventually, she reached the point where she insisted that she could do her work without my help."

Another parent wrote that her son required extended care beyond what was normal for his chronological age because of fine motor difficulties. "By the time my daughter was four she was dressing and bathing on her own," says the parent. "When she realized her older brother couldn't dress himself without help or cut his food without assistance, she told me she couldn't do these things for herself anymore. I tried to explain to her why her brother couldn't do these things for himself yet, but she was too young to really understand. To encourage her to once again dress and bathe herself, I started using a chart. Every time she got dressed or bathed on her own, I gave her a sticker. For every three stickers, I gave her an inexpensive trinket. Before I knew it, things had returned to normal and we were able to stop using the chart system."

For children with fine motor disabilities, talk with your pediatrician about occupational therapy in which children can learn to button clothes, tie shoes, zip clothing, and improve writing skills. For children who have difficulty bathing because they can't hold a bar of soap and use a wash cloth, buy liquid soap with a pump and a sponge with a wooden or plastic handle. Transfer shampoo and conditioners to pump bottles that prevent children from spilling or pouring too much on their hair. An occupational therapist can provide helpful hints for all types of fine motor difficulties your child may experience.

## Parental Isolation and Curtailed Social Activities

Some parents feel a degree of confinement in terms of interests and activities they enjoy. They may not be able to attend as many social functions or participate in activities outside the home like they used to.

Parental isolation may occur when it consistently becomes difficult to find a reliable babysitter to care adequately for your child (all of your friends go out together on a weekly or semiweekly basis, but you are not able to go). Feelings of isolation also may develop when you are unable to attend certain functions due to your child's behavior—you begin to feel alienated from other parents. This may be especially true when your child's relationships with peers suffer. Parents often become friends with the parents of their children's classmates. These friendships are often formed through scouting, team sports, and school functions. If your child experiences difficulties getting along with classmates or teammates, other parents may unconsciously or consciously alienate you from their group. If your child has difficulties with team sports and is unable to participate due to poor coordination skills or attention problems, you lose the opportunity to form friendships with other families who attend school games and practices.

But you don't have to settle for parental isolation according to one mom, who says, "I wanted my son to be involved in Boy Scouts, yet I didn't feel comfortable sending him off to meetings alone as I was never sure what his behavior would be like. So I made the decision to be the den leader. That way my son could participate and I could keep an eye on him. As a result, I've worked closely with other parents and have made some new friends. Bobby is not able to play the team sports he would like to participate in, but I do take him to the school games when he wants to go. Many of the Boy Scouts play sports, so I see some of the families at the games and I sit with them. I also do other volunteer work around the school."

Isolation may also occur when friends invite you and your spouse to their home for dinner and you don't return the invitation because you are so uncomfortable with your child's behavior. Eventually the invitations stop. "This has happened to us many times over the last ten years," says one mom. "Taking people out to dinner instead isn't quite the same in many peoples' minds. I think they are offended, but trying to have a dinner party with our two children in the house won't work even with a babysitter. When our children finally reach that magical age, I'm going to invite every one I know over to my house for a sit-down dinner." Invitations don't have to be for a sit-down dinner. Try outdoor entertaining during the warmer months. Invite your friends over for a barbecue, pool party, or another informal get-together. Encourage guests to bring their children along and make it a family gathering.

## Parental Stress and Related Health Problems

Stress can also threaten the body's welfare. As parents we face stressful, and sometimes overwhelming, situations almost daily with our child who has AD/HD. Writes one mother from Aurora, Illinois, "I can't help but feel I should be reading your book instead of contributing to it. There are so many times my frustration with the noise, confusion, and destruction involved with AD/HD have me so overwhelmed. I often have to remove myself from some situations by time and space, try to relax (deep breathing in my own time-out), and then consider my next move. My natural reaction would be rashness, anger, and loss of control. On my worst days, my son is spinning while my daughter hangs on my legs crying. I have irritable bowel syndrome and have lost substantial weight attempting to deal with the stress levels present in my home and my life."

Not surprisingly, many parents who submitted tips for this book also enclosed letters. A few courageous parents were willing to share more than a handful of parenting tips. One of them permitted me to excerpt her letter with the hope that it will help others avoid what she has faced. As you read the following, keep in mind that although no definitive statistics are available at this time, the substance abuse, depression, and other problems she describes are alarmingly common.

I grew up in an affluent setting, was well educated, got married, and was finally enjoying my teaching career. I was a good teacher in difficult circumstances. I had good rapport with students and parents, was well respected, and I had good control in my classroom. I felt as if I could handle anything. I was confident and successful.

When I became pregnant, I was excited, but scared. It was a difficult pregnancy and I almost lost my baby. The thirty-six hours of excruciating labor further added to my doubts. My beautiful son, Anthony, was finally in my arms and I was filled with wonder, anticipation, and fear.

In the past, I thought nothing of relaxing with a glass of wine or two. It calmed me down, and I enjoyed how it made me feel. After nine months of abstaining from alcohol, I couldn't wait to receive the celebratory wine that accompanied the first hospital dinner.

As soon as I was home, alone with my son, I discovered an extremely irritable, colicky baby who wouldn't stop crying. The sadness of being at home alone while my friends were teaching made it worse. Our pediatrician recommended drinking a beer to help my breast milk and to calm my nerves. This sounded like a great idea and I wholeheartedly participated.

Anthony was either very happy or very miserable and that affected all of those around him, especially me. It was difficult to go out and I often felt that he would never stop crying. I asked myself, "Is this what motherhood is all about?" I couldn't understand how I could handle thirty-six sixth graders, but one baby, my precious son, could cause me to feel such powerlessness, frustration, and disappointment in both him and me.

So I began to self-prescribe the medicine, alcohol, which could temporarily dull the pain and emptiness and mask the feelings of inadequacy. While munching on a sandwich at lunch, a beer (or two) would be a regular accompaniment. After Anthony would go down for a nap, I would reward myself for such hard work and treat myself to a glass of wine.

As Anthony grew we were thrilled with his development, but his temperament was even more extreme. The hopes of him "growing out of it" diminished, but we had no clue that this behavior was related to AD/HD. I thought his problems were attributed to "bad" mothering and this was my punishment.

I desperately needed a break, so I began a part-time job when Anthony started preschool. This was a great time for me, and I was allowed to gather back some of my own value and worth. I easily gave birth to a beautiful daughter. When Anthony turned three, we moved to another city, and I settled into the role of wife and mother of two. I began to see such a difference in my two children. Sara was a delightful, happy baby who was easy to please. However, Anthony didn't like her at all, and an intense sibling rivalry developed from the start. I was beginning to feel those unacceptable feelings mothers aren't supposed to feel: anger, resentment, and loss of a "normal" child.

As my depression increased and my self-esteem and confidence decreased, my dependence on alcohol grew. I would drink over any stress. Although I rarely got drunk or lost control, I still craved the relief that the alcohol would provide. To those around me I was doing well, but inside I was crumbling.

Now I don't want the reader to believe that I am blaming or excusing my behavior. No one made me drink that glass of wine. People encounter far greater stress and cope in healthier ways than I did. I understand that alcohol dependency is influenced by many factors. Those include a strong hereditary component and a history of abuse, both of which pertain to me. I also read an article describing the relationship between drug and alcohol abuse and living with a difficult or disabled child. The findings did cite a strong correlation. Although it's not an excuse to drink, it shows that I was not alone in how I coped with my stress and anxiety.

When Anthony turned three several things had gone from bad to worse. His behavior was more overt; his anger was immense, self-esteem low, [and] he was having trouble at school and with his peers. I drank even more heavily, as our home became a battleground. I started to suspect AD/HD, but at this point the negative consequences of my depression and drinking were beginning to show, so my input at school and with my husband was disregarded. I was the "identified patient" and although my problems at home did contribute to Anthony's symptoms, it was frustrating that no one looked past this. This delayed Anthony's diagnosis and the treatment he so desperately needed.

In the summer of 1992, with the help of family and a caring therapist, I entered a treatment facility for alcoholism. I had reached my bottom, and it was finally time to surrender. My family needed a whole, healthy mother and wife, and I began to learn the tools to be effective in this role. I have had to deal with my past pain and the role I allowed my son's AD/HD to play in my mental health. I now cope with the strength of a twelve-step group, therapy, a women's support group, and CHADD [Children and Adults with Attention-Deficit/Hyperactivity Disorder]. I haven't felt the need to take another drink since I entered treatment. Anthony's AD/HD is still very difficult to handle at times, but I understand his pain and see his courage.

He was finally properly diagnosed last year, began medication and counseling and we experienced a dramatic improvement. He is a successful, hardworking third-grader, who still struggles with the symptoms of AD/HD, but he is on his way. Finally knowing what we are dealing with makes things much easier.

Being in recovery, and providing the advocacy, support, and strength my son needs, has been a difficult balance to achieve and one I struggle with daily. I know for me to be the best for my family, I need to first take care of myself. I realize it's easy to become enmeshed in our AD/HD children and, although these children need and require additional support, they especially need our help so they can someday be able to meet their own needs. I believe by modeling to my family when things get really tough that I seek help and support, then Anthony will hopefully feel comfortable doing the same.

Therefore, I urge all parents who are struggling to successfully raise an AD/HD child to be aware of the stress involved and to find healthy outlets to reduce the stress. Also, if you recognize yourself in my story, I hope and pray you can borrow a piece of courage and ask for help.

## Marital Stress

"A strain on a marriage? I've thought that there would never be a time that we wouldn't be discussing our son's problems and how to manage it and him," says Mary from Troy, New York. Is this the right school? Is this the best response to his behavior? It went on and on. Guilty feelings on some days when you didn't even seem to like your child. I'm surprised we're still married and I am still sane."

Mary says three things helped her cope:

- "**Talking with a neighbor** whose older child was being evaluated for AD/HD. Just sharing feelings helped tremendously."
- "**Working with a wonderful child psychologist** to help us with our son's behavior. She not only helped him but me. When I'd walk into her office and flop in the chair, she would say, 'He's been driving you up a wall, right?' Just her simple statement made me feel that she really understood how I was feeling."
- "**All-day, five-day-a-week school**. Initially, we started out with one-half-day kindergarten because I really felt that was what is best for kids. But in my son's case, structure was more important. I was told that these children do best with a lot of structure. So at the school's suggestion we went to full day. He's doing better in school and after school also."

"My advice is to communicate with your spouse," says Debra from Crown Point, Indiana. "Pull together on what actions to take and carry through on those actions consistently. Meet with teachers, doctors, and other professionals together, whenever possible. Find a support group for children with AD/HD."

"My husband has ADD and both of our children have AD/HD," explains Gail, who is from Montana. We didn't know my husband had attention deficit disorder until a few years ago. Now, I understand why he's always acted the way he does (doesn't finish projects he's started, is always doing three different things at the same time, never seems to be paying attention when people try to talk with him, unorganized—I could go on and on), but it's difficult parenting two children with AD/HD when your spouse can't follow through on things that you agree on. He has little patience for the children. The very things he hates in them are the same symptoms he displays. I feel like I am in a no-win situation. My husband doesn't realize what effect his ADD has on our family and on me, and he's not willing to try medication or therapy. We've tried marriage counseling, but half the time he forgets about the sessions or shows up a half-hour late. He has a winning personality and is a good talker. Usually by the time we leave a session, he's the 'good' guy and I'm the person who causes all the problems in our home. The stress and anxiety between us and with the children is very obvious. In the meantime, I try to keep a positive attitude by remembering that my husband and children are not intentionally trying to make me miserable. I found that if I mentally dwell on the characteristics I don't like, I tend to get angrier and angrier. One's thoughts can sneak up and create havoc, so I no longer permit myself to dwell on the negative. If my husband starts a project and doesn't finish it, for instance, I either finish it myself or hire someone else to do it."

"I work full time. It's distressing to get a call at two in the afternoon from your child's teacher telling you how out of control your child was that day," says Diane, the mom of an only child. "While you are talking to the teacher, a problem arises at work, and then your husband calls to tell you he has to work late. When you get home, your child is still wound up and he demands dinner right away.

"I have not been on a vacation in six years! My husband works a lot of long hours at night. I have a spa membership I have only used a few times in the last few years. I have a stationary bike in my dining room that I rarely get a chance to use. How are we supposed to cope? The only time I can find peace in my home is in the morning. A cup of coffee on the porch swing at 6 a.m. is the closest thing to heaven I can find on earth. If I don't get my 6 a.m. break, the day is off to a bad start. I collect my thoughts at this time."

Julie, from Newark, Ohio, has a son with AD/HD and says, "My husband and I have had many stress-filled talks about 'what to do with him.' Whenever our son is having particularly difficult problems at school, I become so frustrated that I make myself ill. My blood pressure would be much lower if I did not have a child with AD/HD. I can directly trace my gastrointestinal problems to incidents involving my son.

"My husband and I make a concerted effort to seek out calm and peace. We live out in the country where it is peaceful. We vacation where it is quiet and calm. Other people may think we are boring because of this, but they do not realize that it is necessary for our mental health—we have all the excitement we can handle just with our son."

## Taking Care of Mom and Dad

It's easy to understand how parents can become stressed out or burned out. Couples often feel isolated, not just mom. They find they have little time to go out and have fun with friends, and even less time for each other. Mothers fight stress and depression from juggling everything, and fathers find extra work to do at the office. Friends and relatives often blame the parents for the problems in the home. Marriages are pushed to the limit, causing a breakdown in communication and sometimes collapsing under the strain. One parent wrote about her marriage of twenty years, which was ending in divorce. "My husband says he's had it. He wants a divorce so he can have a chance at some happiness and peace before he's too old. He's forty-five and our son with AD/HD is fourteen. Well, I've had it too, but moms aren't suppose to walk out. It's not motherly."

So what can parents do to preserve their sanity, keep their marriages intact, and not buckle under the pressure? Here are some suggestions:

- **Keep the lines of communication open** with your spouse. Neither of you is to blame for your child's disability, so support each other. Make a date with your spouse every week or every other week and go out and enjoy yourself. Do not talk about your child on your night out. This time is reserved for you and your relationship. Remember that relationship, in many cases, was there before your child.
- **Compliment yourself** out loud daily, either in private or in front of your child.
- **Remind yourself daily that your child did not choose to have AD/HD**, nor does he do things intentionally to make your life miserable. I have a note posted on my bathroom mirror, written as though from my son, that I read the first thing every morning. It says, "Please remember, this was NOT my choice, Mom."
- **Never look at yourself as a bad parent.** In fact, you are probably a much better parent than most, although you may not feel like it

at times. Instead, look at yourself as a good parent of a child who has a disability. Remind yourself that your family is not like most families and, considering the challenges you face, you're doing remarkably well.

- **Hang a copy of the serenity prayer** somewhere where you can see it and read it every day. Mine is in my kitchen next to the sink. When you read it, carefully think about what it says ("God grant me the serenity to accept the things I cannot change, Courage to change the things I can, and the Wisdom to know the difference"). You cannot change the fact that your child has AD/HD, but some of his actions you can help change slowly. Recognize and accept what you can and cannot change in him.

- **Do something nice for yourself every day** because you deserve a break (take thirty minutes to read a book, soak in the tub, watch television, pursue a hobby, work a crossword puzzle, write a letter, or polish your nails), even if it means getting up earlier or postponing your bedtime.

- **Look for funny or humorous things** that your child does and then laugh out loud with him. I remember one morning when my oldest son, then four, was throwing a major temper tantrum in my bathroom. He kept throwing himself up against the bathroom vanity. I turned away in an attempt to ignore him, when suddenly the screaming and yelling stopped. When I looked over at him, I burst out in uncontrollable laughter. He had caught his bib overalls on the knob on the drawer and was literally hanging by his shoulder strap, feet off the ground. For a brief second, I felt his embarrassment and shock, but then he, too, burst out laughing. We laughed for weeks over that incident. (My children are now 21 and 17, and I could write a book on just the things they did when they were younger that now make me literally laugh out loud. My boys, of course, do not recall all of the incidents, but they sure remember enough of them. Many nights we have sat and talked about those incidents and laughed and laughed. Does it really matter now that when my son was seven he sprayed black paint on our tan front door, or that when he was four he flushed toilet paper down all the toilets until they were overflowing? It seemed like a crisis at the time, and in some ways it was because it was so frustrating, but now it is just plain funny.)

- **Don't take everything seriously**. Look at the long-range implications of a given act. If there are none, then ask yourself, "What am I upset about?"
- **Evaluate your day**. Take delight in those things you did right. If you handled a situation poorly, decide how you'll handle it the next time but don't dwell on mistakes.
- **Don't try to be a perfect parent**. Perfect parents don't exist. Even if other families look picture-perfect to you, remember that those families have their own challenges to face.
- **Talk with a caring, nonjudgmental friend or therapist**. You need someone to talk with when you truly believe you can't handle life with your child any longer.
- **Locate an AD/HD support group** for parents in your area and attend the meetings. This is an excellent place to vent frustrations and meet others parenting children with AD/HD.
- **Find an energetic teenager** (preferably one between sixteen and nineteen years old) who enjoys children. This teenager can help lighten your load a few evenings a week until your child's bedtime. The sitter can entertain your child while you clean house, prepare dinner, run errands, spend some time alone with your spouse, or just relax. Many children with AD/HD cannot be left unattended.
- **Exercise at least three times a week**. This can be an opportunity to spend time with your spouse as well. Exercise has been shown to reduce stress. A daily walk of a mile or two in your neighborhood can make you feel so much more fit and relaxed.
- **Delegate tasks to other members of the family**. Parents must share responsibilities equally.
- **If you find you are fighting depression**, drinking, or using drugs to cope and get through the day, talk with your spouse and seek professional help immediately. Don't wait until the situation gets further out of control.
- **Use behavior management techniques** every moment of the child's day.
- **Take a vacation from your child** as often as possible. If you can't get away for a week, then get away on a weekend. And don't feel guilty about being away from your child. You'll come back with renewed strength, a better outlook on life, and more patience.

- **Set realistic expectations for your family life**. Letting go of the dream you once had is the first step toward acceptance—things will never be perfect, so don't expect perfection from yourself or your child.
- **Focus on the positive qualities your child possesses**, rather than the negative. Make a list of your child's strengths and review the list when you become discouraged. Also, work on positive language. For example, substitute "energetic" for "hyperactive," "assertive" for "demanding," "decisive" for "impulsive," etc.
- **Lower your expectations**. It's okay not to have a perfectly clean house every day.

Remember always that there are families who are struggling in far worse ways than you may be able to imagine. Your child is a challenge, but could you imagine life without her? Of course not!

For more information on how AD/HD affects families, read my chapter on family dynamics in my book *AD/HD and Teens: A Parent's Guide to Making It Through the Tough Years* (Taylor, 1995).

# Afterword

**M**ANY YEARS have passed since the first edition of this book was released, but not that many that I can't recall all of the challenges that were placed in my path as a parent. There was a time when I would crawl into bed at night and cry: I cried for my sons, and I cried out of pity for myself because I was so tired! Tired of behaviors that I was working to change, tired of trying to find another way, tired of appointments with doctors and therapists and teachers, and tired of yet another diagnosis and new medications. And, believe me, there were days, many days, when I would have liked to have just scrapped the whole idea of chart systems and rewards and consequences and thrown in the bucket. But I couldn't. I had to believe that all this extra parenting stuff would, in the end, make a difference for my children. And, most important to me, I cried because I worried about what a thousand tomorrows from now would bring for my children. But never, ever did I give up!

Dear readers, I have walked in your shoes! I know how long the days and nights can be. I know the pain and the fears and the work involved. I know the sacrifices that must be made, sometimes over and over and over, but I also know all the joys that can come from this parenting experience.

My oldest son, Christopher, was diagnosed with AD/HD at the tender age of 2½ and was eventually deemed by his doctor as one "of the worst cases" he had experienced to date. The first indications of hyperactivity-impulsivity surfaced around the age of twelve months, and by the age of eighteen months, he had been in the emergency room for stitches several times.

Everything in the house was locked up, and I mean everything, and not with childproof locks because he was able to disable those. I could not let him out of my sight for even a minute. As he grew, his creative and explorative mind got him into trouble, often putting him into physical danger. (He moved quickly! And sometimes I just wasn't quick enough.) By the time he was four, he began showing a great interest in computers and seemed to intuitively know how those darn things worked. So we bought him his own computer, which in the late 1980s was a major expense. He was thrilled. And we were thrilled for him—until the day we found that he had taken it apart. We couldn't understand why he would destroy something that he clearly enjoyed so much. When we replaced one of our computers a year after that, we gave him the discarded one. That too was eventually dismantled, as was the next. But one day, when we found him working on one of the dismantled computers, he said he was "working to make it run again." We left him alone to do just that.

By the time Christopher was in fifth grade he was teaching younger children in the after-school program how to use a computer. He was compensated and brought home a weekly paycheck. We were delighted to find that he did this well, but he was still very hyper and impulsive and quite a handful. When Christopher entered high school, he not only knew a lot about computers, but he had learned how to hack them. We didn't know of this ability until the school called to tell us that he had hacked into their system. He thought it was funny; we were horrified. My greatest fear was that his impulsivity would get him into serious trouble with the legal system.

Christopher is now twenty-one years old. No one who knew him as a child can believe where he is today. Nor can they believe how much he has changed. My once hyperactive-impulsive bundle of joy, whose future I was so concerned about, is an information technology manager at a hotel (part of his job is to keep hackers and crackers out!), owns a small web hosting company, and works part-time at a popular office supply store. All his energy, which was running wild as a youngster, is now focused. He has ambitions and goals, and I believe he has the determination and ability to achieve whatever he sets his mind on. We did not know then that his first computer was actually an investment in his future. And little did we know that his dismantling of computers and his rebuilding was teaching him a lifetime skill.

We suspected Blake had AD/HD at a very young age. Although he was somewhat hyperactive and occasionally impulsive, we realized that his greatest challenge would be his inability to attend. When he entered preschool at age four, it became even more obvious that he was in his own world. We watched him carefully and eventually he was diagnosed with AD/HD after he eloquently described to his doctor the way his mind worked. We fostered his talent in drawing, and he took many awards through grade school. By middle school, his extra energy needed to be channeled. Football turned out to be a perfect solution for some of it. He made varsity after his freshman year (although a few times he failed to notice that he was supposed to be out on the field during a game), faithfully making practice and working out as was demanded of him. Now seventeen, he is still deciding what career to pursue after graduation, but he is planning on continuing his education.

There was a time when it felt like everything I was doing was in vain. But looking back, I realize that, everyday that I worked on my parenting skills and kept my children on track until they could learn to do so on their own, progress was being made. It never jumped out at me, because one behavior problem seemed to be replaced by another over the years, but true progress is often most easily recognized by outcome, I believe. I couldn't be more proud of my children. Given the challenges they have had to face, I commend them.

So the next time you are feeling overwhelmed and worried about the future, please know that your efforts will pay off. Please don't ever give up.

## In Conclusion

We are all fortunate to be parenting a child with AD/HD in the 2000s. Never before have parents had the resources they have now. We can turn to many excellent books for information, parent support groups that offer intellectual and emotional support, and national organizations that provide educational information to parents and teachers. There are also magazines and newsletters and national conferences and local workshops for parents and educators. Plus, a growing number of professionals now specialize in AD/HD. If you haven't read the foreword and introduction to this book, be sure to do so. Both Drs. Cady and Squire work with children and teenagers who have AD/HD. (Please be sure to check the bibliography and the appendix for a listing of some of the resources available to you.)

Many of today's health and parent organizations (both local and national) would never have been formed if it hadn't been for courageous adults with disabilities or their families. How is it that one family accepts their child's disability so fully that they want to reach out to other parents facing the same challenges, while another family struggles in silence?

It is because of their acceptance and attitude! One family meets the challenges head-on because, despite the challenges, they see their child as a remarkable human being of immeasurable value. They find hope in learning about the disorder and giving support to other parents attempting to cope with it. They do not sit and wonder who's to blame. Rather, they live life fully, realizing that what happened yesterday cannot be changed. Your attitude can make this job of parent either rewarding or rewardless. The choice is yours.

As parents we must make commitments to our children because they desperately need all our love, patience, understanding, and strength if they are to become healthy, functional adults. Our role as parents will not always be easy. We may face many challenges as our children grow and mature. But remember, AD/HD is an obstacle placed in our path. The size of that obstacle is determined by the beholder. If we see it as overwhelming, it will be just that. If we can look at it as only a detour, we can find ways to adapt and adjust. Our purpose as parents is to provide our children with the opportunities to be the best they can, to raise healthy children in mind and spirit, and then to send them on their way with our blessings. As parents of children with AD/HD, our parenting road is just bumpier than most, but that road is not impossible to travel. Take it one day at a time. When you wake up in the morning do so with renewed spirit. Ask for strength to make it through the day with love and patience, and forget about yesterday. The recovering alcoholic takes it one day at a time. We would be wise to do the same.

I encourage all parents to take a good look at their child. If your child has an interest in a special area, do what you can to enhance and support that interest. That one talent, special interest, or hobby can be the bright light in the life of a child who faces daily frustrations. Hobbies and special talents are areas where children with AD/HD can excel, gain competence, and build self-esteem. Believe me, as a parent your heart will soar with joy when you witness your child succeeding and excelling in an area special to him or her. Often those memories are enough to get you through that next demanding day with a smile on your face and love in your heart.

I hope that you can release any negative thoughts, discover your child's qualities, and share him with the world by standing behind him, not in front of him. Reach out to others who are raising a child with AD/HD. Let them find a comforting friend in you. Become an advocate in the schools and community. Please join me. Together we can make a difference!

# Resources

## Parent Support Groups in the United States

**ADDA (Adult ADD)**
P.O. Box 543
Pottstown, PA 19464
484-945-2101
www.add.org

**Attention Deficit Information Network, Inc.**
58 Prince
Needham, MA 02492
781-455-9895
www.addinfonetwork.com

**Children and Adults with Attention Deficit Disorders (CHADD)**
8181 Professional Place, Suite 201
Landover, MD 20785
301-306-7070
800-233-4050 (to request information packet)
www.chadd.org

**National Resource Center on AD/HD: A Program of CHADD**
www.help4adhd.org

# Parent Support Groups in Canada

**CHADD National Office**
Standard Life Postal Outlet
P.O. Box 43021
Edmonton, Alberta, Canada T5J 4MB
866-434-9004
613-731-1209 (local)

CHAPTERS

TADA Edmonton Chapter of C.H.A.D.D. Canada
Standard Life Postal Outlet
Box 43021
Edmonton, Alberta, Canada T5J 4MB
780-406-5212

Calgary Chapter of C.H.A.D.D.
147 Edgeland Road NW
Calgary, Alberta, Canada T3A 2Y3
403-225-8512

Lethbridge Chapter of C.H.A.D.D.
2002 20 Avenue S
Lethbridge, Alberta, Canada T1K IG5
403-329-4789

Vancouver Chapter of C.H.A.D.D.
P. O. Box 74670
Vancouver, British Columbia, Canada V6K 4PA
604-222-4043

C.H.A.D.D.
825 Carling Avenue
Ottawa, Ontario, Canada KIS 2E7
613-72-8482

# General Resource List

**America Academy of Child and Adolescent Psychiatry (AACAP)**
3615 Wisconsin Avenue SW
Washington, DC 20016
202-966-7300
www.aacap.org/index.htm

**American Psychiatric Association (APA)**
1000 Wilson Blvd., Suite 1825
Arlington, VA 22209
www.psych.org/index/cfm

**American Psychological Association**
750 1st Street NE
Washington, DC 20002
800-374-2721
202-336-5510
www.apa.org

**CADRE (Consortium for Appropriate Dispute Resolution in
    Special Education)**
Direction Services, Inc.
P.O. Box 51360
Eugene, OR 97405
541-686-5060
800-695-0285
www.directionservice.org

**Center for Effective Collaboration and Practice**
1000 Thomas Jefferson Street NW, Suite 400
Washington, DC 20007
202-944-5400
888-467-1551
www.cecp.air.org

**Center for Mental Health Services**
Substance Abuse and Mental Health Services Administration
Rm. 12-105 Parklawn Building
Rockville, MD 20857
301-443-8956
www.samhsa.gov

**Center on Positive Behavioral Interventions and Support**
1761 Alder Street
1235 University of Oregon
Eugene, OR 97403
541-346-2505
www.pbis.org

**Council for Disability Rights**
205 West Randolph, Suite 1645
Chicago, IL 60606
312-444-9484
www.disabilityrights.org

**ERIC Clearinghouse on Disabilities and Gifted Education**
Council for Exceptional Children
(Project is no longer in operation, but a substantial website of disability-
    related material is still available)
www.ericec.org

**Families and Advocates Partnership for Education (FAPE)**
(Project is out of operation, but website provides information on IDEA
    for parents)
www.fape.org

**International Dyslexia Association**
Chester Building #382
8600 LaSalle Road
Baltimore, MD 21286
800-222-3123
410-296-0232
www.interdys.org

**JOB Accommodation Network**
West Virginia University
P.O. Box 6080
Morgantown, WV 26506
800-526-7234
800-232-9675 (information on the ADA)
www.jan.wvu.edu

**Learning Disability Association of America**
4156 Library Road
Pittsburgh, PA 15234
412-341-1515
www.LDAamerica.org

## Learning Disabilities Association of Canada
323 Chapel Street, Suite 200
Ottawa, ON K1N 7Z2
Canada
613-238-5721
www.LDAC-taac.ca

## National Alliance for the Mentally Ill
Colonial Place Three
2107 Wilson Blvd., Suite 300
Arlington, VA 22201
800-300-6710
www.nami.org

## National Association of Private Special Education Centers
1522 K Street NW, Suite 1032
Washington, DC 20005
202-408-3338
www.napsec.com

## National Association of Protection and Advocacy Systems
900 Second Street NE, Suite 211
Washington, DC 20002
202-408-9514
www.napas.org

## National Center for Learning Disabilities
311 Park Avenue South, Suite 1401
New York, NY 10016
888-575-7373
212-545-7510
www.ncld.org/research/index/cfm

## National Center for the Dissemination of Disability Research
Southwest Educational Development Laboratory
211 East Seventh Street, Suite 448
Austin, TX 78701
800-266-1832
512-476-2286
www.mcddr.org

**National Council on Disability**
1331 F Street NW, Suite 850
Washington, DC 20004
202-272-2004
www.ncd.gov

**National Clearinghouse on Postsecondary Education for Individuals with Disabilities**
George Washington University
HEATH Resource Center
2121 K Street NW, Suite 220
Washington, DC 20037
202-973-0904
800-544-3284
www.heath.gwu.edu

**National Dissemination Center for Children with Disabilities (NICHCY)**
Box 1492
Washington, DC 20013
800-695-0285
www.nichcy.org

**National Institute for Learning Disabilities**
107 Seekel Street
Norfolk, VA 23505
877-661-6453
757-423-8646
www.nild.net

**National Institute of Mental Health (NIMH)**
Public Inquiries
6001 Executive Blvd.
Room 8184
MSC 9663
Bethesda, MD 20892
866-615-6464
301-443-4513
www.nimh.nih.gov/healthinformation/adhdmenu.cfm

**National Mental Health Association**
2001 N. Beauregard Street, 12th floor
Alexandria, VA 22311
703-684-7722
800-969-6642
www.nmha.org

**National Mental Health Information Center**
P.O. Box 42557
Washington, DC 20015
800-789-2647
www.mentalhealth.org

**Nonverbal Learning Disorders Association**
2446 Albany Avenue
West Hartford, CT 06117
800-570-0217
www.nlda.org

**Office of Special Education Programs**
Office of Special Education and Rehabilitative Services
U.S. Department of Education
400 Maryland Avenue SW
Washington, DC 20202
800-USA-LEARN
202-245-7459
www.ed.gov

**Parent Advocacy Coalition for Educational Rights (PACER)**
8161 Normandale Blvd.
Minneapolis, MN 55437
952-838-9000
800-537-2237 (toll free in Greater Minnesota)
www.pacer.org

**Parents Helping Parents: The Parent Directed Family Resource Center for Children with Special Needs**
3041 Olcutt Street
Santa Clara, CA 95054
www.php.com

**SADD National (Students Against Destructive Decisions)**
P.O. Box 800
Marlboro, MA 01752
877-SADD-INC
www.saddonline.com

**SpeciaLink**
The National Centre for Child Care Inclusion
P.O. Box 775
Sydney, Nova Scotia, Canada B1P 6G9
902-562-1662
866-902-6333
www.specialinkcanada.org

**Suicide Hotline**
800-SUICIDE (800-784-2433)

**TOUGHLOVE International**
P.O. Box 1069
Doylestown, PA 18901
215-348-7090
www.toughlove.org

**U.S. Social Security Administration**
800-772-1213
www.socialsecurity.gov

**Zero to Three**
(National Center for Infants, Toddlers, and Families)
2000 M Street NW, Suite 200
Washington, DC 20036
800-899-4301 (for publications)
202-638-1144
www.zerotothree.org

## Other National Organizations

**American Speech-Language-Hearing Association**
10801 Rockville Pike
Rockville, MD 20852
800-498-2071
www.asha.org

**Anxiety Disorders Associations of America**
8730 Georgia Avenue, Suite 600
Silver Springs, MD 20910
240-485-1001
www.adaa.org

**Autism Society of America**
7910 Woodmont Avenue, Suite 300
Bethesda, MD 20814
800-328-8476
301-657-0881
www.autism-society.org

**Child and Adolescent Bipolar Foundation**
1187 Wilmette Avenue
PMP #331
Wilmette, IL 60091
www.bpkids.org

**Depression and Bipolar Support Alliance**
730 N. Franklin Street, Suite 501
Chicago, IL 60610
800-326-3632
312-642-0049
www.dbsalliance.org

**MAAP Services, Inc**
(Services for Autism and Asperger Spectrum)
P.O. Box 524
Crown Point, IN 46308
219-662-1311
www.maapservices.org

**Obsessive Compulsive Foundation, Inc.**
674 State Street
New Haven, CT 06511
203-401-2070
www.ocfoundation.org

**Tourette Syndrome Association**
42-40 Bell Blvd.
Bayside, NY 11361
718-224-2999
www.tsa-usa.org

## Gifted Children

**The Council for Exceptional Children**
1110 North Glebe Road, Suite 300
Arlington, VA 22201
703-620-3660
www.cec.sped.org

## Homeschooling Resources

**American Homeschool Association**
P.O. Box 3142
Palmer, Alaska 99645
800-236-3278
www.americanhomeschoolassociation.org

**Home School Legal Defense Association**
P.O. Box 3000
Purcellville, VA 20134
540-338-5600
www.hslda.org

**National Home Education Network**
P.O. Box 1652
Hobe Sound, FL 33475
www.nhen.org

## Parent Training and Information Centers

*The following are state programs that are funded by the government and are wonderful resources for parents of children with AD/HD.*

## ALABAMA

Special Education Action Committee, Inc.
3207 International Drive, Suite C
P.O. Box 16174
Mobile, AL 36616
334-478-1208
800-222-7322 (Alabama only)


## ALASKA

Alaska P.A.R.E.N.T.S., Inc.
(Parents as Resources Engaged in Networking and Training Statewide)
540 International Airport Road, Suite 200
Anchorage, AK 99518
907-563-2246
800-478-7678 (Alaska only)


## ARIZONA

Pilot Parent Partnerships
2150 East Highland Avenue, Suite 105
Phoenix, AZ 85016
602-468-3001
800-237-3007 (Arizona only)


## ARKANSAS

Arkansas Parent Support and Information Network
Arkansas Disability Coalition
10002 W. Markham, Suite B-7
Little Rock, AR 72205
501-221-1330
800-223-1330 (Arkansas only)

CALIFORNIA

**Northern California Coalition for Parent Training and Information, Region I**

Disability Rights Education and Defense Fund
2212 Sixth Street
Berkeley, CA 94710
510-644-2555

**Northern California Coalition for Parent Training and Information, Region II**

Matrix, A Parent Network and Resource Center
555 Northgate Drive, Suite A
San Rafael, CA 94903
415-499-3877
800-578-2592

**Northern California Coalition for Parent Training and Information, Region III**

Parents Helping Parents
The Family Resource Center for Children with Special Needs
3041 Olcott Street
Santa Clara, CA 95054
408-727-5775

**Northern California Coalition for Parent Training and Information, Region IV**

Exceptional Parents Unlimited
4120 North First Street
Fresno, CA 93726
209-229-2000

Parents Helping Parents—San Francisco
1 Vincente Street
San Francisco, CA 94116
415-564-0722

Team of Advocates for Special Kinds, Inc.
100 West Cerritos Avenue
Anaheim, CA 92805
714-533-8275

## COLORADO

Peak Parent Center, Inc. (Parent Education and Assistance for Kids)
6055 Lehman Drive, Suite 101
Colorado Springs, CO 80918
719-531-9400
800-284-0251

## CONNECTICUT

Connecticut Parent Advocacy Center, Inc.
338 Main
Niantic, CT 06333
860-739-3089
800-445-2722 (CT parents only)

## DELAWARE

Parent Information Center of Delaware, Inc.
700 Barksdale Road, Suite 3
Newark, DE 19711
302-366-0152

## DISTRICT OF COLUMBIA

COPE Parent Training and Information Center
(Creating Opportunities for Parent Empowerment)
300 I Street NE, Suite 112
Washington, DC 20002
800-515-COPE
202-543-6482

## FLORIDA

Parent Education Network Project
Family Network on Disabilities of Florida, Inc.
5510 W. Gray Street
Tampa, FL 33609
813-289-1122
800-285-5736 (Florida parents only)

## GEORGIA

Parents Educating Parents
Georgia Arc Network
3680 Kings Hwy.
Douglasville, GA 30135
770-577-7771
800-322-7065

## HAWAII

Learning Disabilities Association of Hawaii
200 North Vineyard Blvd., Suite 310
Honolulu, HI 96817
808-536-2280

## IDAHO

Idaho Parents Unlimited, Inc.
600 N. Curtis Rd.
Boise, ID 83706
208-342-5884
800-242-4785

## ILLINOIS

Illinois Parent Centers on Disability Designs for Change
6 North Michigan Avenue
Chicago, IL 60602
312-857-9292
800-851-8728

**INDIANA**

IN*SOURCE
(Indiana Resource Center for Families with Special Needs)
809 N. Michigan
South Bend, IN 46601
219-234-7101
800-332-4433 (Indiana parents only)

**IOWA**

Iowa Pilot Parents
33 North 12th Street
P.O. Box 1151
Fort Dodge, IA 50501
515-576-5870
800-952-4777 (Iowa parents only)

**KANSAS**

Kansas Families Together, Inc.
501 Jackson, Suite 400
Topeka, KS 66603
913-233-4777
800-264-6343

**KENTUCKY**

Kentucky Special Parent Involvement Network
2210 Goldsmith Lane, Suite 118
Louisville, KY 40218
502-456-0923
800-525-7746

**LOUISIANA**

Project PROMPT
4323 Division Street, Suite 110
Metairie, LA 70002
504-888-9111
800-766-7736 (Louisiana parents only)

## MAINE

Special-Needs Parent Information Network
P.O. Box 2067
Augusta, ME 04338
207-582-2504
800-870-7746 (Maine parents only)

## MARYLAND

The Parents' Place of Maryland, Inc.
7257 Parkway Drive, Suite 210
Hanover, MD 21076
410-712-0900

## MASSACHUSETTS

Federation for Children with Special Needs
95 Berkeley
Boston, MA 02116
617-782-2915
800-331-0688 (Massachusetts parents only)

## MICHIGAN

Citizens Alliance to Uphold Special Education
3303 West Saginaw, Suite F-1
Lansing, MI 48909
517-886-9167
800-221-9105 (Michigan parents only)

Parents are Experts/Parents Training Parents Project
23077 Greenfield Road, Suite 205
Southfield, MI 48075
810-557-5070

## MINNESOTA

PACER Center, Inc.
4826 Chicago Avenue South
Minneapolis, MN 55417
612-827-2966
800-53PACER (Minnesota parents only)

## MISSISSIPPI

Parent Partners
3111 N. State Street
Jackson, MS 39216
601-366-5707

## MISSOURI

Missouri Parents Act
2100 S. Brentwood, Suite G
Springfield, MO 65804
417-882-7434

## MONTANA

Parents Let's Unite for Kids
MSU-Billings, SPED
1500 North 30th Street, Room 267
Billings, MT 59101
406-657-2055
800-222-7585 (Montana parents only)

## NEBRASKA

Nebraska Parents' Center
1941 S 42nd Street, #122
Omaha, NE 68131
402-346-0525
800-284-8520 (Nebraska parents only)

## NEVADA

Nevada Parents Encouraging Parents
6910 Edna Avenue
Las Vegas, NV 89114
702-248-6711
800-216-5188

**New Hampshire**

Parent Information Center
151 A Manchester Street
P.O. Box 2405
Concord, NH 03302
603-224-7005
800-232-0986

**New Jersey**

Statewide Parent Advocacy Network
35 Halsey Street
Newark, NJ 07102
201-642-8100

**New Mexico**

Education for Parents of Indian Children with Special Needs Project
Southwest Communications Resources, Inc.
P.O. Box 788
Bernalillo, NM 87004
505-867-3396
800-765-7320 (New Mexico parents only)

Parents Reaching Out-Project ADOBE
1000A Main Street NW
Los Lunas, NM 87031
505-865-3700
800-524-5176 (New Mexico parents only)

**New York**

Advocates for Children of New York, Inc.
105 Court Street
Brooklyn, NY 11201
718-624-8450

Parent Network Center
250 Delaware Avenue, Suite 3
Buffalo, New York 14202
716-853-1570
800-724-7408 (New York parents only)

Resources for Children with Special Needs, Inc.
200 Park Avenue South, Suite 816
New York, NY 10003
212-677-4650

### NORTH CAROLINA

Exceptional Children's Assistance Center
907 Barra Row
Davidson, NC 28036
704-892-1321
800-962-6817 (North Carolina parents only)

PARENTS Project
300 Enola Road
Morganton, NC 28655
704-433-2662

### NORTH DAKOTA

Pathfinder Family Center
Arrowhead Shopping Center
16th Street and 2nd Avenue SW
Minot, ND 58701
701-852-9426

### OHIO

Child Advocacy Center
1821 Summit Road, Suite 110
Cincinnati, OH 45237
513-821-2400

Ohio Coalition for the Education of Children with Disabilities
Training Center
933 High Street, Suite 106B
Worthington, OH 43085
614-431-1307

## OKLAHOMA

Parents Reaching Out in Oklahoma
1917 South Harvard Avenue
Oklahoma City, OK 73128
405-681-9710
800-PL94-142 (Oklahoma parents only)

## OREGON

Coalition in Oregon for Parent Education Project
999 Locust Street NE
Salem, OR 97303
503-373-7477

## PENNSYLVANIA

Mentor Parent Program
P.O. Box 718
Seneca, PA 16346
814-676-8615
800-447-1431 (Pennsylvania parents only)

Parent Education Network
2107 Industrial Highway
York, PA 17404
717-845-9722
800-522-5827 (Pennsylvania parents only)
800-441-5028 (Spanish, Pennsylvania only)

## PUERTO RICO

Asociación de Padres Pro Bienestar de Niños con Impedimentos de P.R., Inc.
P.O. Box 21301
San Juan, PR 00928
809-763-4665

## RHODE ISLAND

Rhode Island Parent Information Network, Inc.
175 Main Street
Pawtucket, RI 02860
401-727-4144
800-464-3399 (Rhode Island parents only)

## South Carolina

Parents Reaching Out to Parents of South Carolina, Inc.
2712 Middleburg Drive, Suite 203
Columbia, SC 29204
803-779-3859
800-759-4776 (South Carolina parents only)

## South Dakota

South Dakota Parent Connection
3701 W. 49th, Suite 200B
Sioux Falls, SD 57106
605-361-3171
800-640-4553 (South Dakota parents only)

## Tennessee

Support and Training for Exceptional Parents
1104 Tusculum Blvd., Suite 401
Greenville, TN 37745
615-639-0125
800-280-STEP (Tennessee parents only)

## Texas

Partners Resource Network, Inc.
1090 Longfellow Drive, Suite B
Beaumont, TX 77706
409-898-4684
800-866-4726

Partnerships for Opportunity, Development, Education and Resources
2300 West Commerce, Suite 207
San Antonio, TX 78207
210-222-2637
800-682-9747 (Texas parents only)

Special Kids, Inc.
P.O. Box 61628
Houston, TX 77208
713-643-9576

## UTAH

UTAH Parent Center
2290 East 4500 South, Suite 110
Salt Lake City, UT 84117
801-272-1051
800-468-1160

## VERMONT

Vermont Parent Information Center
1 Mill Street, Suite A7
Burlington, VT 05401
802-658-5315
800-639-7170 (Vermont parents only)

## VIRGINIA

Parent Educational Advocacy Training Center
10340 Democracy Lane, Suite 206
Fairfax, VA 22030
703-691-7826
800-869-6782 (Virginia parents only)

## WASHINGTON

Washington PAVE (Parents Are Vital in Education)
6316 South 12th Street
Tacoma, WA 98465
206-565-2266
800-5-PARENT (Washington parents only)

Specialized Training of Military Parents
12208 Pacific Hwy SW
Tacoma, WA 98499
206-588-1741
800-298-3543

Touchstones—More Alike than Different
Parent Advocacy and Access Project
6721 51st Avenue S
Seattle, WA 98118
206-721-0867

**WEST VIRGINIA**

West Virginia Parent Training and Information
371 Broaddus Avenue
Clarksburg, WV 26301
304-624-1436

**WISCONSIN**

Parent Education Project of Wisconsin, Inc.
2192 South 60th Street
West Allis, WI 53219
414-328-5520

**WYOMING**

Parent Information Center
5 North Lobban Avenue
Buffalo, WY 82834
307-684-2277

**PALAU**

Palau Parent Network
P.O. Box 1583
Koror, Republic of Palau 76740
01-680-488-3513

**VIRGIN ISLANDS**

Virgin Island Family Information Network on Disabilities
#2, Nye Gade
St. Thomas, USVI 00802
809-775-3962

# Online Resources

www.bridges4kids.com Everything from book reviews to Ask the Attorney

www.addedreality.com

www.adders.org (UK)

www.add.about.com

www.LDonline.com

*A Guide to Children's Medications*, from the American Academy of Pediatrics.
www.aap.org/family/medications.htm

"Facts for Families," a series of fact sheets that include information for
children, health insurance, how to seek help, and other topics from
the American Academy of Child and Adolescent Psychiatry.
www.aacap.org/publications/factsfam/index.htm

*Attention Research Update* (subscribe to free e-mail newsletter).
www.helpforadd.com

## Publications

ADDitude Magazine
P.O. Box 500
Missouri City, TX
888-762-8475
www.additudemag.com

# Bibliography

## General Resources

Adelman, Howard S., and Linda Taylor. *An Introduction to Learning Disabilities.* Glenview, IL: Scott, Foresman, 1986.

Alexander-Roberts, Colleen. *AD/HD and Teens: A Parent's Guide to Making It Through the Tough Years.* Dallas, TX: Taylor, 1995.

Amen, Daniel G. *Healing ADD: The Breakthrough Program that Allows You to See and Heal the Six Types of Attention Deficit Disorder.* New York: Putnam, 2001.

*American Psychiatric Association.* Diagnostic and Statistical Manual of Mental Disorders (DSM-IV-TR). 4th ed., Text Revision. Washington, DC: American Psychiatric Association, 2000.

Armstrong, Thomas. *ADD/AD/HD Alternatives in the Classroom.* Alexandria, VA: Association for Supervision and Curriculum Development, 1999.

———. "Driven to Distraction." *Parenting*, October 1990:32, 34, 38.

———. *In Their Own Way: Discovering and Encouraging Your Child's Personal Learning Style.* Los Angeles: Jeremy P. Tarcher, 1987.

*Attention Deficit Disorder (ADD).* Reston, VA: Council for Exceptional Children.

Bain, Lisa A. *A Parent's Guide to Attention Deficit Disorders.* New York: Bantam Doubleday Dell Publishing Group, 1991.

Barkley, Russell A. *Taking Charge of AD/HD.* New York: Guilford, 2000.

Cummings, Rhoda W., and Cleborne D. Maddux. *Parenting the Learning Disabled: A Realistic Approach.* Springfield, IL: CC Thomas, 1985.

Fowler, Mary Cahill. *Maybe You Know My Kid: A Parent's Guide to Identifying, Understanding and Helping Your Child with Attention-Deficit Hyperactivity Disorder.* Secaucus, NJ: Carol Publishing, 1999.

Friedman, Ronald, and Guy T. Doyal. *Attention Deficit Disorder and Hyperactivity.* 2nd ed. Danville, IL: Interstate Printers & Publishers, 1987.

Garber, Stephen W., Marianne Daniels Garber, and Robyn Freedman Spizman. *If Your Child Is Hyperactive, Impulsive, Distractible . . . Helping the ADD (Attention Deficit Disorder)/Hyperactive Child.* New York: Villard, 1990.

**283**

Goldstein, Sam, and Michael Goldstein. *Hyperactivity: Why Won't My Child Pay Attention?* New York: Wiley, 1992.

Hallowell, Edward M., and John J. Ratey. *Driven to Distraction: Recognizing and Coping with Attention Deficit Disorder from Childhood through Adulthood.* New York: Simon & Schuster, 1995.

Hartman, Thorn. *Attention Deficit Disorder: A Different Perception.* Grass Valley, CA: Underwood, 1997.

———. *Focus Your Energy: Hunting for Success in Business with Attention Deficit Disorder.* New York: Pocket Books, 1994.

Ingersoll, Barbara D., and Sam Goldstein. *Attention Deficit and Learning Disabilities: Realities, Myths and Controversial Treatments.* New York: Doubleday, 1993.

*Learning Disabilities.* Washington, DC: National Information Center for Children and Youth with Disabilities.

Lippert, Joan. "Help for Your Hyperactive Child." *Healthy Kids 4–10 Years,* Winter 1990:40–44.

McNamara, Barry E., and Francine J. McNamara. *Keys to Parenting a Child with Attention Deficit Disorder.* Hauppauge, NY: Barren's Educational Series, 2000.

Moss, Robert A. *Why Johnny Can't Concentrate: Coping with Attention Deficit Disorder.* New York: Bantam, 1990.

Parker, Harvey C. *The ADD/Hyperactivity Workbook for Parents, Teachers and Kids.* Plantation, FL: Impact Publications, 1994.

Phelen, Thomas W. *All about Attention Deficit Disorders: A Comprehensive Guide.* Glen Ellyn, IL: Child Management, 1993.

Silver, Larry B. *The Misunderstood Child: Understanding and Coping with Your Child's Learning Disabilities.* New York: Times Books, 1998.

Taylor, John F. *Helping Your Hyperactive Child.* Rocklin, CA: Prima Publishing & Communications, 1997.

## Resources for Parents

Alexander-Roberts, Colleen. *AD/HD and Teens: A Parent's Guide to Making It Through the Tough Years.* Dallas, TX: Taylor, 1995.

———. "Smart Discipline," *Christian Parenting Today.* May/June 1995: 35–37.

Crawford, Veronica. *Embracing the Monster: Overcoming the Challenges of Hidden Disabilities.* Baltimore: P. H. Brooks, 2001.

Flick, Grad L. *Power Parenting for Children with ADD/AD/HD: A Practical Parent's Guide for Managing Difficult Behaviors.* West Nyack, NY: Center for Applied Research in Children, 1996.

Garber, Stephen. *Facts about Medication and Other Strategies for Helping Children, Adolescents, and Adults with Attention Deficit Disorders.* New York: Villard, 1996.

Hallahan, James, James M. Kauffman, and John Wills Lloyd. *Introduction to Learning Disabilities.* Boston: Allyn & Bacon, 1999.

Hallowell, Edward M. *When You Worry about the Child You Love: Emotional and Learning Problems in Children.* New York: Simon & Schuster, 1996.

Hallowell, Edward M., and John Ratey. *Answers to Distraction.* New York: Pantheon, 1994.

————. *Delivered from Distraction: Getting the Most Out of Life with Attention Deficit Disorder.* New York: Ballantine, 2005.

————. *Driven to Distraction: Recognizing and Coping with Attention Deficit Disorder from Childhood through Adulthood.* New York: Simon & Schuster, 1995.

Hartman, Thom. *Attention Deficit Disorder: A Different Perception.* Grass Valley, CA: Underwood, 1997.

————. *ADD Success Stories: A Guide to Fulfillment for Families with Attention Deficit Disorder.* Grass Valley, CA: Underwood, 1995.

————. *The Edison Gene: AD/HD and the Gift of the Hunter Child.* Rochester, VT: Park Street Press, 2003.

Ingersoll, Barbara D. *Daredevils and Daydreamers: New Perspectives on Attention-Deficit/Hyperactivity Disorder.* New York: Doubleday, 1998.

Kilcarr, Patrick J., and Patricia O. Quinn. *Voices from Fatherhood: Fathers, Sons, and AD/HD.* New York: Brunner/Mazel, 1997.

Lynn, George T. *Survival Strategies for Parenting Your ADD Child: Dealing with Obsessions, Compulsions, Depression, Explosive Behavior, and Rage.* Grass Valley, CA: Underwood, 1996.

Monastra, Vincent J. *Parenting Children with AD/HD: 10 Lessons That Medicine Cannot Teach.* Washington, DC: American Psychological Association, 2005.

Nadeau, Kathleen, Ellen Littman, and Patricia Quinn. *Understanding Girls with Attention-Deficit Hyperactivity Disorder.* Silver Spring, MD: Advantage, 1999.

Pliszka, Steven R., Caryn L. Carlson, and James M. Swanson. *AD/HD with Comorbid Disorders: Clinical Assessment and Management.* New York: Guilford, 1999.

Quinn, Patricia O., and Kathleen G. Nadeau. *When Moms and Kids have ADD (AD/HD).* Washington, DC: Advantage, 2004.

Reiff, Michael I. *AD/HD: A Complete and Authoritative Guide.* American Academy of Pediatrics, 2004.

Reiff, Sandra. *The AD/HD Book of Lists: A Practical Guide for Helping Children and Teens with Attention Deficit Disorders.* San Francisco: Jossey-Bass, 2003.

Silver, Larry B. *Dr. Larry Silver's Advice to Parents on Attention-Deficit Hyperactivity Disorder.* New York: Times Books, 1999.

Sonna, Linda. *The Everything Parent's Guide to Children with ADD/AD/HD.* Avon, MA: Adams Media, 2005.

Steinberg, Mark, and Siegfried Othmer. *ADD: The 20-Hour Solution.* Bandon, OR: Robert D. Reed, 2004.

Taylor, John F. *Helping Your ADD Child: Hundreds of Practical Solutions for Parents and Teachers of ADD Children and Teens (with or without Hyperactivity)*. Roseville, CA: Prima Health, 2001.

Weingartner, Paul L. *AD/HD Handbook for Families: A Guide to Communicating with Professionals*. Washington, DC: Child & Family Press, 1999.

Wender, Paul H. *AD/HD: Attention-Deficit Hyperactivity Disorder in Children and Adults*. Oxford University Press, 2002.

Wilens, Timothy E. *Straight Talk about Psychiatric Medications for Kids*. New York: Guilford, 1999.

Windell, James. *Children Who Say No When You Want Them to Say Yes: Failsafe Discipline Strategies for Stubborn and Oppositional Children and Teens*. New York, NY: MacMillan, 1996.

Wyckoff, Jerry, and Barbara C. Unell. *Getting Your Child from No to Yes: Without Nagging, Bribing, or Threatening*. New York: Meadowbrook, 2004.

## Children's Activities

Bergstrom, Joan M. *School's Out: Now What? Creative Choices for Your Child*. Berkeley, CA: Ten Speed, 1990.

Hickman, Danelle, and Valerie Teurlay. *101 Great Ways to Keep Your Child Entertained While You Get Something Else Done: Creative and Stimulating Activities for Your Toddler or Preschooler*. New York: St. Martin's, 1992.

## Choosing a Doctor

Ripley, Suzanne. *A Parent's Guide: Doctors, Disabilities, and the Family* 1, no. 2 (May 1990). Washington, DC: National Information Center for Children and Youth with Disabilities.

Ward, Michael. *Self-Determination Revisited: Going Beyond Expectations*. NICHCY Transition Summary, no. 7 (September 1991). Washington, DC: National Information Center for Children and Youth with Disabilities.

## Chores

McCollough, Bonnie Runyan, and Susan Walker Monson. *401 Ways to Get Your Kids to Work at Home*. New York: St. Martin's, 1981.

## Communicating with Children

Faber, Adele, and Elaine Mazlish. *How to Talk So Kids Will Listen and Listen So Kids Will Talk*. New York: Avon Books, 1999.

———. *How to Be the Parent You Always Wanted to Be.* New York: Hyperion, 1992.
———. *How to Talk So Teens Will Listen and Listen So Teens Will Talk.* New York: William Morrow, 2005.

## Developing Social Skills

Duke, Marshall, and Stephen Nowicki. *Helping the Child Who Doesn't Fit In.* Atlanta: Peachtree, 1992.
Greene, Melissa Fay. "The Left-out Child." *Family Life* September/October 1990: 104–8.

## Gifted Children

Alexander-Roberts, Colleen. "Gifted Kids with Attention-Deficit Hyperactivity Disorder: What You Should Know and How You Can Help," *OURS,* September/October 1992: 16–19.
Dunn, Rita, Kenneth Dunn, and Donald Treffinger, *The Giftedness in Your Child: Unlocking Every Child's Unique Talents, Strengths, and Potential.* New York: Wiley, 1992.
Walker, Sally Yahnke. *The Survival Guide for Parents of Gifted Kids: How to Understand, Live With, and Stick Up for Your Gifted Child.* Minneapolis, MN: Free Spirit, 2002.

## Organizational Skills

Crary, Elizabeth. *Pick Up Your Socks and Other Skills Growing Children Need.* Seattle, WA: Parenting Press, 1990.

## Parenting Adopted Children

Melina, Lois R. *Raising Adopted Children: A Manual for Adoptive Parents.* New York: Harper & Row, 1986.
Schaffer, Judith, and Christina Lindstrom. *How to Raise an Adopted Child.* New York: Crown, 1989.

## Positive Discipline

Dinkmeyer, Don, and Gary D. McKay. *The Parent's Handbook.* Circle Pines, MN: American Guidance Service, 1989.
Kersey, Catherine C. *Don't Take It Out on Your Kids: A Parent's and Teacher's Guide to Positive Discipline.* Washington, DC: Acropolis, 1990.
Phelan, Thomas. *1-2-3-Magic: Training Your Preschoolers and Preteens to Do What You Want.* Glen Ellyn, IL: Child Management Press, 1985.

Robin, Arthur, and Sharon Foster. *Negotiating Parent-Adolescent Conflict.* New York: Guilford, 1989.

Varni, James W., and Donna G. Corwin. *Growing Up Great: Practical Steps for Parenting Your 6 to 10 Year Old.* New York: Berkley, 1993.

Windell, James. *Discipline: A Sourcebook of 50 Failsafe Techniques for Parents.* New York: Collier, 1991.

Wyckoff, Jerry, and Barbara C. Unell. *Discipline without Shouting or Spanking: Practical Solutions to the Most Common Preschool Behavior Problems.* Minnetonka, MN: Meadowbrook Press, 2002.

## School Related

Bean, Reynold. *How to Help Your Children Succeed in School.* Los Angeles: Price Stern Sloan, 1991.

Berger, Gilda. *The Gifted and Talented,* New York: F. Watts, 1980.

Bloom, Jill. *Help Me to Help My Child: A Sourcebook for Parents of Learning Disabled Children.* Boston: Little, Brown, 1991.

Canter, Lee. *Homework without Tears: A Parent's Guide for Motivating Children to Do Homework and Succeed in School.* New York: HarperPerennial, 1988.

Fiske, Edward B. *Smart Schools, Smart Kids: Why Do Some Schools Work?* New York: Simon & Schuster, 1991.

Gearheart, Bill R. *Learning Disabilities: Educational Strategies.* 5th ed., Columbus, OH: Merrill, 1988.

Greene, Lawrence J. *1,001 Ways to Improve Your Child's Schoolwork: An Easy-to-Use Reference Book of Common School Problems and Practical Solutions.* New York: Dell, 1991.

Higbee, Kenneth L. *Your Memory: How It Works and How to Improve It.* New York: Marlowe, 1996.

Jones, Claudia. *Parents Are Teachers, Too: Enriching Your Child's First Six Years.* Charlotte, VT: Williamson, 1988.

———. *More Parents Are Teachers, Too: Encouraging Your 6- to 12-Year Old.* Charlotte, VT: Williamson, 1991.

Kelley, Mary L. *School-Home Notes: Promoting Children's Classroom Success.* New York: Guilford, 1990.

Levine, Melvin D. *Keeping a Head in School: Students Book about Learning Abilities and Learning Disorders.* Cambridge, MA: Educators Publishing Service, 1990.

Mercer, Cecil D., and Ann R. Mercer. *Teaching Students with Learning Problems.* Upper Saddle River, NJ: Prentice Hall, 2005.

Novick, Barbara, and Maureen Arnold. *Why Is My Child Having Trouble at School?: A Parent's Guide to Learning Disabilities.* New York: Putnam, 1995.

Rief, Sandra F. *How to Reach and Teach ADD/AD/HD Children*. West Nyack, NY: Center for Applied Research in Education, 1993.

Scheiber, Barbara, and Jeanne Talpers. *Unlocking Potential: College and Other Choices for Learning Disabled People*. Bethesda, MD: Adler & Adler, 1987.

Sonna, Linda Agler. *The Homework Solution: Getting Kids to Do Their Homework*. Charlotte, VT: Williamson, 1990.

*Teaching Children with Attention Deficit Disorder*. Reston, VA: Council for Exceptional Children.

Thiel, Ann, Richard Thiel, and Penelope B. Grenoble. *When Your Child Isn't Doing Well in School*. Chicago: Contemporary, 1988.

Townsend-Butterworth, Diana. *Your Child's First School: A Handbook for Parents*. New York: Walker, 1992.

Wade, Theodore E. *The Home School Manual: For Parents Who Teach Their Own Children*. 5th ed., Auburn, CA: Gazelle Publications, 1991.

## Building Self-Esteem

Youngs, Bettie B. *How to Develop Self-Esteem in Your Child: 6 Vital Ingredients*. New York: Fawcett Columbine, 1991.

## Sibling Rivalry

Faber, Adele, and Elaine Mazlish. *Siblings without Rivalry: How to Help Your Children Live Together So You Can Live Too*. New York: Avon, 1998.

## Special Education

*Providing an Appropriate Education to Children with Attention Deficit Disorder*. Reston, VA: Council for Exceptional Children.

*Questions Often Asked about Special Education Services*. Washington, DC: National Information Center for Children and Youth with Disabilities.

*Rights and Responsibilities of Parents of Children with Handicaps*. Reston, VA: Council for Exceptional Children.

## Social Skills

Drew, Naomi, ed. *Learning the Skills of Peacemaking: An Activity Guide for Elementary-Age Children on Communicating, Cooperating, Resolving Conflict*. Rolling Hills Estates, CA: Jalmar Press, 1987.

## Temper Tantrums

Hall, Nancy. "Taming Temper Tantrums." *Working Mother* July 1993:42–43, 46.
Welch, Martha G. *Holding Time: How to Eliminate Conflict, Temper Tantrums, and Sibling Rivalry and Raise Happy, Loving, Successful Children.* New York: Simon & Schuster / Fireside, 1988.

## Books for Children and Adolescents

Caffrey, Jaye Andras. *First Star I See.* Fairport, NY: Verbal Images Press, 1997.
Carpenter, Phyllis, and Marti Ford. *Sparky's Excellent Misadventures: My A.D.D. Journal by Me (Sparky).* Washington, DC: Magination Press, 2002.
Corman, Clifford L., and Esther Trevino. *Eikee: The Jumpy, Jumpy Elephant.* Burlington, VT: Waterfront Books, 1995.
Cummings, Rhoda, and Gary Fisher. *The School Survival Guide for Kids with LD (Learning Differences).* Minneapolis, MN: Free Spirit Publishing, 1991.
Drew, Naomi. *The Kids' Guide to Working Out Conflicts: How to Keep Cool, Stay Safe, and Get Along.* Minneapolis, MN: Free Spirit Publishing, 2004.
Galvin, Matthew. *Otto Learns about His Medicine: A Story about Medicine for Children with AD/HD.* New York: Magination Press, 2001.
Gehret, Janet. *Eagle Eyes: A Child's Guide to Paying Attention.* Fairport, NY: Verbal Images Press, 1996.
Gordon, M. *Jumpin' Johnny, Get Back to Work: A Child's Guide to AD/HD/Hyperactivity.* DeWitt, NY: GSI Publications, 1991.
Gordon, Michael. *My Brother's a World-Class Pain: A Siblings Guide to AD/HD/Hyperactivity.* Dewitt, NY: GSI Publications, 1992.
Ingersoll, Barbara. *Distant Drums, Different Drummers: A Guide for Young People with AD/HD.* Bethesda, MD: Cape Publications, 1995.
Janover, Caroline. *Zipper, The Kid with ADHD.* Fairport, NY: Verbal Images Press, 1997.
Moss, Deborah. *Shelly the Hyperactive Turtle.* Kensington, MD: Woodbine House, 1989.
Munsch, Robert. *Love You Forever.* Willowdale, Ontario, Canada: Firefly, 1986.
Nadeau, Kathleen G. *Learning to Slow Down and Pay Attention: A Book for Kids about ADD.* Washington, DC: Magination Press, 1997.
Nemiroff, Marc. *Help Is On the Way: A Child's Book about ADD.* Washington, DC: Magination Press, 1998.
Quinn, Patricia O., and Judith M. Stern. *Putting on the Brakes: Young People's Guide to Understanding Attention-Deficit Hyperactivity Disorder (AD/HD).* New York: Magination Press, 2001.
Zimmett, Debbie. *Eddie Enough!* Bethesda, MD: Woodbine House, 2001.

# Index

abilities, concentrating on, 117
academic difficulties, 22–24, 140
academic expectations, 172
accommodations, 137, 216
acquaintances, telling about child's problem, 56–57
actions, accepting responsibility for, 13–14
activities: after-school, 130–131; educational, 142; extracurricular, 130; individualized, 170; parent-teacher, 204–205; social, 170, 244–245; soothing, 75; summer, 101; transitions from, 102; vocational assessment, 215
activity leaders, 55–56
Adderall, 222, 226, 228–229
Adderall XR, 228–229, 233
AD/HD (attention-deficit/hyperactivity disorder): acceptance of, 9–10; causes of, 3; characteristics of, 2; co-morbid conditions, 5–6; diagnosis and treatment, 3–5; finding information on, 10; look-alikes, 221; medication, 7–9; prevalence of, 3; support group, 253
*AD/HD and Teens: A Parent's Guide to Making It Through the Tough Years,* 217, 254
adolescents. *See* teenagers with AD/HD
adopted teenagers, 214–215
adoptive parents: of difficult babies, 28; family differences from adopted

children, 214; keeping journals, 46; sharing medical information, 50
advocating self, 213
after-school activities, 130–131
airplanes, traveling by, 106–107
Amen, Daniel, 233, 234
amino acid manipulation, 4, 220
amphetamine class, 222, 227, 228–229
anger issues, 79, 82–83
annual goals, 182
anticonvulsants, 231
antihistamine, 230
antipsychotics, 230, 231
anxiety, 5, 6, 22
appetite boosting, 230
appointments, questions to ask when scheduling, 47
appropriate behaviors, praising, 33
arguments, 126, 210
arithmetic, 171
articles on AD/HD, 135
assessments, 5, 176, 182–183
assets, concentrating on, 64
assignments: checklists for, 165; folders for, 153; giving, 167–168; major assignments, 156–158; notebooks for, 167; pads for, 145, 146; unclear, 147
assistance, seeking, 166
assistive technology devices, 187
The Association for the Gifted, Council for Gifted Children, 145
atomoxetine (Strattera), 222–223, 227, 232

# About the Author

**OLLEEN ALEXANDER-ROBERTS** is the author of *ADHD and Teens* and *The Essential Adoption Handbook*. She is the mother of two young adults who face the daily challenges of AD/HD. A freelance writer and national speaker on AD/HD, she resides in Maumee, Ohio, with her son.